FACE TO FACE
WITH CHILDREN

FACE TO FACE WITH CHILDREN

The Life and Work of
Clare Winnicott

Edited by

Joel Kanter

Forewords by

Jeremy Holmes

Brett Kahr

KARNAC

LONDON   NEW YORK

First published in 2004 by
H. Karnac (Books) Ltd.
6 Pembroke Buildings, London NW10 6RE

British Library Cataloguing in Publication Data

A C.I.P. for this book is available from the British Library

ISBN: 1-85575-997-7

10 9 8 7 6 5 4 3 2 1

Edited, designed, and produced by Communication Crafts

Printed in Great Britain

www.karnacbooks.com

COPYRIGHT ACKNOWLEDGEMENTS

Jason Aronson for permission to reprint "D.W.W.: A Reflection", from S. Grolnick & L. Barkin (Eds.), *Between Fantasy and Reality: Transitional Objects and Phenomena* (New York: Jason Aronson, 1978) [chapter 13].

British Association of Social Workers for their kind permission to reprint "Casework Techniques in the Child Care Services", *Case Conference*, 1 (9): 3–15 (1955), and *Social Casework*, 36 (1): 3–13 (1955) [chapter 6]; "Face to Face with Children", from J. King (Ed.), *New Thinking for Changing Needs* (London: Association of Social Workers, 1963) [chapter 7]; and "Communicating with Children—II", *Social Work Today*, 8 (26): 7–11 (1977) [chapter 9].

Alan Cohen for permission to reprint "Child Care in Oxfordshire: Interview with Alan Cohen" [chapter 5].

Institute of Psychoanalysis, for permission to reprint "Fear of Breakdown: A Clinical Example", *International Journal of Psycho-Analysis*, 61: 351–357 (1980) [chapter 17].

Kay McDougall for permission to reprint "The Development of Insight", from C. Winnicott, *Child Care and Social Work* (Hitchin, Hertfordshire: Codicote Press, 1964) [chapter 11].

National Council of Voluntary Child Care Organizations for permission to reprint "Communicating with Children—I", *Child Care*

Quarterly Review, 18 (3) (1964) [chapter 8]; "The 'Rescue Motive' in Social Work", Letters in *Child Care Quarterly Review, 9* (3): 120 (July 1955), and *10* (1): 12–13 (January 1956) [chapter 10].

New Era in Education for permission to reprint "The Problem of Homeless Children", with D. W. Winnicott (*The New Era in Home and School*, September–October 1944) [chapter 2].

The Squiggle Foundation for permission to reprint "DWW: His Life and Work" [chapter 14].

Taylor & Francis for permission to reprint "Introduction" from D. W. Winnicott, *Deprivation and Delinquency* (London: Tavistock, 1984) [chapter 4].

The Winnicott Trust and Paterson Marsh Ltd for permission to reproduce "Development Toward Self-Awareness" from *Challenges, Frustrations, Rewards, for Those Who Work with People in Need*, Report on the 1964 Conference (Shrewsbury: Shotton Hall, 1964); and *Toward Insight for the Worker with People* (Shrewsbury: Shotton Hall, 1971) [chapter 12]; "Early Observations on Object Relations Theory" (unpublished letter) [chapter 15]; and "Lois Munro" (unpublished essay) [chapter 16].

World Educational Fellowship for permission to reprint "Children Who Cannot Play", from *Play and Mental Health* (London: New Educational Fellowship, 1945) [chapter 3].

CONTENTS

PREFACE

The challenge of this volume is to allow Clare Britton Winnicott to emerge as a person in her own right, separate from her husband yet intimately involved with him. For those who knew her personally, and Donald as well, this is not a difficult task: her talents were recognized by almost all of them. A leader in child care and social work in Britain, through her work at the London School of Economics and the Home Office she influenced a generation of professionals.

However, as her main task in the last decade of her life involved the enhancement of her husband's professional legacy, most professionals today only know Clare, if at all, as the wife of a leading psychoanalyst. Her final professional writings are centred on Donald's life and work; many of those closest to Clare in her last years knew little or nothing about her substantial professional contributions. And, while overshadowed by an idealized husband, Clare was also overshadowed by a devalued profession: even most social workers look outside their profession for wisdom or insight.

As David Howe commented:

> because social work arises in response to problems of everyday living, its expertise rests in gaining a thorough and sensitive understanding of ordinary matters. The catch for social workers is that if the technical base and strength of occupation consists of a vocabu-

lary that sounds familiar to everyone, it will have difficulty in claim-
ing a monopoly of skill or even roughly exclusive jurisdiction over its
working environment. To the onlooker, the practices of social workers do not appear markedly different from those of ordinary social
intercourse. [Howe, 1986, p. 117]

But, unlike many contemporary psychotherapists and social workers
in academia, Clare was never enamoured with professional jargon; she
was much more comfortable with the "first treasured possession" than
with the "transitional object". A "thorough and sensitive understanding of ordinary matters" can be explained in plain English as well as
complex jargon. Perhaps reflective of her father's evangelical talents,
wisdom is a gift to be shared, not hoarded.

Indeed, in working with the evacuees in Oxfordshire, this capacity
verged on patriotic duty. With the help of "Dr Winnicott" on Fridays,
she had to guide an array of hostel staff without professional training
in caring for 80 troubled children. And she had to teach "Dr Winnicott"
fundamental skills in professional consultation—a perspective that
changed the direction of his professional career.

For the next thirty years, both were in great demand as speakers to
an array of lay persons and community caregivers. These talks com-
prise the vast majority of Donald's published papers, including many
of his most commonly read publications. Similarly, in Clare's case,
almost all of the essays reprinted in this volume began as manuscripts
for oral delivery. By almost all accounts, Clare was a much more
dynamic speaker than Donald, both passionate and direct while
Donald had a tendency towards obscurity and eccentricity. Perhaps
the dynamism of Clare's personality detracted from an intellectual
appreciation of her contributions. Although her paperback monograph *Child Care and Social Work* was treasured by a cadre of social
workers, many have remembered Clare more than her ideas. The very
clarity that is the gift in her lectures and writings allowed listeners and
readers to incorporate her ideas as their own.

While few outside the social work profession have read any of
Clare's writings apart from those about her husband, the readers of
this volume are likely to come from a variety of professional backgrounds, with diverse interests. Some may be interested in child care
or social work, others in psychoanalysis and D. W. Winnicott, still
others in the history of social work. This volume has been organized so
that readers can easily seek out the topics in which they are most
interested. But, as in Donald's writings, interesting ideas pop up in
unexpected papers. The overview of Clare's contributions in the last

section of the introductory essay offers a guide to her most important themes and the related chapters.

As an editor, I have made only very minimal changes to Clare's published writings, occasionally adding more paragraph breaks for clarity and deleting extraneous material for reasons of brevity and relevance. I have almost always preserved the original grammar and emphases, except when it seemed that errors in the original publication were made. (Many of the original sources were shoestring publications with limited editorial resources.)

I also want to call attention to my use of Clare and Donald's first names in chapter 1. I had read Donald's work for over a decade before I learned his first name, assuming that he always was known only by his initials, D.W. And I was even more surprised when I learned, when I met his friends and colleagues, of the informality in his personal relationships—how many of his acquaintances knew him as "Donald". In any case, in writing the introduction, it seemed awkward to identify Donald as "Winnicott" and Clare as "Clare", so I have used a parallel construction of first names throughout the volume.

While many readers may find the biographical sections in this volume of great interest, Clare's writings offer much-needed insight into the difficulties of children experiencing loss and separation. Too often, our child care and child welfare systems have focused on administrative and legal procedures, and the personal experience of the child-in-care is lost. Meanwhile, social work has focused on the child's outer reality to the exclusion of his or her inner world, while psychoanalysis has too often done the reverse. By taking us back to the crisis of the wartime evacuation—apart from the policy controversies of today—Clare's reports eloquently transcend both the analytic abstractions and the bureaucratic concerns that so often engulf us, vividly reminding us of the importance of *both* inner and outer realities. More broadly, with over half the children in the United States and the United Kingdom experiencing parental separation or divorce today, the impact of these losses has become part of the fabric of our daily lives, too often overlooked in our work with children, whether as social workers or as psychotherapists.

While child abuse has often received the most attention in the public dialogue about children's issues, Clare reminds us in chapter 9 herein, that "the pain of separation from those we love is for all of us a devastating experience, but for the dependent child the whole of his world collapses and everything loses meaning". Such simple insights remain as true today as they were sixty years ago.

ABOUT THE EDITOR

Joel Kanter, MSW, LCSW has been a practising social worker since completing his graduate education at Smith College School for Social Work in 1974. A graduate of the Advanced Psychotherapy Training Program at the Washington School of Psychiatry, he is currently a Senior Clinician with Fairfax County (Virginia) Mental Health Services and is in private practice in Silver Spring, Maryland. He has taught, lectured, and written extensively on many topics involving the community treatment of mentally ill clients, including case management, family consultation, and day treatment. His publications in these areas include *Coping Strategies of Relatives of the Mentally Ill* (NAMI, 1984), *Clinical Issues in Treating the Chronic Mentally Ill* (Jossey-Bass, 1985), *and Clinical Studies in Case Management* (Jossey-Bass, 1995) and over twenty chapters and articles.

ACKNOWLEDGEMENTS

When I initiated this project, my original intention was to republish Clare's tiny volume, *Child Care and Social Work*, along with the two or three other essays of which I was aware. I had few contacts in either the United States or the United Kingdom, and I had no idea that a serious biographical investigation was either possible or warranted. Like many others, I "knew" Clare largely as Donald's wife. However, when I shared my manuscript for my initial article on Donald's concept "management" (Kanter, 1990) with "Jock" Sutherland and E. James Anthony, they both strongly supported my inclusion of Clare in both the title and the article itself.

Their encouragement kept this project alive for me until I sought to republish an article by another British social worker as part of an edited collection (Marjorie Sheppard, in Kanter, 1995). Gerry Schamess at Smith College referred me to Jean Nursten in Reading, and she, in turn, introduced me to the late Kay McDougall. During a trans-Atlantic phone call, I mentioned my lingering interest in Clare, and I soon learned of her personal and professional relationships with both Clare and Donald. In addition to their work together at the London School of Economics, I learned that Kay's husband had owned the small press, Codicote, which had published *Child Care and Social Work*.

Kay strongly supported my desire to bring Clare's work to contemporary audiences on both sides of the Atlantic and, with her help, this project was launched. Within weeks, however, the scope of the project expanded significantly. I learned of the repository of Clare's papers at the Wellcome Institute of Medicine, obtained the support of the Winnicott Trust—with the particular assistance of Jennifer Johns—and initiated a week-long visit to England to examine the Wellcome collection and to conduct a handful of interviews for a brief introductory essay.

In the weeks before the trip, a web of contacts began to develop on both sides of the Atlantic, was largely facilitated by Jean Nursten and Kay McDougall. Jean's colleague at the University of Reading, Peter Pettit, a social work historian, told me about Alan Cohen's remarkable collection of interviews with distinguished social workers (see chapter 5 herein). I was soon introduced to Harriet Meek and Jane Petit, two American colleagues who had lived and trained in England. Harriet helped with developing contacts among Clare's social work colleagues and Jane assisted with introductions to psychoanalytic colleagues. And, as I arrived in London, a letter awaited me at my B&B from Juliet Berry and Pamela Mann with a wealth of other potential contacts. All of these colleagues continued to assist me in a variety of ways as the project continued.

Numbers alone cannot convey the spirit of these offers of support. As I began to meet Clare's vast network of colleagues (both in social work and in psychoanalysis), friends, and relatives, I was greatly moved by the posthumous generosity I encountered. Clare had touched many, many lives in significant ways, and over a decade after her death so many wanted to share in return. This generosity was critical to the success of this project. I had no university sponsorship and no research grants, and I had significant responsibilities, caring for two young children. In addition to the many who shared their recollections of Clare (and Donald) with me through interviews, letters, and email, many also gave of their time to help me to assemble useful materials or reference information. Without this often passionate outpouring of support—which said so much to me about Clare—this project would never have achieved fruition.

In this regard, I especially wish to thank the following persons who contributed to this project in special ways, involving personal recollections, sharing documentary materials, exploring research questions that I could not pursue from abroad, and providing detailed editorial feedback: Norma (Duncan) Campbell, Joan Cooper, Margaret Fosbrook, Bob Holman, F. Marjorie (Green) Jones, Sue Johnson, Brett Kahr, Olive Stevenson, George and Janie Thomas, and Joan Vann.

The following friends, colleagues, supervisees, and students also gave freely of their time in sharing their both their personal recollections of Clare (and Donald) and their views on the historical milieu in which she lived: Pati Auterinen, Barbara Barnett, Ursula Behr, Gemma Blech, Dorothy Bradfield, Dorothy Brierly, Mary Bromley, Zofia Butrym, Nora Calton, Sheila Collis, Jill Curtis, Judy Cooper, John Davis, Barbara Dockar-Drysdale, David Donnison, Michael Eigen, Irmi Elkan, Baroness Lucy Faithfull, Sharon Genassi, E. M. Goldberg, Phyllis Grosskurth, Colin Graves, Alma Hartshorn, Peter Hildebrand, Robin Hughes, Arthur Hyatt-Williams, Judith Issroff, Lydia James, Eliot Jaques, Marcus Johns, Betty Joseph, Beti Jones, Barbara Kahan, Pearl King, Harry Karnac, Audrey Lees, Emanuel Lewis, Josephine Lomax-Simpson, Ella (Blumenkahl) Marks, Nancy Martin, Nora Minnies, Janet Matteson, Elspeth Morley, Karen Proner, Eric Rayner, Charlotte Riley, Simon Rodway, Jane Rowe, Stanley Ruszczynski, Hanna Segal, Ray Shepherd, and Diana Williamson.

Yet another group of British colleagues provided support for this project through research, technical support, personal hospitality, and professional insight. These include Arthur Collis, Dilys Daws, John Hudson, John Jackson, Elizabeth Mapstone, Joan Rubenstein, Dave Smith, Riccardo Steiner, and Mary Twyman. I particularly wish to thank the Squiggle Foundation, including Leslie Caldwell, Sarah Cooke, and Jan Abram, who have supported this project in various ways, including allowing Clare's lecture at the Squiggle to be shared in this volume (chapter 14). And I have to especially share my gratitude for the assistance and friendship of Alan Cohen; in addition to allowing the publication of his unique interview with Clare, he provided ongoing research assistance throughout this project.

I also wish to acknowledge the generosity of other scholars and researchers who shared their findings and materials with me. They include James W. Anderson, Gordon Pradl, F. Robert Rodman, Roger Willoughby, and Anne Wyatt-Brown.

Clare also has a remarkable family, and all of her nieces and nephews—Alison Britton, Andrew Britton, Celia Britton, Margaret Britton, and Katherine Grey—most generously shared their recollections of Clare and Donald and the family that Clare had grown up in.

In the United States, an array of colleagues provided a different sort of aid, perhaps less coloured by personal sentiment, reading and discussing Clare's papers and providing feedback on my manuscript. In this regard I wish to especially thank Martha Chescheir, Linda Hopkins, and Bill Meyer, as well as Jeffery Applegate, Jon Fredrickson,

George Hagman, and Shelly Rockwell. I also wish to express my appreciation to the *Clinical Social Work Journal*, and its editors, Jean Sanville and now Carolyn Saari, which has enabled me to share this evolving research with the social work community.

Apart from the aforementioned Wellcome Institute of Medicine, which enabled me to have access to their well-maintained archives, I also received support from the library at the University of Chicago School of Social Administration (where I first discovered *Child Care and Social Work*), the archives of the British Psychoanalytical Society, and the Oskar Diethelm Library at New York Hospital–Cornell Medical Center, which maintains the archives of Donald's papers.

Of course, I have been deeply appreciative of the support from the Winnicott Trust, as represented by Jennifer Johns and the late Ray Shepherd. I had approached the Trust as a literal stranger and I have experienced their willingness to allow me to proceed with this project, which recognizes their founder, as a great honour. The support of the Trust, in turn, facilitated an agreement with Mark Paterson and Associates, the literary agent for the Winnicott Trust. I also want to thank the Editorial Staff at Karnac, especially Leena Häkkinen, as well as Klara King of Communication Crafts, for their assistance in bringing this project to fruition.

Finally, I would like to thank my family for their patience and support as this seemingly interminable project has proceeded. My children, Rebecca and Elana, have been there since the inception, and Jessie and Adam have witnessed the completion. My experience as a parent has resonated with Clare's wisdom about children throughout these years, and, as with Clare's life, the personal and professional are inextricably intertwined. And lastly, my deepest appreciation to my wife Cindy, who has provided the "holding environment" that has enabled me to complete this volume.

FOREWORD

Jeremy Holmes

This book is primarily about the ways in which psycho-analytically informed social work set out to help troubled children in the middle decades of the previous century. As such it represents an invaluable historical record. But I believe it has much wider contemporary relevance and resonance. Pointing backwards to the rediscovery of lost values, it also has significant links with the very cutting edge of twenty-first century social care.

This is my attempt to describe the impact of social work on the novice psychiatric trainee in the 1970s:

A professorial ward round at a famous postgraduate psychiatric institution. The trembling resident presents the case. The professor interviews the patient, skilfully, but with great detachment. There follows a long and erudite discussion about diagnosis and psychopathology. A conclusion is reached and recorded. The professor departs, accompanied by acolytes. The resident, ward nurse and psychotherapeutically trained social worker remain behind. Silence falls. Then, as though from another world of discourse, the voice of the social worker is heard asking gently, but insistently, "but how

Visiting Professor, Psychoanalysis Unit University College London; Honorary Consultant Psychotherapist, Tavistock Clinic.

shall we set about trying to help—as opposed to categorize, medical-
ize, diagnose, Procrusteanize—this suffering person?" [Holmes,
1991]

This was my 1970s introduction to the social worker as a key member
of the psychiatric team. In those days the psychiatric social worker was
someone who had good training and skills in psychotherapy yet was
not incarcerated in a psychoanalytic ivory tower, and she was able to
use them, together with her personal strengths and practical wisdom,
in the applied setting of the clinic.

The inevitable feminine of the personal pronoun, and the evident
gender stereotyping of the Grand Round scenario, are inescapable. In
those days the overwhelming majority of British social workers were
women, direct descendants of the middle-class "do-gooding" lady
almoners of the hospitals and voluntary "Care Committee" workers of
the 1930s–1950s. In its preoccupation with child development and
concentration on the emotional and practical needs of those in distress,
social work appeared to reinforce at a social level the stereotype of
domestic "women's work", while acquiescently vacating the high
ground of doctoring, diagnosis, and academic prestige to men—albeit,
as it often happened, "their" men.

Insofar as she is seen as "Winnicott's [D.W.W.] wife", this is true
too of Clare. But Miss Britton (as she was until the age of 45) also
illustrates and embodies a very different set of images of social work: a
vehicle for the liberation and self-expression of independent-minded
women; a valuation of the developmental needs of children as an
essential contribution to just, humane, and mature society; a recognition of the emotions as well as the intellect as a touchstone of humanity; a containing and reflective counter-weight to a male world
dominated at best by action and exploration, at worst by unspeakable
cruelty and destructiveness.

Joel Kanter's sympathetic introductory chapter covers these and
other aspects in depth. The comments below should be seen as footnotes to his excellent summary. I shall pick out four themes that seem
to me to make Clare's work relevant to contemporary preoccupations:
the relations between the sexes, applied psychoanalysis, the nature of
professionalism, and the values underlying social care.

Marriage.   The first follows immediately from the discussion of gender stereotyping. As doctor, psychoanalytic president, life-and-soul
extrovert, much-lauded author, and theorist, D.W.W. seems to em-
body typical "male" attributes. By contrast, Clare's modest back-

ground presence, unflashy teller of apparently everyday stories of conversations with her child clients, not to mention being an unfailing provider of seven o'clock dinner for D.W.W., suggest a womanliness that might be expected of a typical social worker. But, as emerges so clearly in this volume, the reality was somewhat different. D.W.W. was chaotic, intuitive, academically unsystematic, often lacking in common sense, and, in his private life, often a poor judge of men. Clare was organized, efficient, and down to earth, both in her practice and her thinking. She had a distinguished career in her own right and would today almost certainly have achieved a Chair in Social Work at the LSE.

Their successful marriage brought into play "masculine" and "feminine" elements, as well as the grown-up and childlike sides of *both* of them. They were able to retain separateness and individuality despite—or perhaps as a consequence of—their deep mutual involvement. Clare drew on D.W.W.'s creativity and civilized it into a form that was useable in her everyday dealings with children and those of her students. D.W.W. needed Clare to translate his ideas into practice, to provide the tinder-box where sparks of original thought could be struck, the anvil upon which new ideas could forged. While remaining within a conventional gender division of labour, they were able to express rather than suppress their "shadow" selves.

This suggests a different approach to the deconstruction of gender that has been such a preoccupation of the last two decades of the twentieth century. Feminism rightly asserts vis-à-vis the masculine that "anything you can do I can do just as well (and many things better)". But behind that there lies a void, leaving the question of the relationship between the sexes still unanswered.

The example of Clare and D.W.W. suggests that "marriage", if seen—metaphorically as well as literally—as an intercourse of equals, can be a way of breaking down traditional patterns of male authority and female submission. The "issue" of such a marriage (notwithstanding that Clare and D.W.W. were childless) can be both a benignly regressive "harmonious mixup" (to use a phrase coined by D.W.W.'s psychoanalytic contemporary Michael Balint), and a sublimatory sphere in which, through work, culture, and conversation, men and women can exchange their intrinsic attributes without feeling depleted.

Applied psychoanalysis.   Both D.W.W. and Clare, before becoming psychoanalysts, had had successful careers in different professions: D.W.W in paediatrics, Clare of course as a social worker. Perhaps because of this they both had the knack of using psychoanalytic ideas in everyday non-psychoanalytic clinical settings. Clare was clear that engagement, making contact with troubled children, striking up an authentic conversation, and reinforcing their sense of self were all essential tasks to be completed before any formal interpretative work could be usefully done. Like D.W.W., she too knew that children are often best approached indirectly—through a game, conversation during a car journey, comment on a pair of fashionable shoes, or even snuggling up in front of the TV together. For her, "support" and interpretation were not, as held in some psychoanalytic circles, mutually exclusive, but mutually reinforcing. Deep truths can emerge from the ordinary and are often themselves utterly simple. She did not see psychoanalytically informed social work (or, for that matter, psychiatry) as somehow watered down or inferior to the five-times-a-week "real thing", but, rather, a way of engaging in the everyday lives of ordinary people, but with the added depth and dimension that comes from a psychoanalytic perspective.

The best aspects of the impractical yet invaluable supervision that D.W.W. offered Clare and her fellow social workers with evacuated and adopted children in the war were carried over into her own supervisory work in training social workers, whose case reports she comments on so beautifully throughout this volume. That perspective, which gives meaning to care work and provides the conditions under which a professional task becomes a creative act, sorely needs to be rediscovered if social work is to regain its attraction for the idealistic young.

Professionalism.   This brings me to my third theme: social work as a profession. The LSE was a hotbed in the maelstrom of the early 1970s where students questioned to their very foundations traditional intellectual and social authority. One of the consequences of that and other social change in the last two decades of the twentieth century has been to sweep away traditional social work practice, and especially the casework that lay at the heart of Clare Winnicott's professional identity. Professionals of all sorts are today viewed with suspicion. The rights of the "user"—no longer a "patient" or "client"—reign supreme.

While there is much that was necessary about this seismic cultural shift, for social work it has had unforeseen negative consequences. Rather than becoming agents of social change, manning the barricades alongside their clients, the role of social workers today is if anything more than ever bound up with social control. In the mental health field in the United Kingdom, social work expertise covers risk assessment, intimate knowledge of mental health legislation, and generally acting as a broker for deprofessionalized practical services. The long-term, intimate, subtle, deeply involved developmental experience that case-work at its best could offer has become a thing of the past, incomprehensible to the young generation, nostalgically mourned by their elders.

For Clare Winnicott, the professional relationship brought out the best in its practitioners: a relatively unconflictual zone where people could express their love, toughness, intellect, compassion, and humanity in the service of others. At the same time social work practice—if properly nurtured, supported, reflected upon—was a maturational experience for the professional herself. The Clare Winnicott that comes through this in volume embodies the essence of that professionalism. As she writes about her work with children and their carers, she conveys a sense of being instinctively professional (if that is not an oxymoron) —respectful of boundaries, focused on the task in hand, able to muster all necessary knowledge and experience in the service of the client. At the same time she is utterly herself, calm, warm, encouraging, playful, funny, and able to be surprised by what her clients can teach her, and the responses they evoke in herself.

Values.   That brings me finally to the values that inform Clare Winnicott's thinking and to their contemporary relevance. Here too we find her unique blend of common sense and psychoanalytic insight. Her view of the psyche and of social life was essentially dynamic in that she saw both as a resultant of a balance of forces: on the one hand those that tend towards individuation, authenticity, and maturation; on the other, the stress, disruption, and loss that challenge the self with disintegration and false accommodation to a traumatic reality.

She was acutely aware that harmonious relationships could prevail, but that maturity involves being able to cope with discord as well. Nothing is so perfect that it can last for ever. What makes her writings interesting to us today is that, unlike many of her psychoanalytic contemporaries she did not reify any particular psychoanalytic construct—such as transference interpretations—as a route towards successful therapy. She was, rather, interested in the psychotherapeutic *process*, and how it can help people towards authenticity and a sense of self. For her, establishing a therapeutic conversation was what mattered, not what the content of that conversation happened to be. She saw that the moment a child can communicate in words something of his inner world, a foothold has been established. Recovery flows from speaking the truth about feelings and being sensitively heard, not judged, organized, or advised. And, of course, it is the possibility of being heard that is the catalyst that allows the feelings to flow and the words to form.

The voice that comes through these pages is imbued with the values that make a good therapist. It combines authority with modesty, a simplicity that is not afraid to tackle complex or seemingly intractable problems, an authenticity that flows from experience but is informed by the ideas and theories that enable that experience to be reflected upon and digested. Clare Winnicott knew what was good and what was wrong, which were the defences needed to survive in a difficult world, and those that could usefully be discarded. She managed to be both her own woman and a devoted wife to one of the outstanding psychoanalysts of his day. Her harmonious additions bring depth and completeness to the mercurial melodies of her husband.

Clare met D.W.W. while working with orphans and evacuees who were the innocent child victims of war. Today's social work clients are casualties of family breakdown in an increasingly fragmented, ever-changing, regression-inducing, global society. Borderline clients, refugees, and victims of torture need both social work and psychotherapy if they are to survive psychologically, let alone flourish. Clare Winnicott will no doubt continue to be remembered because of whose wife she was. With the help of this volume, however, D.W.W. and Clare's complementarity becomes clearer and shows the way for the much-needed revival of partnership between psychotherapy and social work. Without that mutual support and understanding, the *whole picture*—the integration that is the hallmark of the authenticity Donald and Clare strove for—will remain for ever elusive.

FOREWORD

Brett Kahr

Clare Britton was a successful and influential social work professional, both nationally and internationally. A beautiful, talented, and sane woman, it is no wonder that Donald Winnicott fell in love with her when he met her in Oxfordshire during the Second World War: Clare could provide Donald with a peace of mind that he had never known during his marriage to his first wife, Alice, who was a psychologically vulnerable woman. Donald felt very much looked after by Clare, and he often told friends and colleagues that he would have died ten years sooner had he not married Clare Britton.

Donald once wrote to Clare: "Your effect on me is to make me keen and productive and this is all the more awful—because when I am cut off from you I feel paralysed for all action and originality" (quoted in Clare Winnicott, 1978, p. 32 [see chapter 13 herein]). We even have some empirical evidence of the impact of Donald's marriages on his professional and scientific creativity. During his twenty-five years of marriage to Alice, Donald published only one book, whereas during the nineteen years of marriage to Clare, he published enough material

School of Psychotherapy and Counselling, Regent's College, London; The Winnicott Clinic of Psychotherapy, London to fill eighteen volumes, and there is still unpublished material written in the 1950s and 1960s that could swell this number to at least twenty, or perhaps more.

But, in praising Clare as a source of succour and creativity to Donald, I realize that I have already adopted a very "Donaldocentric" approach to the life of Clare Winnicott, and of course, virtually every psychoanalytic scholar has done so, until now. The beauty of Joel Kanter's work as an editor of Clare Winnicott's professional papers and as her biographer is that he has restored Clare to her rightful place in the history of social work, child care, and psychoanalysis as an independent, original thinker, and not just as the appendage of Donald Winnicott.

Joel Kanter's research on the life and work of Clare Winnicott deserves special praise. He has not only rescued almost all of Clare Winnicott's papers from archival obscurity, many of which are included in this volume, but he has presented them in a careful and thoughtful manner which facilitates readability. And he has undertaken a behemoth task of writing her entire biography without the aid of any previous biographical work at all. With the skill of a detective, Kanter has tracked down a wide range of friends, colleagues, and relatives who knew Clare Britton Winnicott intimately, and he has presented their reminiscences in a very cogently written narrative. Joel Kanter's endeavours are all the more impressive since, residing in the United States of America, he has carried out his research at a considerable distance—a distinct challenge for any researcher of a British psychoanalytic and social work practitioner.

I have derived great pleasure and knowledge from reading this volume. I first met Joel Kanter some years ago, and I found him unusually warm and helpful. Most scholars tend to keep their research discoveries close to their chests until publication, but Joel, by contrast, proved an extremely gracious and generous researcher, always willing and eager to share his archival treasures with a fellow Winnicott scholar prior to publication. I know that I learned much more about Clare Winnicott from Joel than he learned about Donald Winnicott from me. I applaud Joel Kanter on his achievement for having completed the biography of Clare Winnicott, and for having edited Clare Winnicott's papers with such skill and aplomb, a challenging task for any full-time clinician.

The Clare Winnicott papers provide a testament to a unique woman who devoted herself to the furtherance of children, so much so that the usually paedophobic British monarchy awarded her the

OBE, a prize that her husband certainly deserved but never received. The papers of Clare Winnicott reveal the mind of a child care expert who, of course, could think with Donald Winnicott in a creatively interdependent manner but who could be quite creative and original in her own right. I recommend this volume most warmly to all of us who work with children and to those of us who care about children. I extend my warmest congratulations to Joel Kanter for restoring Clare Winnicott to her proper place in the history of child care, in the history of social work, and in the history of psychoanalysis.

FACE TO FACE
WITH CHILDREN

CHAPTER ONE

Clare Winnicott: her life and legacy

Joel Kanter

We must have clicked at once—Clare was a rebel and so was I—but she was a much cleverer one than me. . . . A memory—it was October and I had a new tweed suit that I was longing to wear. So one morning with a chill in the air I put it on, arriving at the office first. When Clare came—wearing a thin summer dress—she stopped short and exclaimed "Gwennie, what on earth are you wearing THAT for?" I protesting, said "well, it is October and getting chilly". "Don't be daft", said Clare, "look at the sun, it's still summer and I'm going to make it last as long as possible. I'm not shedding my summer dresses 'til I have to."

I think I remember that because it says something important to me about Clare. She lived every part of life to the full. She took from life with both hands. No doors were closed to her. She looked in them all and usually found something to enjoy . . . the theatre, music, concerts, "Match of the Day", poetry, Torvill and Dean, Wimbledon . . . It was because she took so much from life and enriched herself that she was able to give so much to us her friends and all whom she came in contact. . . . Hers was somehow a very complete life.

Gwen Smith[1]

1

Wife of Donald Winnicott, analysand of Melanie Klein, sister of distinguished academics, teacher and mentor to a generation of leaders in British social work, a wartime innovator in helping evacuated children, founder of England's first social work programme in child welfare, awardee of the Order of the British Empire for her leadership in training child welfare workers, editor of her husband's writings: Clare Britton Winnicott's life encompassed a remarkable richness of relationships and accomplishments.

Yet, to most psychoanalysts and social workers, Clare Winnicott is only known, if at all, as the spouse of a prominent psychoanalyst. However, as her friend Gwen Smith suggested, Clare's life was more than the sum of her relationships and accomplishments: these were woven into a luxurious tapestry by her unique intelligence, common sense, and passion. As the *London Times* commented, Clare "radiated vitality, being always intensely interested in what was happening around her, and possessed a special blend of seriousness and fun, augmented with a subtle mischievousness".[2]

This volume, a collection of Clare's papers, talks, and interviews, is an expression of both Clare's professional work and her personal life—in many respects, the two are perhaps inseparable. Although this is most apparent in her relationship with Donald Winnicott, Clare's professional interests were also enriched by her relationships with her talented siblings. Similarly, her personal life was enriched by the many colleagues and students who became close personal friends.

Strangely, this intriguing intermingling of the personal and the professional played a role in the belated introduction of her thinking to a contemporary audience. As an American social worker who first came to know Clare through the out-of-print and unpublished materials assembled in this volume, I found myself in a unique position as I began the editing process and learning about her life. Meeting and interviewing dozens of colleagues, friends, relatives, students, supervisees, and analysands, I almost always found that intense personal memories of Clare overshadowed a more objective appreciation of her professional contributions.

However, once this fog of affection and appreciation had lifted, these associates often acknowledged the extent of Clare's professional influence. For example, Olive Stevenson, a student of Clare's who became one of the leading figures in contemporary British social work, noted that "when I think how little contact I'd really had with her over the years, I'm amazed at the extent to which what she had taught me became absolutely seminal to my own thought and writing as well as my own practice".[3]

Unlike her husband, Donald, and her analyst, Melanie Klein, Clare rarely conceptualized her ideas apart from the immediate challenge of the classroom, lecture hall, or supervisory consultation. Thus, the materials in this volume largely emerged from the texts or transcripts of oral presentations. Once these presentations had been completed, Clare had little motivation to conceptualize her ideas for unseen audiences. Although she skilfully managed her husband's literary estate, apart from her memoirs of Donald she only published one paper in the United States, and she seemed uninterested in securing a wider audience for her writings in Britain. Even colleagues who worked closely with her editing of Donald's work were unaware of her considerable written contributions.[4]

In these collected papers, Clare eschews professional jargon and theoretical abstractions, directly addressing the emotional turmoil of children's experiences of loss and separation, often within the chaos and inadequate resources of the public child welfare systems. These concerns have a timeless quality: the anguish of street urchins in a Dickens novel, the suffering of a child during Britain's wartime evacuation, or the torment of an American child of a drug-addicted mother. And the essence of the task of social workers and psychotherapists with such children endures across time and space.

In the first section of this introduction, I introduce the reader to Clare's personal and professional life, providing a context for appreciating her contributions in this volume. Following this, I identify and discuss some of the central contributions of her work. From a historical perspective, these contributions had a significant impact on her husband's professional work as well as on the British child care system. Similarly, her contributions can offer contemporary social workers and psychotherapists new insights into their practice.

Early life

Born on 30 September 1906 in the northern seaside town of Scarborough, Elsie Clare Nimmo Britton was the oldest of four children. Her father, James Nimmo Britton, housepainter or plumber from Glasgow, had joined the Baptist church and become a minister in that denomination. He was an energetic and creative clergyman who displayed a talent for oratory and organization.

In the years of his first ministry in Lincolnshire in his early twenties, Revd Britton increased the church's membership from 20 to 300. After doubling the membership of another church in Lincoln, he moved to Scarborough in 1903; there he was described as an "effective preacher" who "lit up his subject with the gift of humour and got his point home" (Albemarle Baptist Church, 1965). After helping the congregation construct a new building, he moved to the London borough of Clapham in 1912, and while there, he again doubled his church's membership.

Revd Britton's evangelistic talents achieved fruition when he was invited to assume the ministry of the Avenue Baptist Church in Southend-on-Sea in 1922. He came to this congregation with the "reputation of being a great preacher to young people and one of the outstanding evangelists of the denomination" (Jeremy, Barfield, & Newman, 1982, p. 64). A church member described him as follows:

> Mr. Britton has a manner and style of his own. He never beats around the bush. Pithy sentences and telling phrases follow one another with the weight and rapidity of hammer blows. It is good to watch his face; there is character written all over it. How quizzical it looks with its forehead lines and mobile brows. Merriment is depicted, but there are more signs of quiet, consecrated thought. There is an assurance about his utterances which communicates itself to his hearers. He believes in work among the young people. A congregation, as such, gives him little satisfaction, except as material for the formation or strengthening of a Church. [ibid., p. 64]

A church history expanded on this characterization of Clare's father:

> Avenue members quickly found that their new minister was not only a spiritual power-house, but a physical dynamo of a man, full of restless energy, who expected from himself and from his co-workers nothing less than a total commitment to the work in hand. In his first message to the church he wrote: "It is much better to make things happen than to hang back to see what is going to happen. Waiting is far more wearying than working. I was at a school sports a few days ago, and the boys who won were boys who meant to win from the first spring they took when the gun went." . . .
> He characteristically took the title of his first sermon at Avenue from David Livingston's well-known saying: "Anywhere so long as

it be forward." During that opening address to his new church, Revd Britton said: "Marking time has always seemed to me to be a heartbreaking form of expending strength. Forward—at the double—accords much more with my mood." . . .

Having thus given notice to his people of what they were to expect if they were going to keep up with him, he opened a ministry of 13 years during which 845 new members were added to the church and hundreds more discovered a new meaning to life. They were to be years in which it would be exhilarating to be involved in the work at Avenue, but in which anything less than exhaustion was not good enough. The challenge to greater exertion and larger sacrifice was ever-present, and not forgotten even as the Minister signed his (1927) Christmas greetings: "Yours trying hard, J. N. Britton." [ibid., pp. 64–65]

As a teenager and young woman, Clare was more likely to have been affected by her father's creative ministry—his facilitation of a "holding environment" for his parishioners beyond Sunday morning—than by the numerical growth of the parish. The church was especially known for the "enormous vitality of its work amongst young people"; the Sunday School met each Sunday afternoon, and over 50 teachers used "every nook and cranny" of the church to serve more than 600 children (ibid., p. 71). Boys' Life and Girls' Life Brigades—which offered spiritual, educational, and recreational activities for the children—were begun, and Revd Britton also encouraged the formation of tennis, football, and cricket clubs and a large children's choir (ibid., pp. 71–72). According to Nora Calton, a friend of Clare's from this period, Clare was an active participant and leader in Sunday School and the Girl's Life Brigade.[5]

Clare also observed her father's unique skill in facilitating the leadership skills of dozens of parishioners. For example, he encouraged one member to organize a Young Men's Club. Within several years, the membership had grown to over 130 men, who combined worship, Bible study, and recreational and social action activities. They raised funds both to maintain their own facility and to bring groups of underprivileged children from East London for visits to their seaside community. The church history notes that "J.N.B."—as he was known by his parishioners—was "inevitably always in the background", ensuring "that in addition to all the fun the Club maintained its position as a source of spiritual energy" (ibid., p. 74).

The church as a whole also addressed social concerns. During the 1926 General Strike, Revd Britton "filled the Church for a special serv-

ice attended by both sides of industry and challenged both management and men to live by the text: 'What shall it profit a man if he gain
the whole world and lose his own soul?'" (ibid., p. 69).

As the Depression began, the church hosted 1,500 women from the
"cheerless conditions" of East London for a dinner and day at the
seaside; later, as conditions worsened, Revd Britton helped the church
to open a building that was to serve during the day as a "club" for
unemployed men, and he appealed to his parishioners to help the
unemployed find some sort of work. Then, as the threat of war increased, he "joined many members of his church in praying and working for peace" (ibid., pp. 69–70).

In the midst of this activity, Revd Britton also authored an assortment of religious publications. One booklet—*To Be or Not to Be*—is
notable for its attempt to appeal to the rational interests of its intended
audience of adolescents. Illustrating a clarity of expression seen in the
writings of Clare and her brothers, the tract opens as follows:

> I suppose there is not the slightest need to tell any boy or girl reading
> this booklet that no one ever becomes a great athlete or a good
> scholar by mere accident. You never suddenly wake up and find that
> without any effort you have become a gymnast or a scholar. To
> succeed at either demands, as you know, clear-cut decision, patient
> practice, and dogged determination. [J. N. Britton, n.d., p. 3]

Like Clare's future husband, Revd Britton "overtaxed" himself, expending "ceaseless energy" attending hundreds of meetings and functions each year. "Constantly in demand" as a "preacher, layer of foundation stones and crusader against the evils of the day", he had to
"grudgingly endure" two extended periods of sick-leave before he
retired from the Avenue Baptist Church in 1935. However, in the
following decade, before his death in 1945, he served as the first National Commissioner of Evangelism of the Baptist Union and as a
Chaplain to an anti-aircraft battery during the war (Jeremy, Barfield, &
Newman, 1982).

Clare's mother was born Elsie Clare Slater. She was the daughter of
William Slater, also a Baptist minister. During her childhood, his
church was in the Nottingham area, where he was a community leader
who served as County Secretary, a school board member, and a member of the Poor Law Board of Guardians (a relief agency). During a
bitter coal strike, possibly in 1893, he organized relief for the miners'
families. He was described by his son-in-law as "strongly evangelical,
a man of wide sympathies and sound judgment [who] won his way

into the hearts of all who knew him" (from *Memoirs of Ministers and Missionaries*, n.d.). When Clare's father retired from the ministry at the Avenue Baptist Church, Revd Slater assumed various ministerial responsibilities while a search was conducted for a new minister (Jeremy, Barfield, & Newman, 1982, p. 75).

Clare's mother, Elsie Slater Britton, was actively involved in church activities and, in 1949 she was elected the first woman deacon of the Avenue Baptist Church (ibid., p. 91). Margaret Britton, her oldest granddaughter, recalls that she was a kind, virtuous woman with "very high ideals". Although she looked forward to visiting her grandmother, she acknowledged that her virtuousness could be "a little bit frightening, because she was so good". She recalled that she and her brother were careful to behave well in their grandmother's presence.[6]

Another of Clare's nieces, Celia Britton, reported that her father (Jimmy) never seemed very enthusiastic about visiting his mother.[7] Similarly, a close friend of Jimmy's reported that he often avoided opening letters from his mother for weeks, as they would be filled with religious homilies and entreaties.[8]

Yet Clare's childhood friend, Nora Calton, described the family as an "ideal close-knit family, in which [all members] . . . were highly intelligent, ambitious, forthcoming and strong characters" who were also "great debaters". She described Clare as "very proud" of her family, but one can easily imagine tensions between Clare's vivaciousness and her parents' emphasis on Christian virtue.[9]

As noted earlier, the family moved several times during Clare's childhood. When Clare was 6, they moved from Scarborough to Clapham, in South London, where they lived throughout the First World War. In 1917 Clare's maternal aunt, Jessie, was widowed. She had married in 1915 and had probably moved in with the Brittons soon afterwards, while her husband served in the Army. Over time, Aunt Jessie assumed an important maternal presence in the Britton family; she lived with them until Elsie Britton's death in 1956.[10]

In addition to the loss of Clare's uncle, the war had a dramatic impact on the family's standard of living. Clare's brother Karl recalled that he and his friends were once mistaken by a stranger as European refugee children; out of sympathy, this passer-by offered these shabbily dressed youngsters an orange.[11]

Having moved to Southend-on-Sea in 1922, Clare completed high school in 1925. Her activities over the next several years are unknown, but her *curriculum vitae* indicates that she attended Selly Oak College, a

Baptist-affiliated teacher-training college in Birmingham, from 1929 to 1930.

After completing her training, Clare moved to the Nottingham area (where she had relatives) and then to Norwich, where she worked as a club leader and organizer in YWCA centres from 1931 through 1937. These positions were a transitions between her family's evangelical background and her future career as a professional social worker. Clare later recalled that "... in a way my family had always been interested in social work. My father had run a club for unemployed people and my grandfather had taken quite a big part in the social situation where I lived. I think it was in the family. . . . before the war, I went and worked in Y.W.C.A. clubs simply because a friend of my mother was in charge of a Y.W.C.A. centre and she invited me to go and work in the centre. And I did" (chapter 5 herein).

There is little information about Clare's life in the 1930s, but her nieces, Celia and Alison Britton, both recall hearing that she was "wild" during these years.[12] The meaning of "wild" is unclear, but one imagines that Clare was viewed by her religious parents as a "free-spirited" young woman. Undoubtedly, Clare's upbringing in a minister's family affected her deeply. On one hand, as an adult, she never affiliated with any church. The Baptist doctrine preached by her father explicitly promoted a submissive obedience:

> ... if you decide to join [the church] ... you are no longer free to do as you like. You are only free to do as he gives command. Your decision to join at once brings you under his control. That is what your decision to make Jesus the Captain of your life means. . . . For instance, it means that everything in your life which He disapproves must go. . . . It is love of your great Leader which makes you willing to give up the most cherished things, willing to endure hardest things, and willing to try the most difficult things. [J. N. Britton, undated, pp. 6–8]

Throughout her life, Clare refused to submit to any sort of ideology or doctrine, maintaining an independence of thought in the face of ideological passions in both social work and psychoanalysis. Yet, like her future husband, she was somehow intrigued by those who passionately expressed the very sort of doctrinal purity that also offended her.

At the same time, Clare also identified with many elements of her parents' social concerns, religious lifestyle, organizational skills, and personal characteristics.

She recalled that her father "was a liberal . . . and public-minded. He was chairman of committees and things in the local authority . . . chairman of the hospital committee . . . and things like that. He would certainly not mind using political pressure if he felt it was appropriate."[13]

Clare's passionate, even evangelical, concern for children and those in need, her clarity and forcefulness of self-expression, her appreciation of the importance of play and recreational activities, her sense of humour, her tireless energy, her appreciation of extra-familial networks in the developmental process, and her organizational skill in inspiring and empowering others to assume responsibility—the origins of all of these essential qualities are traceable to her religious upbringing and parental identifications.

Siblings

No account of Clare's life is complete without an appreciation of her siblings, James (Jimmy), Karl, and Elizabeth (Liz). Clare had close relations with all three throughout her life; all were educated professionals who devoted much of their lives to various forms of teaching, and her brothers had especially distinctive careers.

James (known widely as "Jimmy"), the second child, became a secondary-school English teacher and published a creative curriculum guide for teaching composition (J. Britton, 1934). When the war began, he joined the Royal Air Force and was stranded with a small platoon on Crete when the Germans invaded that island. He led this platoon on a daring retreat across the island's mountains and they were eventually rescued (J. Britton, 1988).

After the war, he became an editor for an educational publisher, and in 1954 he joined the faculty of the University of London Institute of Education. In the wake of the publication of his renowned volume, *Language and Learning*, in 1970, he developed an international reputation as a leader in the movement to advance the role of active language in learning and education and helped found the International Federation for the Teaching of English (Martin, 1994).

Incorporating ideas from education, literature, philosophy, linguistics, child development, and psychology, Jimmy's work examined the expressive use of language in the context of the child's overall life experience (J. Britton, 1970). He became a leader in the educational movement of "language (or writing) across the curriculum", which has had considerable influence on teaching in both Britain and the United States (Goodman, 1992; Wyatt-Brown, 1993).

In his numerous books and essays, Jimmy cited the writings of both Clare and Donald; notably, his seminal work, *Language and Learning*, compares Clare's ideas about social work with Martin Buber's ideas about teaching (J. Britton, 1970). Although the former focused on the most troubled children and the latter on "normal" children, Clare and Jimmy shared an acute interest in how children communicate—not only in a transactional manner, but in both the expressive and poetic modes of language.

The writings of both continue their father's tradition of clarity of expression; both speak directly to their reader with a minimum of jargon or obscure abstractions. Similarly, in the classroom or lecture hall, both were perceived as talented, even charismatic, teachers. The following observation about Jimmy's teaching style by his colleague, Nancy Martin, could equally have applied to Clare as well:

> His synthesizing narrative mode enabled his ideas to move quickly into people's personal experience and lodge there. One can trace the way the ideas he worked on affected people's thinking and practice, but a large part of his influence is other than this—much more diffi- cult and intangible. [Martin, 1994]

Jimmy and Clare were also deeply interested in literature and poetry. Both were avid readers of poetry, and both included selections of children's poetry in their writings. Jimmy also wrote poetry, and he published a collection shortly before his death in 1994 (J. Britton, 1994).

Donald, too, shared these interests. Late in his life, Donald wrote a poem about the darker side of his mother, and he shared a copy with Jimmy—an act suggestive of an intimate friendship (Phillips, 1988). While one author has explored the impact of Donald's ideas on Jimmy's work (Wyatt-Brown, 1993), Jimmy may have also exposed Donald to ideas from an array of leading thinkers, including Buber, George Kelly, Michael Polanyi, and Edward Sapir. However, such influences are nearly impossible to confirm, because, as Jimmy wrote, "I did not write a great deal about him (Donald), or him about me".[14]

Donald and Clare also assisted Jimmy in his work. He invited both to lecture at London University and at the London Association for the Teaching of English.[15]

Karl, the third child, studied philosophy with Wittgenstein at Cam- bridge and spent much of his career as a Professor of Philosophy at the University of Newcastle. He authored several books in his field, in- cluding an important volume on John Stuart Mill (K. Britton, 1953).

While Clare was in Oxfordshire during the war years, they frequently visited each other, as Karl lived nearby. In 1945, when Karl's wife was in hospital for several weeks after the birth of her third child, Clare came to care for her seven-year-old niece and five-year-old nephew. Also, in 1945, Karl's diary entry indicates that he assisted Clare in the writing of her first solely authored professional paper, "Children Who Cannot Play" (chapter 3 herein).[16]

When Clare moved to London in 1947, her contact with Karl lessened, yet she often visited during holidays, and they corresponded throughout their adult lives, sometimes consulting with him about important life decisions. Karl died in 1983.

Elizabeth (known as "Liz"), Clare's youngest sibling, was an art teacher in a London high school. In her 1945 paper "Children Who Cannot Play" (chapter 3 herein), Clare devotes a paragraph to the development of creativity in art education, apparently a reference to her sister's profession. Also, when Clare published her husband's work *The Piggle* (D. W. Winnicott, 1978), she included a drawing by Liz of Donald's consulting-room. Soon after Donald died, Liz moved into a basement apartment in Clare's home. When she purchased a smaller home nearby, Liz moved with her. Tragically, just before Christmas 1978 Liz was critically injured by a speeding car as she stepped off the curb near their home. After spending several months in a coma, she died in February 1979.[17]

Noting that Clare was the first child, Jimmy commented that "when war between the generations broke out—as it sometimes does in the best families—(Clare) was our redoubtable leader". He recalled a family legend which suggested that:

> Liz and I [Jimmy] were more alike than Clare and Karl. Karl and Clare loved to admire and enjoy their Christmas presents and Liz and I always wanted to take them to pieces to see how they worked . . . so it was a family in which alliances were made in different directions for different purposes.[18]

Beginnings in social work

In 1937, Clare began a formal training in social work by enrolling on the one-year Social Science course at the London School of Economics (LSE). Unlike contemporary social work education, this course focused solely on the theoretical underpinnings of social work, including sociology, psychology, political science, social policy, and economics. Students on this course chose from an array of lectures available in these disciplines. There were no classes or agency placements in social work practice. The depression-era milieu at the LSE was highly political and largely socialist, and Clare was undoubtedly influenced by it.

After graduation in 1938, Clare began work in Merthyr Tydfil, Wales, with the Commissioners for Special Areas as club organizer for unemployed juveniles. This steel-making region was devastated by the Depression. With unemployment at over 50%, poverty was endemic. Clare administered the "Boot and Shoe Fund", which provided children's footwear for these families, but little else is known about her activities during this period.[19]

In her 1945 paper "Children Who Cannot Play" (chapter 3 herein), Clare was probably referring to her tenure in Wales when she discussed the importance of "organizing groups of children for communal play and teaching them the traditional games and songs that are their heritage". She then went on to describe her work with a "very inhibited" young woman in a girls' club. She encouraged the girl to share her talent in weaving with the club's leader, and then with other girls—a process that greatly enhanced her self-confidence and social relationships.

In 1940, Clare returned to the LSE to study social work on the thirteen-month Mental Health Course. At that time, this was Britain's leading programme in psychiatric social work. Because of the outbreak of war in 1939 the course had been suspended for a year, but it was subsequently relocated in Cambridge. The various programmes were scattered across the campus, and the 12 students on the Mental Health Course were isolated from the rest of the LSE programmes in an old house.[20]

As F. Marjorie (Green) Jones, one of Clare's classmates, recalls, the academic year was divided into four quarters. The first quarter was spent attending classes in Cambridge. Then the class was split, and one group trained at Mill Hill Emergency Hospital in London while the other spent the term at the Oxford Child Guidance Clinic. The former placement focused on work with adults, and the students participated in seminars with Aubrey Lewis, a renowned psychiatrist. The latter focused on work with children, and seminars were taught by Mildred Creak, a prominent child psychiatrist who also was a colleague of Donald Winnicott's (Kahr, 1996). Then the groups exchanged placements for another three months before returning to Cambridge for a final term of study and examinations.

The Mental Health Course was directed by Sybil Clement Brown, a leading social worker who preceded Clare in her appointment as Director of Child Care Training at the Home Office. Margaret Ashdown taught adult casework, and Nancy Fairbairn taught child guidance. Lectures included content on mental illness and its treatment, social policy, "mental deficiency", child psychiatry, psychology, physiology, and criminology. Students also could attend lectures by other faculty at the London School of Economics or at Cambridge.

Only a few of the courses offered content on psychoanalytic theory. These included a stimulating series of lectures on child development by Susan Isaacs, perhaps Britain's leading child psychologist, who became acquainted with Donald Winnicott at the Institute of Psycho-Analysis in the 1930s (Kahr, 1996).[21] Mildred Creak lectured on child psychiatry and introduced students to the ideas of Freud, Jung, Adler, and Klein. The intensive nature of the one-year course precluded any extensive study of psychoanalytic theory or practice.

The war, at the height of the Battle of Britain, also pervaded the learning experience of the students on the Mental Health Course. As Marjorie Jones recounts:

> I well remember standing outside an Air Raid Warden's Post in Cambridge in November 1940, watching a large number of German bombers going over and wondering where they were going. The next morning, we heard that they had devastated Coventry.

She described the three-month internship in London as

> pretty hairy; we spent a high proportion of the nights in air raid shelters! The patients came from all over London, so we spent a lot of time traveling to visit their relatives at home to get background history and give support. Fortunately, at that time, the air raids were largely at night so we didn't have that problem, but all the getting round London was very tiring.[22]

During that academic year, the war also affected Clare in several personal ways. Her maternal grandparents' home near Southend-on-Sea was damaged by a bomb blast in 1940, and they were evacuated to Luton. The Avenue Baptist Church in that same town—where Clare had spent much of her later adolescence and young adulthood—was also severely damaged by bombing. Soon afterward, in early 1941, her maternal grandmother died, and in May 1941 her brother Jimmy was evading capture by German troops on Crete (J. Britton, 1988).

Jones specifically recalls three students on the course as "academically brilliant": Clare, Betty Joseph, and Lulie Shaw.[23] Joseph is a well-known Kleinian psychoanalyst in London[24] and Shaw went on to a long, distinguished career as a senior lecturer on social work at Bristol

University. Comparing herself to Clare, Shaw smilingly told a colleague that Clare was a "naughty little schoolgirl", suggesting a high-spirited and feisty streak.[25]

Jones regarded Clare as "having a brilliant brain, markedly acute and perceptive. She certainly had no problems in assimilating the content of the Course and she played a very positive and active role in discussion. She had no difficulty in getting distinction in every subject in the final examination." Interestingly, she perceived Clare as "younger" than her classmates, who were mostly in their "upper twenties". Clare was almost 34 when the course began. Like many other friends and colleagues in other settings, Jones was impressed by Clare's youthful appearance and demeanour.

Oxfordshire

Clare's work with evacuated children in Oxfordshire was the defining experience of her life: not only did she meet Donald Winnicott, her future husband, there, but her talents as a social worker emerged at a time when Britain was undergoing a dramatic change in its child welfare policies and programmes. The work of Clare and others during the war established precedents that altered the course of children's services for the half-century.

Over six million people were evacuated from England's cities to the countryside during the early years of the war, especially after the Blitz in September 1940. Families agonized about these separations: should they put their child's physical safety ahead of their psychological needs for attachment? Fathers were away in the Forces, and mothers were pressed into employment. In contrast to the United States, concern about invasion and the bombings made the war a source of omnipresent anxiety. Even with the massive evacuations, nearly 8,000 children were killed in Britain (Holman, 1995).

These urban evacuees, primarily working-class, were often unwelcome to the middle-class families who were required to accept them. Many brought psychological problems with them; even more developed difficulties when faced with long periods of parental separation and, in some instances, parental death. Throughout the country, rudimentary social work services were created to serve the needs of these children. When home placements failed, hostels (group homes) were established that could provide special care.

Unlike many of her fellow graduates from the London School of Economics' course in psychiatric social work, Clare deliberately avoided employment in child guidance clinics or mental hospitals. Out at a pub with her fellow students, she told them: "I've enjoyed this course enormously, but the last thing I'm going to be is a P.S.W. (psychiatric social worker). I want to be in the hurly burly of what's going on in the world." She "wanted to be in the thick of social work, not stuck away in a clinic".[26]

Clare first worked with the evacuation scheme in the Reading area with the National Association for Mental Health and then moved to the English Midlands Region to work with a regional health authority (chapter 5 herein).

Within a few months she received instructions to consult part-time in Oxfordshire, an assignment that changed the course of her life:

> I was sent to work in the Oxfordshire evacuation scheme, one day a week, by the person who was running my office. It was only a one-day-a-week assignment, to work with Dr Winnicott who was coming down once a week to be a consultant to the hostels which were set up for difficult children. The children who couldn't be kept in an ordinary billet were put into hostels . . . there were five hostels with difficult kids in. And I was told to go and work there once a week and sort things out.
>
> I think the person who was my boss then actually briefed me by saying, "There's a difficult doctor working in that area. He comes down once a week. He doesn't believe in social work because he likes to do it all himself. But it's really in quite a mess and you must go and straighten the whole thing up." That's what I was told. So I did; I turned up one Friday to the hostel where he was visiting and listened, wondering where I could come in and what I could do in this situation.
>
> And I think one of the things that I did achieve, fairly soon, was to help the staff in the hostels to make use of his expertise, his knowledge, in a way that they were not able to do. They used to say, "He comes down and talks to the children. He plays his pipe to them and we like him very much, but he doesn't ever tell us what to do." So I said, "Well let's never ask him what to do. Let's do the best we can in the present situation and then when he comes again tell him what we did and see if he's got any comment to make on it, and if we can therefore learn something from what we did." And that's how it really evolved. And he always said, "You gave me a role and turned the job into a professional job."
>
> One thing I did was to stop him eating all the children's rations in one meal! The staff were inclined to save all the best food for him, and I just slipped in one day "I suppose you know you're eating the

children's butter ration for a week?" He was absolutely horrified! So
that's how I started in the hostel scheme. [chapter 5 herein]

Soon Clare was working full-time in Oxfordshire, caring for over 80
children scattered among the five hostels. Donald visited on Fridays to
consult with these hostels, but their jointly authored wartime article,
"The Problem of Homeless Children", explicitly states that "in practice", the psychiatric social worker controlled "the whole of the work"
and was the "one individual at the centre of the scheme"(chapter 2
herein). Clare even assumed much of the responsibility for the hostel
maintenance and supplies:

> I was asked to take on the administration of the hostels ordering
> equipment, seeing and reporting back building things that wanted
> doing, and I did accept that. And it was tremendously important to
> me that I did accept it because my credibility in the hostel situation
> was greatly enhanced by the fact that I had access to resources, other
> than just human resources. I mean I could get more equipment for
> them, or I could put orders in for more equipment. [chapter 5 herein]

Beyond these administrative tasks, Clare provided continuity to the
hostels as staff came and went, played a key role in the placement and
transfer of children, consulted regularly with hostel staff, and was the
only person who knew "each child at every stage" (chapter 2 herein).
As noted in Clare and Donald's 1944 article, the social worker saw
the child:

> in his school and billet, and then in the hostel, and possibly in more
> than one hostel. If there is a change in hostel wardens, it is the
> psychiatric social worker who gives some feeling of stability during
> the period of change. . . . She is also in contact with the child's home,
> visiting the parents whenever possible. [chapter 2 herein]

In contrast, this article explicitly states that the psychiatrist's role was
limited to weekly consultation with the hostel staff, occasional interviews with difficult children, and the provision of medical authority in
problematic situations.

Years later, Clare elaborated on their collaboration:

> my first task [was] trying to evolve a method of working so that all of
> us, including Winnicott, could make the best possible use of his
> weekly visits. The staff living in the hostels were taking the full
> impact of the children's confusion and despair and the resultant
> behaviour problems. The staff were demanding to be told what to do
> and it took time for them to accept that Winnicott would not, and in
> fact could not, take on that role, because he was not available and

involved in the day-to-day living situation. . . . Gradually it was recognized that all of us must take responsibility for doing the best we could with the individual children in the situations that arose from day to day. Then we would think about what we did and discuss it with Winnicott as honestly as we could. . . . These sessions with him were the highlight of the week and were invaluable learning experiences for us all including Winnicott. . . . His comments were nearly always in the form of questions which widened the discussion and never violated the vulnerability of individual members. After these sessions, Winnicott and I would try to work out what was going on from the mass of detail that had been given to us, and we would form some tentative theories about it. [chapter 4 herein]

Irmi Elkan, a psychiatric social worker who worked with Donald at Paddington Green Children's Hospital in London, joined Donald on one of his Friday visits to the Oxfordshire Hostels. She recalled that Donald and Clare's approach to this work "made a lasting impression" on her:

Donald and Clare practiced what they preached. They accorded the hostel foster parents the same respect that most of us accord all parents. They accepted them as equal partners whilst not ignoring personal difficulties and limitations. They made known their conviction that foster parents, like any other parents, should not be expected to bring up more than one family of children.[27]

Clare's colleague and friend, Gwen Smith, who shared an office and living quarters with Clare in Oxford, described the texture of their work with the evacuation scheme:

We were called "temporary civil servants" and weren't liked by the permanent ones . . . we conformed to no pattern. We were not obviously responsible to anyone. We didn't sign on at 9 and off at 5 and we only could be found anywhere between Henley on the South and Banbury on the North.

We protested violently when we found an urgent case in someone's in-tray not to be reached 'til the day after tomorrow or when a family we were visiting was visited the next day by another department without any cross-reference. This sort of thing happened many times and we started discussions with the Chairman of the Council, the Earl of Macclesfield, on the need to coordinate and have reference between departments and have one person in charge of children's work. These discussions, which I like to think were taking place in other parts of the country too—I always like to think—were the beginnings of what led to the Curtis Report in which Clare later became involved.

Clare several times rang at midnight—at least it always seemed to be midnight—when one of the boys had run away from the hostel and once when the warden's wife ran away with the newly appointed deputy warden—and I followed her car in mine along the blacktop roads and waited for the "thumbs-up" sign that all was well and she could cope.

Once a week, we went on night duty together in County Hall to man the telephones in case there was a "Red Alert". I don't think that either of us knew quite what to do if there was a "Red Alert". We either sat up 'til 3 A.M. or went to bed and were called at 3 A.M.—it was ghastly. Clare was particularly scathing about [our] grubby little office.[28]

In addition to her work with evacuees, Clare also assisted other children in need in Oxfordshire. These children included the mentally retarded ("sub-normal"), juvenile delinquents ("fit-person cases"), and those placed into foster care and homes for the poor ("work-houses"). In some of these situations, Clare was asked by her superiors to address the needs of these other groups; in others, she assumed the initiative to address problems that came to her attention (chapter 5 herein).

In one situation, Clare was called to consult with a nursery that suffered from an epidemic of bedwetting. Anxious about her lack of expertise with such problems, she listened carefully to the staff's account of the highly structured daily routine, gently commenting that the children "don't get much time to themselves, do they?" When she realized that the children in this institution were restricted to their chairs all day if they "got messy", she gently helped the staff to discover that they needed to relax the institution's structure (chapter 5 herein).

In a dramatic case report, Clare tells how she consulted with hostel staff in supporting a therapeutic regression of a troubled adolescent girl after the death of her abusive and alcoholic mother. Once the girl had stabilized and found a comfortable home, Clare aggressively advocated for this girl when government officials attempted to disrupt her placement (chapter 5 herein).

Each of these interventions illustrated Clare's interest in facilitating environmental changes that had a therapeutic impact on the inner world of children, and, in turn, these changes within the children would decrease the tension in their living situations. This awareness of the inner life of the child was illustrated in Clare's 1950 discussion of "transitional objects", written several years before Donald's classic paper (Winnicott, 1953), where she discussed the ruthless removal of treasured possessions from evacuated children (C. Britton, 1950).

Although her exposure to psychoanalytic theory during the war is unclear, her 1945 paper "Children Who Cannot Play" conveys her emerging familiarity with object relations theory:

> the mother, however, must do more than give to the child; she must be able to accept his love in return, thereby proving to him his own goodness and loveableness. Her acceptance of his love also helps him to feel secure through his own bad moments of feeling angry and destructive. [chapter 3 herein]

This passage suggests a familiarity with the ideas of Melanie Klein—a familiarity most probably gained through her collaboration with Donald. Her focus on how interpersonal relations influence the child's inner world is reminiscent of Klein's acknowledgment of social factors in her 1940 paper "Mourning and Its Relation to Manic-Depressive States", perhaps Clare's favourite paper by her future psychoanalyst (Grosskurth, 1986).[29]

While her work with Donald most certainly affected Clare, this collaboration dramatically influenced Donald's perspective on professional teamwork. Confirming the aforementioned observation of Clare's Oxfordshire supervisor that "he likes to do it all himself", Donald remarked in a January, 1943, unpublished address entitled "A Doctor Looks at the Psychiatric Social Worker" that he "deliberately worked for fifteen years without employing a psychiatric social worker". He went on to share his belief that in "psychotherapeutic practice, *teamwork is bad*" (Donald's emphasis).

Yet, in this talk, Donald acknowledged that his views on collaboration had recently evolved, and he went on to offer a dozen examples of the value of social work interventions. He stated that the "social worker's main function, like the (doctor's), is to bear emotional burdens", which he viewed as a "heavy job". Perhaps referring to Clare's management of eighty troubled evacuees as well as the other responsibilities she assumed, Donald noted that "the psychiatric social worker has to be told to go away and take a proper holiday lest she become a case herself".

The post-war years

Clare continued to work with needy children in Oxfordshire after the war. This work included continuing to monitor the hostels set up for children who had no homes to return to after the war (C. Britton, 1946) as well as more conventional peacetime work with foster care and adoption. At a 1954 United Nations seminar on social casework, Clare presented case notes of her work in 1946–47 with a two-year-old boy in foster care. As the boy moved between foster homes on his way to a permanent adoptive placement, Clare recognized the significance of a toy duck, which helped him to maintain a sense of personal security as he made the transition from a foster home to an adoptive family.

Also, at some point between 1945 and 1947, Clare worked as a "civil liaison officer" in the Civil Resettlement Unit of the War Office in Kingston-on-Thames. In this capacity, she assisted returning British soldiers who had been prisoners of war and had endured traumatic experiences in their captivity.[30] Irmi Elkan recalled Clare drawing parallels between these soldiers and deprived children, noting that these ex-prisoners would have trouble "eating their main course unless their fair share of pudding" was placed in front of them.[31] Ursula Behr, a member of Clare's first class at the LSE in 1947, recalls a similar story: in her recounting, the ex-prisoners couldn't bear watching leftover food discarded.[32] Olive Stevenson recollects Clare discussing how these men could not discuss any serious matters as mealtimes approached.[33]

During this period, Clare's talents became more widely recognized, and in 1946 she began teaching an evening course with Leslie Bell, entitled "The Child in the Family and the Community", at the University of London. Clare's part of the course concerned child development and included such topics as "how the first relationships are made", "the child's need to test the solidarity of the family group", "the significance of play in . . . development", "the need for widening social contacts", the (adolescent) "interest in self and anything which enhances self importance" and "the importance of [the child's] own social group in finding independence".[34] At this early stage in her career, Clare's focus on the child's interaction with his or her environment, both familial and extra-familial, at all stages of development was already explicit.

In the autumn of 1946 Clare also joined the Education Department of the National Association of Mental Health (apparently on a part-time basis) to plan and implement short courses for residential staff and child care workers (Britton, 1946).

The crisis of war and the evacuation stimulated many creative initiatives in work with children, notably Dorothy Burlingham's and Anna Freud's work at the Hampstead nurseries (1942, 1944) and John

Bowlby's (1944) work in Cambridge with aggressive children. Donald and Clare's work in Oxfordshire also became well known across Britain. After their 1944 article in *The New Era in Home and School* (chapter 2 herein), their 1947 article on the Oxfordshire "scheme" was the lead article in the first issue of *Human Relations*, an interdisciplinary journal published by the Tavistock Institute of Human Relations (Winnicott & Britton, 1947). In his classic volume, *Maternal Care and Mental Health*, John Bowlby (1951) discussed the Oxfordshire work at considerable length, highlighting it as an effective model for serving troubled children.

The personal experiences of most British families with childhood separation and, in 1945, the death of a foster child precipitated a well-publicized Home Office inquiry in 1946 known as the Curtis Committee. This high-profile committee examined 229 witnesses, including John Bowlby, Susan Isaacs, Donald Winnicott, and Clare Britton. The report of this committee (The Curtis Report), formally entitled "The Report of the Care of Children Committee", identified over 100,000 children in need of placement in England and Wales and recommended that each Local Authority establish a Children's Committee under the leadership of a "Children's Officer", who would organize services for each community (Holman, 1995, 2001). The Curtis Report was well received by the British public and led to the passage of The Children's Act of 1948. This Act helped to integrate children's services, which had until then been haphazardly provided by an assortment of governmental and voluntary agencies.

A major recommendation of the Curtis Report involved training social workers and residential staff to work in this evolving system of care. To this end, the Home Office and the social work programme at the London School of Economics collaborated in 1947 to establish Britain's first programme for training social workers for these new children's departments. As Clare had established a reputation as a leader in this emerging field, she was appointed as the first "Lecturer in Charge" of the new "Child Care Course".

The "Child Care Course" and the London School of Economics

From 1947 through 1958, the Child Care Course at the London School of Economics, under Clare's direction, educated a generation of social workers who worked with children in need across the United Kingdom, many of them becoming leaders in the emerging child care field (Holman, 1998, 2001). As was the practice in British social work education, the Child Care Course was an intensive one-year postgraduate programme that integrated classroom instruction, individual tutorials, and field work with several agencies. Potential students submitted applications to the Home Office, which provided grants to cover fees and living expenses; in turn, students were expected to return to work in the Children's Departments of the local authorities.

The curriculum designed by Clare included classes in child development, paediatrics, legal issues in child welfare, and sociology. Clare taught a class entitled "Care of the Deprived Child". Donald, too, taught on this programme from its inception, offering ten lectures annually in a class entitled "The Inter-relation of Physical and Psychological Aspects of Development"; in 1955, he began offering an additional five lectures on "Adult Personality Patterns".

The Child Care Course also included individual tutorials, often with Clare, and brief periods of practice experience with agencies and residential care programmes. Only a dozen or so students were enrolled each year, and Clare interacted with each participant in a personal way.

Each year, Clare hosted parties for the students. Initially, these were held at her flat in Chelsea, with Donald in attendance; after their 1951 marriage they were held at their Chester Square home. These occasions were quite memorable for their informal festivity. One student recalls arriving early and finding Clare and Donald working together in the kitchen, making a batch of marmalade.[35] Another recalls Donald playing the piano and leading everyone in song.[36]

Clare's actual teaching was pragmatic and avoided theoretical abstractions. For example, she preferred the evocative phrase "first treasured possession" (Stevenson, 1954) to Donald's distinctive but abstruse "transitional object".[37] Although she began her first analysis (with W. Clifford M. Scott) in 1948, she assigned few readings from the psychoanalytic literature. She wanted her first groups of students to remain focused on their work in child care and not become overly intrigued with psychotherapeutic interventions.[38]

The central elements of Clare's teaching can be gleaned from a detailed set of lecture notes taken by Norma (Duncan) Campbell in 1957 from the class "Care of the Deprived Child". Early in the first lecture, Clare called attention to the gap between "theoretical comprehension and practical application" and to the uniqueness of each individual: it is "terrifically important that people are different". She stressed the need for a balance between scientific objectivity and personal involvement. In this first lecture, she also expressed her concern about "labelling" children and interpreting their behaviour instead of remaining focused on the practical task of helping children "find a home".

In subsequent lectures, she offered her categorization of the different types of children who enter the child care system, some history of British child care, an overview of family relationships, a discussion of "normal" dependency in the mother–infant relationship, and an overview of early childhood development.

In contrast to reports from students in earlier classes, Campbell's 1957 notes indicate that Clare directly lectured on some of the central concepts of psychoanalytic theory, including the importance of unconscious "phantasies", the classical psychosexual stages (oral, anal, and oedipal), and the Kleinian cycle of love, aggression, hate, guilt, and reparation.

She also offered students recommendations for supplementary readings, including Ribble's *The Rights of Infants* (1941), Middlemore's *The Nursing Couple* (1941), D. W. Winnicott's, *The Child and the Family* (1957a) and *The Child and the Outside World* (1957b), and articles by Rene Spitz (1945) and Olive Stevenson (1954).

Expressing a consensus of Clare's students and faculty colleagues, Irmi Elkan described Clare as a:

> superb and inspiring teacher. She combined intense liveliness with sensitivity and thoughtfulness. Her ability, through vivid examples, to convey how children feel and how their feelings can be understood through their behaviour, often made a lifelong impression on students. Many of them have, in turn, become leaders and initiators in the Child Care field. With so gifted a teacher as Clare, one might easily overlook the amount of conscientious hard work that went into the achievement. Clare worked very hard and was never unprepared. She said unless she spend some hours "steeping" herself in reading and thinking about her topic, she could not feel confident that she would deliver a good lecture or seminar.[39]

Bob Holman (2001), a student who went on to a distinguished career as a child care officer, researcher, social work educator, community organizer, and author, described Clare as "small and enthusiastic. She moved around the room, full of vitality. She presented profound ideas in simple ways and illustrated complex material with vivid case examples from her own experience. Above all, she conveyed that child care officers were engaged in a tremendously important job and that it was within their powers to improve the lives of deprived children" (p. 111). Describing Clare's lectures as "carefully prepared and well-delivered", Holman reported that Donald "shuffled into the room without any notes and drew 'a squiggle' on the blackboard". He asked the students what they saw in it and "produced lessons from children he had been seeing in his practice. He was not as easy to follow as Clare . . ." (p. 163). Most students at the LSE who had both as instructors had similar reports of their respective styles.[40]

Mary Bromley, a student in 1961–62 at Oxford University where Clare was a guest lecturer, recalls her skills as a teacher in more specific terms:

> Clare Winnicott gave a series of lectures which left a great impression on me. "Lecture" is not quite the correct term as she was very relaxed and approachable, talking with us and enabling us to participate. She had great strengths as a teacher in that she never appeared to talk "theory" at us. The discussions were always practice-based and her illustrations were real, not textbook. She had a gift of going to the heart of the matter and opening our eyes to an understanding of people around us.
>
> Two illustrations stay with me over the years. The first was, in describing the importance of accepting and assessing children as individuals and meeting their needs, an example of a mother who had several children and in a busy schedule took the time to treat them all individually by asking what shape sandwiches they each wanted and going to the trouble of always making them to each child's choice. On the surface, a simple act, but an excellent example of how small daily acts give a child a sense of respect, esteem and acceptance.
>
> The second was a story of meeting a young woman on a train. She was tired and anxious, her baby becoming more and more fretful and the pair of them really working each other up. Clare asked permission to hold the baby to give the mother a break. She then rewrapped the baby who by this time was flinging arms and legs all over the place. She wrapped her tightly in her blanket and the baby, feeling secure, calmed down and went to sleep. The story illustrated babies' need for security, but also a mother's need for support at the right time.
>
> She never told a story to show how good she was, just to illustrate a point, but I now was left with the impression of wisdom rather than solely academic knowledge.[41]

Through her leadership of the Child Care Course, Clare became known across the United Kingdom and was frequently invited to lecture and teach. These opportunities included giving an address at the 1954 United Nations Seminar on European Social Services alongside such luminaries as Florence Hollis. Her paper, "Casework Techniques in the Child Care Services" (chapter 6 herein), was well received, and it was published concurrently in *Case Conference* in Britain and in *Social Casework* in the United States.[42]

Although Clare's teaching skills and leadership of the Child Care Course were widely recognized, larger trends in social work education led to the dissolution of the Child Care Course at the LSE in 1958. In the 1950s, social work practice and education in Britain was divided into a variety of specialized fields, including family, medical, and psychiatric social work, child care, and probation (Younghusband, 1978). Each of these fields of practice had its own professional organizations, journals, standards, and training schemes. This professional fragmentation led to an array of difficulties, and in the early 1950s a movement developed to unite the professional organizations and implement a generic approach to social work education. Such generic training was already widespread in the United States, where in 1955 a similar array of social work organizations had merged and formed the National Association of Social Workers. Charlotte Towle's (1945) classic text, *Common Human Needs*, provided the intellectual underpinning to this generic approach to social work practice.

In 1954, the London School of Economics, with the help of a major grant from the Carnegie Foundation, established Britain's first generic training programme, the Course in Applied Social Studies, also known as the "Carnegie Experiment", under the leadership of Richard Titmuss and Eileen Younghusband (Hartshorn, 1982).[43] Although Clare served on the planning committees for this course, she hoped that the specialized Child Care Course could somehow coexist with this generic initiative. The specialized courses in Child Care and Mental Health at the LSE were nationally recognized, and both had vocal constituencies that advocated their continuance.

Yet there were considerable ideological and financial pressures to consolidate these courses with the generic course. With the Carnegie grant for the new course set to expire in 1958, Richard Titmuss, the Head of Department, advised the LSE staff in April 1956 that "a scheme for the process of unification" would have to be worked out in the next year (Hartshorn, 1982, p. 108). This process was extremely stressful for the whole faculty at the LSE, as no one could predict the programmatic and personnel implications of these incipient changes (Donnison, 1965).

Unfortunately, Clare had become critically ill with meningitis several months earlier, and she had to withdraw from her teaching and other faculty duties. As a result, she was not involved in critical faculty discussions about the courses.

Clare's admiring students were stunned by her sudden absence, and the course floundered for weeks while a temporary replacement was sought. One day, her students were surprised to find Donald taking over her lectures.[44] Similarly, during this illness, Donald filled in for Clare at speaking engagements across the country.

Although she recovered sufficiently by the autumn to begin her course work at the Institute of Psycho-Analysis, Clare took a year's leave of absence from the LSE and did not return until the autumn term of 1957. Irmi Elkan, who was invited to teach in the Child Care Course during Clare's leave, recognized Clare's "natural leadership qualities" and noted that Clare "felt freest and functioned at her best when she had sufficient elbow room to develop her own ideas and her own style. She became very unhappy during a period at LSE when her autonomy and the autonomy of her Course began to be threatened."[45]

David Donnison (1965), another colleague, noted that Clare "didn't enjoy administration and she hated conflict" (p. 259). He said she "sometimes learned by accident of major decisions" at the LSE and "then was compelled to react more aggressively than she would have wanted" (p. 272).

In January 1957, a decision was made to continue the Applied Social Studies and Mental Health Courses and to consolidate the offerings of the Child Care Course into the new generic programme at the end of the 1957–58 year. Sadly, Clare was not told personally about this change; she learned of it in a LSE faculty meeting.[46] This news came as a major blow to Clare, who lost her cherished role as the leader of Britain's pre-eminent graduate training programme in child care; instead, she became a part-time lecturer in the Applied Social Studies Course.

During the last year of the Child Care Course, Clare attempted to avoid consolidation with the Applied Social Studies Course and negotiated a plan with Kay McDougall, the Senior Lecturer of the Mental Health Course, to merge with that programme instead. Around New Year's Day, 1958, she wrote to Professor Titmuss about this plan, arguing that the Child Care and Mental Health Courses already shared four main lecture classes, and the internship needs of the Mental Health students with interests in child guidance overlapped with those of the Child Care students. However, Clare herself recognized in this letter that this last-minute plan was unlikely to be implemented. She encouraged Professor Titmuss to resolve the matter quickly and commented that "if we don't like the decision, we shall get over it".[47]

Years later, Clare offered a somewhat different version of these events:

> I started to plan the [Applied Social Studies] course. I worked five years on committees planning the thing, and then was not invited into it! It never occurred to me that this would happen. Never occurred to me! It didn't. So we were left with a separate child care course and child care students being trained in the generic. An impossible situation. Two lots of students that never spoke to each other. So when I was asked to continue it for another year, I said, "No, not on. Can't go on like this." So we dropped to twenty places for training at LSE, because I dropped out of the course. They would have let me go on indefinitely, but it just wasn't fair to anybody. Absolutely mad! I was not wanted on the generic course and I was out of it. I was ill for a year as a result.
>
> Then I took another year's leave of absence and then I thought, "Yes, I shall go back." I was asked many things. To go back and run the whole thing, by Professor Titmuss. But by this time, I was beginning to take my psycho-analytic training and I said "No." I might come back because I wanted to make a link with the old child care. I really went back for the sake of linking child care into the new thing. For the sake of the poor students. I was very unhappy there for a long time. In fact never enjoyed it, although I did teach on it. Some things I enjoyed. The students you always enjoy, but it was a difficult thing for me.[48]

Although it is impossible to reconstruct the objective details of this period, Clare's hurt and anger over these changes were quite explicit.

The demise of the Child Care Course had a special impact on Clare and Donald; this Course had allowed them to continue a professional collaboration that had begun in Oxfordshire. Apart from the obvious contact with students through lectures and parties, Donald also developed a collegial relationship with Kay McDougall, the Lecturer-in-Charge of the Mental Health Course. She also edited and published a small creative journal entitled *Case Conference*, in which Donald published at least three papers (D. W. Winnicott, 1954, 1955, 1970).

Donald and Clare also frequently travelled together across Britain, lecturing and teaching at conferences and meetings of child care agencies and organizations. They played a notable role in the formation and development of the Association of Child Care Officers (ACCO). The initial meeting of this group in 1948 was convened by some of Clare's first students at the LSE, and Donald soon volunteered the use of his consulting-room at Paddington Green Hospital for committee meetings of this "penniless" group, a custom that was to continue for over ten years (ACCO, 1970; Jacka, 1973).

Clare was invited to the organization's first formal Executive Committee meeting in April 1950 to discuss training and membership issues. She strongly and successfully advocated that ACCO membership should be open to all child care workers, whether or not they had received any formal social work training or qualification.[49] In 1966, both Clare and Donald were awarded the only honorary memberships granted by this organization (Jacka, 1973). With their support, ACCO grew from 12 members in 1948 to over 2,500 by 1969.

Given the intense conflicts he negotiated in the British Psychoanalytical Society (BPS), it seems likely that Donald greatly appreciated the respect and admiration he received in the child care and social work world. Perhaps unlike his fellow analysts, social workers were comfortable "dropping by" Clare and Donald's Chester Square home. Joan Cooper, a colleague of Clare's at the Home Office in the 1960s, offered this typical recollection: "At the end of a day's clinical work at Paddington Green Hospital, Donald, exhausted, would come home and lie flat on the floor, relaxing. Clare would be in the kitchen preparing the evening meal. If I missed my train at Victoria Station, I would sometimes drop in to learn to relax—but not to eat. Their quiet little suppers were important to them."[50]

In his grief over the demise of the Child Care Course, Donald wrote a paper in June 1958, initially entitled "A Comment on Generic Teaching", a title later modified to "Where Angels Fear to Tread or A Comment on Generic Teaching". In this unpublished paper he criticized what he viewed as social work education's irrational embrace of a "generic" approach. He argued that it was naive to believe that a year's generic training could adequately prepare social workers to function in child care, probation, as well as in medical and psychiatric social work. He also expressed his fear that the personal and educational needs of students interested in different fields would be neglected in both the admission process and the training itself.

When the Child Care Course was ended in 1958, Donald continued to give fourteen lectures on the Mental Health Course and ten on the Applied Social Studies Course until the year before his death in 1971.

Clare, too, continued to teach on the Applied Social Studies Course at the LSE until 1964. From 1958 to 1960, along with Irmi Elkan and

Zofia Butrym, she taught a core course for all Applied Social Studies students on the "Principles and Practice of Social Casework", and from 1958 to 1964 she gave twelve lectures annually on "Casework and the Child Care Service" to students with special interests in this area.

During this period, Clare was also completing her analytic training at the Institute of Psycho-Analysis while she continued to lecture and write in the child care field. She was a guest lecturer and external examiner at several universities across Britain. Freed of administrative responsibilities, she wrote several of her best-known papers during these years. At Kay McDougall's urging, she collected six papers for publication in a 1964 monograph entitled *Child Care and Social Work*.[51] Also, as Clare was now teaching on a generic social work course, her writings in this period moved beyond child care to address more general social work concerns; these papers included "The Development of Insight" and "Development Toward Self-Awareness" (chapters 11 and 12, respectively, herein), and "Casework and Agency Function" (C. Winnicott, 1962).

Interestingly, until 1958 Clare had identified herself at the LSE and in her other professional activities as "Miss Clare Britton", even though she had married in 1951. Although her marriage to Donald Winnicott was known by her Child Care students and intimates on the faculty,[52] some faculty members were unaware of her marriage until 1958, when she began to identify herself professionally as "Mrs Clare Winnicott".[53] Her reasons for this change are unknown; one can only surmise that her marital identity became more important after the loss of the Child Care Course—a programme she had begun before her marriage.

Marriage

The transformation of Donald's and Clare's relationship from a professional to a personal one is impossible to reconstruct with any accuracy. During the war, Donald was married to his first wife, Alice, and his time in Oxfordshire was limited. Clare's friend, Gwen Smith, commented that it "soon became clear that Friday had become a 'red-letter day'".[54]

Similarly, Irmi Elkan recalls Clare's coolness toward her when she joined Donald on his weekly visit to Oxfordshire in 1942. She had the distinct impression that Clare did not appreciate having to share Donald's attentions with another young female colleague. However, when Ms Elkan attempted to excuse herself to allow Clare and Donald a private moment later in the day, Clare joined Ms Elkan and initiated a friendly chat.[55]

In September 1943, Clare wrote Donald about his recent invitation to work with him at Paddington Green, asking him, "but are you *really* serious?" (Rodman, 2003, p. 97). Still employed in Oxfordshire, she again writes to Donald in December 1943 about an unsolicited job offer from the National Association of Girls Clubs, to be their Principal Officer for training youth leaders. This letter offers a clearer sense of the ambiguity in their relationship:

> This is rather out of the blue as I haven't applied for the job. I merely said at some stage that I was *interested* in this sort of work. There is no doubt about it that this is a big responsible job—and I am not likely to get such a "good" offer again (much more money for one thing!) Plenty of scope—and a job that I feel *needs* doing badly. Also, between you and me, quite honestly I think I *could* make a useful contribution to the Youth Mvt.:—I could *give*—that's the point and in a small way, I'd be important—and somehow I *need* all that. I could do the job and *believe* in what I was doing—and that what I could give would be of value. And I long—as don't we all!—to be able to *give* (and take) to the limit of my capacity. That has never happened in the job I'm doing now—for various reasons—but it has happened in other jobs—so that I know that I am *capable* of giving. So that the one thing that *does* seem clear, is that I must find a better job (i.e. better from *my* point of view).
>
> Of course I know that it is important to get married—as you once said to me—but that is so very difficult because of never meeting anybody. (I am *seriously* thinking of joining the Marriage Bureau in Bond Street—do you think it's a good idea?) . . .
>
> What do I want of you in all this? Perhaps you know better than I—but I know that I'm not asking you to *solve* all my problems for me—I *promise* I will never ask you that! But try as I will, I can't make a decision about this job without reference to you—all day I have tried—but then suddenly I felt that you wouldn't mind if I wrote—and it seemed right to do so. And you see, something that *does* affect my decision about the new job—is if you still think I can come to Paddington Green—if you still think it is a good idea—and want it. Is it *really* possible? Because I still think I would like to try it. . . . I *know* that I can be the sort of person who could do the Club Training job—and do it well—and make a name for myself in that field etc.—what I *don't* know is if I can be the other sort of person who can deal satisfactorily with personal relationships which the other job really means—and *this* is what I want reassurance about—terribly badly. It

really *is* a question of deciding what *sort* of person I am. [Rodman, 2003, pp. 98–99]

Several months later, in 1944, Clare informed her brother, Karl, about yet another job offer involving work with refugee children. She told him that she was concerned that the move would disrupt her relationship with "Dr Winnicott".[56]

One of the seventy-four extant wartime letters from Clare to Donald eloquently expresses the romantic dimension of this relationship:

> My dear—I'm afraid you would be terribly tired on Friday night by the time you get home. . . . I only hope that I haven't made you miserable as well! I hated you to cry & seem unhappy. You know, it wasn't long enough time—possibly that was why it was difficult. I want you to know that I am better—less depressed—& relaxed somehow. So don't worry about what you've done to me etc. because you've given me so much happiness & today & I know it and *feel* it & am grateful. . . . I was very surprised when I said that you'd *drained* me in the last few months. Well. I suppose in a way things couldn't happen to you unless they were so—also somehow I'd taken responsibility of your love for me—as well as mine for you. . . . Love from Clare. [Rodman, 2003, pp. 99–100]

Such letters undoubtedly suggest that this relationship developed a romantic dimension during their collaboration in Oxfordshire. Yet Clare did not accept the appointment at Paddington Green, which would have enabled them to have daily contact in London, nor either of the other two positions, which would have prematurely ended their professional collaboration. Donald's marital and professional lives were entangled in a complex web of relationships that were not easily brushed aside for a new love interest.[57] By remaining in Oxfordshire, the frustrations of this wartime romance could more easily be contained.

After the evacuation scheme dissolved with the war's ending, Clare and Donald's relationship continued. While still working outside London, Clare frequently visited the city, teaching an evening class and consulting with the National Association for Mental Health (NAMH). In November 1946, Clare and Donald were both featured speakers at a NAMH conference on the evacuation. Maintaining a professional persona, Clare poked fun from the lectern at Donald's recommendations:

> Now for the question which Dr. Winnicott brought up. "How do we feel about applying the knowledge gained through hostels to the

wider field of children in homes of all kinds?" Quite frankly, I am
appalled at the thought of even trying to think it out, let alone trying
to apply it! [C. Britton, 1946, p. 43]

Just a few weeks later, in December 1946, Donald wrote to Clare that
"my work is really quite a lot associated with you. Your effect on me is
to make me keen and productive and this is all the more awful—
because when I am cut off from you I feel paralysed for all action and
originality" (chapter 13 herein). This letter suggests the interplay between the personal and professional dimensions of their relationship—
a collaboration that resulted in two of the rare publications that Donald
co-authored with colleagues (chapter 2 herein and Winnicott & Britton,
1947).

Clare's appointment to lead the Child Care Course in the middle of
1947 enabled her to move to London and increase her contact with
Donald. She immediately engaged Donald as a lecturer on this Course,
re-establishing a professional collaboration that, as in wartime, offered
them additional opportunities for personal contact.

Yet openly consummating this relationship in marriage was a slow
and difficult process. By most accounts, Donald had been unhappily
married to Alice, his first wife, who has been described as an eccentric
and unhappy woman who possibly suffered from a psychiatric illness
(Kahr, 1996; Rodman, 2003). She was quite attached to him and did not
want a divorce. The British divorce laws of that era only permitted
divorce in cases of adultery, cruelty, desertion, or insanity.[58] Allegedly,
Donald was reluctant to initiate the divorce process while his elderly
father was still alive. However, soon after his 93-year-old father died
on 31 December 1948, he suffered his first heart attack.[59] Unhappy at
home, he began spending nights at his office during his convalescence
(Kahr, 1996).

On 25 August 1950, Donald approached Karl Britton, Clare's
brother, and initiated a personal discussion of his relationship with
Clare and his difficulty in obtaining a divorce without creating problems for Clare's professional reputation. As the other alternatives involved blaming Alice for the divorce, Donald discussed employing the
common practice of naming an uninvolved woman—often the attor-
ney's secretary—as the third party in an illicit relationship.[60] The personal strain was evident, and less than two weeks later, on 5 September
1950, Donald suffered another heart attack. But eventually these obsta-
cles were overcome, and Donald's divorce was granted on 11 December 1951.

A couple of weeks later, on 28 December 1951, Donald and Clare were married. Perhaps because of Donald's divorced status, a formal church wedding was not conducted, but the day began with a small ceremony at a Baptist Church in South London, led by the Baptist minister who had assumed Clare's father's ministry in Southend-on-Sea many years before. Karl Britton described this ceremony as "quite like a marriage" and reported that Clare's mother, Aunt Jess, and her brother Jimmy were also in attendance. Karl thought Clare "looked splendid in her grey velvet suit".[61]

The family all returned for tea at Donald's home on Chester Square, where they were joined by Clare's sister Elizabeth, her friend, Gwen Smith, Joyce Coles (Donald's secretary), and a colleague of Donald's.[62] Gwen Smith recalled Clare greeting the waiting guests with the remark that "I made him promise to live to be one hundred".[63]

Later that day, Clare and Donald, accompanied by Jimmy and Karl, went to the Registry Office for a civil wedding ceremony.[64] After this, the gathering at Donald's home continued, and they were joined by a cousin of Donald's, Jimmy's wife, and Clare's childhood friend, Nora Calton.

By Clare's eloquent account (chapter 13 herein) and the reports of others, the marriage was a fulfilling and loving partnership. In contrast to their small wedding, "Clare-and-Donald" (as so often identified by many friends and colleagues) quickly widened their social involvements once they were married with relationships with social workers, psychoanalysts, and physicians from across Britain and throughout the world. They frequently entertained in their home, and their parties were enjoyed by a wide circle of acquaintances. On one occasion, when Donald was President of the BPS, they engaged a folk singer and guitarist to entertain their analytic colleagues, who were seated on the floor of the Society's offices. As Pearl King recalled, "it had not been done before, nor has it been done since".[66]

With such activities, Clare and Donald shared with others the sense of play that pervaded their relationship. Reflecting the opinions of many others, Jimmy Britton, Clare's brother, found them "delightful company because they never lost their sense of play".[67] As Clare recalled their relationship, they had:

> never set out to play, there was nothing self-conscious and deliberate about it. . . . We played with things—our possessions—rearranging, acquiring, and discarding according to our mood. We played with ideas, tossing them about at random with the freedom of knowing

that we need not agree, and that we were strong enough not to be hurt by each other. . . . We each possessed a capacity for enjoyment, and it could take over in the most unlikely places and lead us into exploits we could not have anticipated. After Donald's death, an American friend described us as "two crazy people who delighted each other and delighted their friends". [chapter 13 herein]

The radiance of Clare and Donald's relationship was also described by Serge Lebovici, a French psychoanalyst: "At a conference in Rome, I was particularly struck by how much he seemed to be in love with his wife; what she told me did not seem in any way exaggerated, when she spoke of the way he danced with her at conference receptions" (Clancier, 1984, p. 134).

Similarly, Clare recalled how Donald, early in their relationship, had surreptitiously bought a whole pushcart of peonies early one morning and arranged them throughout Clare's living area, for her to discover when she came downstairs for breakfast.[68]

Beyond this romantic aspect, Clare was consciously aware of the importance of providing a "holding environment" for her peripatetic husband. She told a colleague how essential it was that she serve dinner each evening at seven o'clock.[69]

While Clare's glowing account of her marriage is supported by the recollections of many friends and relatives, the couple also experienced some marital tensions. Donald had numerous professional interests and was reluctant to refuse requests for professional involvement. Although Clare supported his professional activities, she also had to struggle for private time when she could be with Donald alone. In 1950, for example, Donald began meeting weekly on Sunday mornings with Masud Khan to edit his written work. Clare resented this intrusion into her only free day with Donald and would insist that they end their activity at noon.[70] In his later years, Donald would often spend his Saturday afternoons chatting with Harry Karnac in his bookshop; Clare would often ring the store to retrieve her husband.[71]

But, as Pearl King noted, Clare and Donald "didn't have to agree . . . and they couldn't hurt each other. The mutual trust between them was something quite fantastic".[72]

Clare also regretted their childless marriage.[73] Although their ages at the time of marriage may have precluded this (Clare was 45), both were keenly aware of adoption resources. For example, soon after their marriage, Donald published a paper entitled "Two Adoptive Children" in a social work journal (D. W. Winnicott, 1954). Years later, in

1973, Clare attended a conference on adoption. After hearing a talk by her former student, Norma (Duncan) Campbell, on childless couples, she approached Ms Campbell to discuss her research at greater length. Recently widowed, Clare seemed to be struggling with her decision many years earlier to remain childless; she seemed to find reassurance in Campbell's observations that childless couples often seemed to have more fulfilling marital relationships than do those with children.[74]

However, both Clare and Donald enjoyed considerable satisfaction from their involvement with Clare's five nieces and nephews. They visited frequently with these young relatives and assisted several in significant ways during periods of personal difficulty.[75]

Psychoanalytic training

Clare's involvement with psychoanalysis evolved over a period of thirty years. Her exposure to psychoanalytic theory in her social work training was cursory, and she expressed no interest in pursuing analytic training or practice on graduating from the LSE in 1941. Undoubtedly, her collaboration with Donald in Oxfordshire greatly enhanced her interest in psychoanalysis, and her 1943 letter to Donald and 1945 paper on play (chapters 15 and 3, respectively, herein) provide clear evidence of her emerging familiarity with object relations theory.

In 1949, Clare began a psychoanalysis with W. Clifford M. Scott, Melanie Klein's first British training analysand. Strangely, Scott was also the analyst of Alice Winnicott, Donald's first wife (Kahr, 1996), and he briefly analysed Winnicott as well, most probably at around the same time as Clare's entry into analysis.[76] But there is no evidence, one way or the other, regarding Clare's awareness of these analyses. Clare was impressed by Klein's 1940 paper, "Mourning and its Relationship to Manic-Depressive States", as mentioned earlier, and she wanted a Kleinian analysis (Grosskurth, 1986). However, she was disappointed in this experience and told Scott that "you're supposed to be a Kleinian—give me a Kleinian interpretation of [my dreams]" (ibid., p. 451). She told Grosskurth she was sick of "wishy-washy analysts and wanted someone like the voice in the Mourning paper".[77]

As Scott prepared to move to Canada in 1954, Clare sought an analysis with Melanie Klein herself. She told Donald of her interest in an analysis with Klein, indicating to him that "I think she's tough enough for me" (ibid., p. 451). Donald may also have reminded Klein that he had analysed her son at her request.

In a letter dated 14 January 1954, Klein wrote rejecting Donald's suggestion that they continue their professional dialogue:

Dear Donald: I am glad that you feel our talk was useful but I don't think that to see you from time to time is advisable for it would disturb your wife's analysis.

I am very concerned to keep her analysis as free from external disturbances as possible—and as we know, this is not at all easy in the circumstances.

I am sure you will agree with me on this point and understand that it is as only for that reason that I would rather not meet you frequently nor correspond.

Of course as far as work is concerned we need not agree about everything and as you say no one has a monopoly of the truth.

With kind regards

Yours

Melanie

[Rodman, 2003, pp. 257–258][78]

Although Clare did acknowledge Klein's "fantastic memory for detail" and her "feeling of strength behind you", she was greatly troubled by many aspects of Klein's technique, including Klein's lack of personal civility, her disregard of environmental influences, her impersonal interpretive style, and her insistence on focusing on only the negative aspects of the transference (ibid., pp. 451–452).

Clare told Grosskurth that she was very dismayed when she returned to analysis from a life-threatening bout of meningitis in 1956. Reflecting on the helpful nurses in the hospital, Clare told Klein that she had "enabled [her] to trust other people". Clare was annoyed when Klein dismissed her comment, suggesting that "this is simply a cover-up for your fear of death" (ibid., p. 452).

In contrast, in her tribute to Dr Lois Munro, her third analyst, Clare recalled meeting her at a garden party in the summer of 1956 at one of her first social occasions after her illness:

Many people spoke to me at the garden party . . . but Dr Munro communicated on a different level. She seemed to emerge from the general background and to metaphorically hold out a hand and pull me into the party and into the present. She spoke in a straightforward way about illness, my illness, about life as a patient in hospital, and the dependence that serious illness imposes. She also spoke about how it feels to be back in the world again where time and conventions operate, after being at the back of beyond where there is no time and nothing matters but the next breath. These were her words, and the impact was immediate. . . . Her reaching out to me at the party . . .

taught me an important lesson: that people who have been through an intense personal experience absolutely need to have this fact acknowledged—naturally and explicitly—if social relationships are to be re-established and maintained in any way this is meaningful. The incident showed Dr Munro's warmth and humanity, and her courageous lack of fear at the human predicament. [chapter 16 herein]

This comparison between Klein's and Munro's response to Clare's traumatic illness suggests that by 1956 Clare was consciously aware of her dissatisfaction with Klein. Yet, her aforementioned comment to Klein suggests that she experienced some benefit from the early years of her analysis.

At around the same time, in the autumn of 1956, Clare began psychoanalytic training at the Institute of Psycho-Analysis as she took a year's leave of absence from her teaching duties. According to Peter Hildebrand, a fellow trainee at the Institute, Clare seemed "rather shy for a woman of such distinction and spoke very little in the seminars and lectures". Hildebrand reported that their large training group was a "rumbustious lot", mostly men around age 30 beginning careers. Clare, of course, was 50 years old at the time she began training. Hildebrand sometimes helped to drive Clare home. After an Institute seminar with Melanie Klein, Clare told him "how struck she was by [Klein's] strength and clarity".[79]

Clare's involvement in her Institute course-work was dramatically different from her participation in any other group activity in her career. Normally an assertive leader, she seemed reluctant to become engaged in the lively dialogues that characterized the training experience.[80] Donald had just been elected to a term as President of the BPS, and she certainly was aware of the tensions between the various factions. It also seems likely that she consciously suppressed her ambivalence about Kleinian theory and Melanie Klein herself.

Clare's *curriculum vitae* for the BPS identified Hanna Segal and Herbert Rosenfeld, two leading Kleinians, as her clinical supervisors. However, Segal reported that Clare's first supervisor had been Michael Balint, who allegedly discouraged Clare from seeking supervision with Segal. According to Segal, Balint had told Clare that if she went to Segal, she would "only tell you every day what to do". Like Hildebrand, Segal reports that Clare never challenged Kleinian theory and allowed Segal to supervise her training case with a classical Kleinian approach.[81]

Yet, at the same time, Clare was having considerable difficulty with both Melanie Klein herself and with aspects of her theory. In her lectures at LSE in 1957, Clare presented a wide range of psychoanalytic perspectives, including drive theory, ego psychology, classical Kleinian theory, and, of course, her husband's ideas.[82]

However, her interest in psychoanalytic theory was not an uncritical eclecticism. In March 1959, Clare gave a paper at a conference on social work education entitled "The Development of Insight" (chapter 11 herein). This presentation was Clare's only paper that includes citations from the psychoanalytic literature. It refers to three analysts outside the Kleinian group: Marjorie Brierley, Ernst Kris, and Anna Freud. She cites Brierley to emphasize the importance of focusing on "objective knowledge" as well as "subjective experience". In a discussion of identification in the learning process, Clare then refers to Kris's ideas about how primitive merger phantasies sometimes underlie "over-identification" with a supervisor or teacher (chapter 11 herein). Finally, she refers to Anna Freud's concept of identification with the aggressor, commenting: "If in the pattern of the individual, fear and not love underlies the process of identification, then for that person identification has ceased to be a vehicle of insight, chiefly because the personality of the individual tends to be subservient to that of the person identified with."

Each citation seems directly aimed at important aspects of Kleinian thinking or practice; in the context of a commentary about social work education, each can also be viewed as a scholarly critique of the interpersonal dynamics of the Kleinian group.[83]

While Clare could comfortably articulate her disagreement with Kleinian orthodoxy in the social work domain, her actual analytic experience was, in Grosskurth's (1986) words, "an extraordinary battle of wills" (p. 451). Clare reported that Donald could not envision a successful completion of the analysis, commenting that "[I] never can see the end of your analysis with Melanie"[84]; "you'll kill Melanie or she'll kill you" (p. 451). Clare felt that she would not be allowed to finish analysis until she had become a Kleinian.[85]

Although she had great respect for Klein's theories—commenting that she used "her ideas all the time—my way" (p. 452)—Clare had considerable difficulty with Klein's clinical technique. She was troubled by Klein's impersonalness: Klein never greeted her or said goodbye. Klein's disregard of environmental factors was also difficult for Clare to accept: on one occasion, Klein told her, "it's no good your talking about your mother. We can't do anything about it now" (p. 451).[86]

Clare also believed that Klein obsessively focused on the negative elements in the transference, discounting expressions of love and reparation: "positive acts were interpreted as a disguise for hate" (Grosskurth, 1986, p. 452). However, she told Grosskurth of one incident when she believed she had actually affected Klein:

> One day, on entering the room, she was startled by a vase of beautiful red and white tulips. She remarked that it must be Mrs. Klein's birthday, and went on to say that they symbolized the fusion of love and hate. "I shall send red and white flowers like that when you die." Klein did not reply—a period of uncharacteristic silence—and Mrs. Winnicott felt that she was deeply moved. "I shall never forget those tulips—never!!!" [ibid., p. 452]

More often, though, the analysis was filled with tension and conflict. In an episode that she shared with a number of friends and colleagues, Clare actually stormed out of Klein's office and broke off the analysis. Grosskurth (1986) reports this incident as follows:

> a year before Mrs. Klein's death, Clare Winnicott brought her a "thoroughly Kleinian dream." "Mrs. Klein will be very pleased with this dream," she remembered thinking at the time. Klein then proceeded to analyze it; and her irritated patient timed the interpretation by her watch: twenty-five minutes. Furiously, Mrs. Winnicott exclaimed, "How dare you take my dream and serve it up to me?" and slammed out of the room. Winnicott tried to mediate. He went to see Klein, who told him, "She's too aggressive to analyze." On his return, he advised his wife, "If you give it up, she'll never let you qualify." After a week Clare Winnicott returned, still truculent: "I have come back on your terms, Mrs. Klein, not on mine. [ibid., p. 452]

Marion Milner recalled Clare's comments slightly differently. In her version, after Klein's long-winded interpretation, Clare "sat up and said 'look, that's my dream. I won't have you put all your ideas all over it'. And walked out. Donald made up the breach, and she went back in order to finish her training."[87]

In the spring of 1960, Mrs Klein's health deteriorated dramatically and she died on 22 September 1960; just weeks before her death she told colleagues to inform the BPS that Clare was now qualified as an analyst (Grosskurth, 1986).

Clare remained critical of Klein's analytic technique for the rest of her life and had little use for the Kleinian group in the BPS. In a 1980 letter to a social work colleague that accompanied a book of poetry, she remarked that "these poems add something for me about relationships and loving. Some of them that is. What a pity he [the poet] had a bad psycho-analyst. Must have been a Kleinian!"[88]

Looking back on this difficult analysis, the complexity of Donald's relationship with Melanie Klein and the Kleinian group probably exacerbated the strain of this experience. Donald had been supervised by Klein in child analysis from 1935 to 1941. Rejecting Donald's wish to pursue an analysis with her, Klein instead referred her young adult son, Eric, to him for analytic treatment during this period. Klein had wanted Donald to analyse Eric under her supervision, but he refused this request.[89]

Donald greatly admired—and even idealized—Klein, but he was quite disheartened by her unwillingness to acknowledge his theoretical contributions. His letters include many attempts to establish a dialogue with Klein and her followers, but there is little evidence that he ever succeeded in this effort (Kahr, 1996; Rodman, 2003). Although Klein's aforementioned letter to Donald recommended ending their collegial relationship while Clare was in analysis, Donald wrote her a rather casual note in March 1957—addressing her as "Melanie"— about a paper Hanna Segal—Clare's supervisor—had read at an analytic meeting (Rodman, 1989, p. 114).

Hanna Segal reported that Klein told her that she (Klein) "was very careful not to argue with Winnicott publicly so as not to upset her patient".[90] Yet, this very unresponsiveness seemed evoke ongoing efforts by Winnicott to communicate with Klein and her followers. For example, early in 1954, perhaps in the first months of Clare's analysis with Klein, Donald wrote three letters to W. Clifford Scott, Clare's first analyst (Rodman, 1989). Later, in October 1958, Donald sent a casual note to Herbert Rosenfeld, Clare's second Kleinian supervisor (ibid., 1987). Finally, he accepted Kay McDougall's solicitation to review Klein's book "Envy and Gratitude" in a 1959 issue of *Case Conference*, a social work journal.[91]

Clare herself recalled that Donald sometimes asked her about Klein's analytic approach: "'Does she ever mention sex?' 'No.' 'Did she ever mention the Oedipus complex?' 'No.' [Clare] recalled him then asserting, 'That is because she knows nothing about it!'" (Grosskurth, 1986, p. 453).

Why, then, did Clare pursue analytic treatment with Klein? Grosskurth (1986) speculated that "it is not hard to entertain the conjecture that both Winnicott and Klein, for conscious and unconscious motives, were using her as a stalking horse" for their own professional disputes

(p. 453). Ms A, one of Clare's first analysands when she began her analytic practice in 1972, recalls her suggesting (perhaps in a post-analytic conversation) that she was uncertain about pursuing an analysis with Klein but was urged to do so by Donald.[92] Yet the notion of Clare as Donald's and Klein's pawn seems quite out of character for this assertive woman.

Hanna Segal, Clare's supervisor and Klein's leading disciple, shared a different perspective, definitively stating that Clare was a "severely depressed" person who had suffered a "depressive break-down" on Scott's departure from England, and "that is when Donald approached Mrs Klein". Worried about his wife, he prevailed on Klein to accept her as a patient, telling her that "you never took me into analysis; do one thing for me—take Clare".[93]

However, there is no indication from any other source that Clare suffered from such a psychiatric illness. Also, Donald's correspondence suggests that Scott remained in England through at least April 1954, several months after her analysis with Klein is likely to have begun. On the other hand, Segal's view may be an accurate reflection of Klein's perception of Clare as a deeply disturbed woman; perhaps Klein could understand disagreement with her views only as an expression of psychopathology.

Reflecting her ignorance of Clare's distinguished social work career, Segal also viewed Clare as a Kleinian analyst who avoided beginning a psychoanalytic practice after she qualified in 1961 because she wanted to avoid conflict with Donald. She suggested that "after Donald died, [Clare] had less conflict about it and went into analysis with another Kleinian, Lois Munro".[94]

Marion Milner, one of Donald's supervisees and a friend of both Clare and Donald, directly asked Clare—whom she viewed as "bitterly anti-Melanie Klein"—"Why did Donald send you to Melanie?" Clare responded by stating: "Oh, he didn't send me, I went."[95] Similarly, Ms E, one of Clare's last analysands, recalls her remarking that she "shouldn't have gone into analysis with Klein; I shouldn't have done this to Donald". Clare added that she'd "heard all about this person and wanted to see for myself".[96]

These comments more probably reflect the essence of Clare's decision to begin an analysis with Klein—that Clare simply saw this as an opportunity to explore her psyche in the company of one of the world's leading psychoanalysts. At the same time, the transferential implications of Clare's choice of analyst are difficult to overlook; Clare must have had enough information about Klein to appreciate, at least unconsciously, how Klein's charisma, dogmatism, and wish for her followers' submission mirrored similar qualities in her father.

Government service

Although Clare completed her analytic training in 1960 and was teaching only part-time on the Applied Social Studies Course at the LSE, she did not pursue an analytic practice at that time. However, she did continue her national leadership in the child care field. In September 1963, she gave an invitational address at the Annual Conference of the Association of Children's Officers, where she addressed the desperate shortage of trained workers in child care. Years later, Clare recalled this meeting:

> [The Children's Officers] were all complaining to me: "Where are your students? You train them and we never see them in our local authorities.... We never get a trained student, a trained worker." And I really took that as a challenge and did go into it quite a lot with my past students. A lot of them couldn't stand it because there was no good supervision, no supervision at all really except on administrative procedure.
>
> So they got stuck with frightfully difficult cases which they couldn't solve and they left the authority. They moved on. They moved round and round and round the country two years here, two years there. Nobody stayed. I really think they moved because they couldn't get any further with their cases unless somebody could help them. There was no one to help them.
>
> And I feel that in that conference, I planted the seed for Training Officers. I mean that to me was the most important speech I ever did. I really planted the seed. I wasn't in the Home Office then, I was still at LSE and I was able to say, "Why do you local authorities keep on expecting the Home Office to turn out workers for you all? Why don't you set about training your own staff? ... that training you can provide in the local authority is the other side of the training we do in the universities. If [the child care workers] are not going to get support when they get out there, they're going to leave."[97]

Beti Jones, the President of the Association of Children's Officers in 1963, recalls the dramatic impact of her talk.[98] Aware that Sybil Clement Brown, the Director of Child Care Studies in the Children's Department of the Home Office (and the Director of the LSE's Mental Health Course when Clare was a student), was due to retire, Ms Jones at-

tempted to persuade Clare to seek this position. While this appointment would allow her to influence the training of child care workers
across the nation, Clare was reluctant to trade the relative freedom of
academic life for the yoke of government service.

However, in 1964 Clare accepted an appointment as Director of
Child Care Studies at the Home Office. In this position, she was able to
organize the nation's efforts to train child care workers on all levels.
These staff included relatively uneducated residential staff, professionally trained caseworkers, and managers and administrators of social
agencies.

This appointment was a dramatic departure from Clare's earlier
work. In leading the Child Care Course, she had been responsible for
only one full-time faculty member, a handful of part-time lecturers,
and perhaps a dozen students. At the Home Office, she managed a
much larger group of subordinates and a substantial budget. And, in
doing so, she directly influenced the training of thousands of child care
workers.

Coordinating the activities of the government, universities, local
authorities and professional organizations—especially the Association
of Child Care Officers (ACCO), the Association of Children's Officers
(ACO), and the Residential Child Care Association (RCCA)—during
her seven-year tenure, Clare dramatically increased the number of
trained workers. For example, in 1964, 174 students in Britain completed training for work as child care officers; by 1971, this number had
grown to 805 (Younghusband, 1978).

Much of this expansion occurred through new university programmes, but even more came through new training opportunities for
already employed child care officers and residential staff. Many of
these workers had no college background, and some courses had to
teach basic skills in reading and writing. Initially, Clare's department
tried to provide part-time training opportunities, but it was difficult to
coordinate a combination of ongoing employment and training for
large numbers of students.

Consequently, in 1968 Clare and the Central Training Council initiated an "emergency" two-year training course for child care workers
who lacked professional backgrounds. First conducted at North West-
ern Polytechnic in London, this two-year course offered a fully funded
twelve-month residential course, which combined academic study in
sociology, human growth and development, social policy, and social
work methods with role plays, tutorials, and supervised fieldwork. In

the second year, students returned to their sponsoring agencies, where they resumed employment with additional supervision and group discussions with the course's tutors. Over 1,900 workers applied for the first course, and 108 were accepted. Similar programmes were started in two other locations, and by 1971 the three courses were training 175 students annually (Younghusband, 1978).

Daphne Statham, a director of one of the emergency courses, recalled how Clare:

> brought in people from a different class background. Some were women who had brought up children, some were people who were changing occupations having been teachers, nurses, in the forces, some had been unemployed and in poverty. They were different from the young graduates. On the courses, they had two years to concentrate on child care and families and they left with the makings of competent child care officers. How different from today when child care gets taught in a few weeks. The important thing is that most of them tended to last at the job [Holman, 2001, p. 115]

Clare's colleagues at the Home Office recalled how she accomplished this with "such enthusiasm and excitement"; how "somehow the traditions of the Home Office gave way to permit this creativity"[99] George Thomas, one of the Training Officers in Clare's department, noted that Clare: "had such generosity of mind and spirit, constantly sharing her knowledge and wisdom—drawing out our potential. Her ability to unlock and unblock people enabled growth to take place. This was infectious."[100]

At the Home Office, Clare's informal national leadership in child care was transformed into a more formal role, and her writings more often addressed matters of policy than of practice. The position, though, was a draining one, and Donald was less than enthusiastic about her increased hours and travel. He did not like living alone and would invite friends to stay at their home while Clare was away.[101]

Near the end of her tenure in this position, Clare wrote:

> Since 1965 my own way of life has changed considerably. Work in a government department is very different from anything else I have known. It is always stimulating to find oneself in a totally new and unknown situation, and I shall never regret my move to the Home Office in 1964, because the experience has stretched me to the utmost, and often painfully. Put in a nutshell, I have had to live in a wider context, and to widen the area of my own identifications to include functions that belong to government, and to appreciate all that these functions stand for to me, and to other people. This may

sound grandiose, but in practice it affects everything one does and is, at any given moment. One has to be in touch with a total situation, which includes many levels of operation, and many points of view, but somehow the totality must be encompassed if there is to be any movement at all. At the same time it is necessary to retain smaller areas of urgent interest, because these are the growing points which enable the whole to remain dynamic [C. Winnicott, 1970b, pp. 503–504]

Even while working within a government bureaucracy, Clare maintained an awareness of the psychological dynamics that affected the social field.

Change and loss

The winds of consolidation in social work that swept through the LSE in the 1950s continued to affect Clare's professional career. In 1970, five British social work organizations, including the Association of Child Care Officers, joined together to form the British Association of Social Workers. In her toast at the last meeting of ACCO in 1969, she said that "it will be difficult on this occasion not to turn my remarks into an obituary notice, but I shall try to avoid doing so" (C. Winnicott., 1970b, p. 74). After noting the achievements of ACCO—an organization in which she and Donald were honoured members—she again struggled with her grief:

And now A.C.C.O. is to come to an end. Is it sad that this is so? Of course, the end of something which has played so vital a part in the lives of so many is inevitably a cause for sadness. An understanding develops between a group of people who work together, and loyalties are built up, and at first these will be missed. However, the end of A.C.C.O. not only marks the beginning of a new era of professional growth, but is evidence of growth toward a wider loyalty to the whole social work profession. [p. 76]

She concluded her toast by commenting that:

The attempt to achieve a unified social work profession has naturally led to a tendency to stress similarities between one kind of social work and another, but against a background of professional unity one of the interesting and important things to do will be to distinguish between different kinds of social problems and different kinds of treatment methods. In my opinion, there are immense differences between work with clients in one kind of situation and another, and immense differences in social workers, which attract them to certain kinds of work and not to others. These differences are interesting and challenging, and open up new areas for exploration and study, once professional unity has been achieved. [p. 78][102]

Certainly, Clare's grief about these organizational changes emerges more clearly than does her enthusiasm for a unified profession. Although she bravely welcomed the new organization, she never became active in its activities, and the personal approach to child care work that she and Donald advocated never found expression in the larger group.

As these organizational changes were occurring within the social work profession, similar integrative forces were pushing for consolidation with the government's social welfare bureaucracy. The Seebohm Committee, an important governmental initiative, issued a 1968 report that called for the integration of the separate local authority Welfare, Children's, and Mental Health Departments into unified Departments of Social Services. Central government responsibility for these Departments was to be exercised by a newly formed Department of Health and Social Security (DHSS). Implementation of these changes took place in 1971 and 1972. One consequence of this reorganization was that the Central Training Council in Child Care, which Clare led, was consolidated into a larger Central Council for Education and Training in Social Work (CCETSW) (Younghusband, 1978).

Meanwhile, as these changes in Clare's professional milieu were brewing, Donald's health was deteriorating. After his initial heart attack in 1949, his health had been fragile, and his heart disease progressed. In November 1968, on a professional trip to New York, he contracted the Hong Kong flu, developed pulmonary oedema and pneumonia, and perhaps had yet another heart attack. He was hospitalized for over five weeks, and there was considerable concern about his survival (Rodman, 2003). Clare remained with him in New York during his hospital stay until his return to England, accompanied by two nurses.

Although he returned to work after several months, Donald's health continued to deteriorate, and he suffered frequent pain from angina. He was well aware of his mortality and spoke of it often with friends and colleagues (Kahr, 1996; Rodman, 2003). Clare attempted to help Donald conserve his strength and maintain some limits on his activities, insisting on a regular 7 P.M. dinner-time each evening.[103] As Milner (1985) recalled, "it has been said that it was only through [Clare] that [Donald] survived the constant over-spending of himself as long as he did" (p. 4).

Meanwhile, on 1 January 1971, just months before her position at the Home Office was abolished, Clare was honoured for her contributions in child care and was awarded the Order of the British Empire (OBE) at Buckingham Palace. Several weeks later, at around 4 A.M. on 22 January 1971, Donald suffered a fatal heart attack in their Chester Square home. Brett Kahr describes their last evening:

> Winnicott spent his last evening alive with his beloved wife, Clare, watching a comic film on television about old cars, entitled "Good Old Summertime". . . . When the film ended, Winnicott murmured to Clare, "What a happy-making film!" In all likelihood, these were the last words that Winnicott spoke to his wife. Clare then fell asleep, and when she awoke she found her husband dead, seated (next to her) on the floor, with his head snuggled on his armchair. [Kahr, 1996, pp. 128–129]

Although Clare had expressed her concerns about Donald's mortality on her wedding day in 1951, she was personally devastated by his death. He was cremated four days later, on 29 January 1971, and a memorial service was held, which attracted many friends and colleagues; after the service, a more intimate group returned with Clare to her home. Letters and tributes streamed in from across Britain and around the world.

In a letter to Joan Vann, an early student at the LSE, the week Donald died, Clare poignantly described her initial grieving: "the sympathy and love of friends *holds* me, in my grief, and this means a lot, so that in the end it may even be tolerable—but this I do not know yet—but I am conscious of being 'held'" (emphases in original[104]).

Over the next year, other commemorative meetings of Donald's death were held at the National Association for Mental Health and the British Psychoanalytical Society. Yet, although Donald was a very public figure, Clare's grief was deeply personal and private. This process was complicated by her retirement from the Home Office several months later; as Clare wrote: "In the short space of six months I had lost my husband and my work. Immediately after Donald's death I had to take a leadership role in the dissolution of the work and the working unit I had built up over a number of years in the Children's Department of the Home Office" (chapter 16 herein).

Admittedly depressed, she re-entered psychoanalysis in September 1971 with Lois Munro, a respected psychoanalyst who has been characterized by some as an "independent" and by others as a "very open-minded Kleinian".[105] Clare found this treatment very helpful, "of necessity specifically concerned with the whole process of mourning".

In contrast with Mrs Klein, her previous analyst, Dr Munro spoke infrequently, but, as Clare noted:

> whether she spoke or was silent she was always a presence, and it was her strength that was experienced and was so much needed in order that new areas of pain could be released, and she had a sure touch in locating pain.
>
> I am very fortunate that the process of mourning had come full circle some months before Dr Munro's death [in December 1973]. We both recognised that the essential task was completed because life and death had become a totality—a timeless experience which goes on existing, and which includes all lives, all deaths. [chapter 16 herein][106]

Yet, even with this analytic treatment, her niece Alison Britton recalls that Clare reported shedding her first tears about Donald's passing in 1974 or 1975; during that period, Alison, then a young woman in her twenties, had moved in with Clare, and they spent many evenings reminiscing about Donald.[107]

In the aftermath of these losses, Clare assumed a new position as Head of the Social Work Department at the London School of Economics. Kay McDougall, her former colleague, had retired, and the Mental Health and Applied Social Studies programmes had recently been fully integrated. Zofia Butrym had been the Acting Head, but a permanent appointment was sought. Clare seemed to view this appointment as a sort of homecoming, returning to an institution where she had spent many productive years. Although she continued to grieve for Donald and acknowledged her depression to both students and faculty, she thought that leading this relatively small academic programme would be a manageable assignment.[108]

Sadly, Clare, perhaps for the first time in her career, was unprepared for what quickly became an overwhelming challenge. "The sixties" were in full bloom: instead of finding a group of admiring students with whom she could enjoy personal contact, she found a rebellious student body that perhaps viewed her as an aging member of the "establishment".

Meanwhile, the faculty was in deep disarray. Traditionally a bastion of psychodynamic casework practice, the department had recently hired George Goetschius, an American expert in community development, who had started a small programme in that field. For both personal and ideological reasons, a huge schism developed within the programme, and Clare was unable to mediate these viewpoints. One of Goetschius' students, the student representative to faculty meetings, viewed her as "bullying" and recalls "extremely unpleasant memories of her both as an academic and as a person".[109]

However, Robin Hughes, a fellow student in the community development option described the situation in more balanced terms:

> the driving ideology of community development (client empowerment, collective action and anti-poverty) sat very uncomfortably with the course ethos, which was that of traditional social work with a strong psychodynamic theoretical base. . . . What they thought they were doing importing someone like George Goetschius I cannot imagine. It was oil and water from the outset . . . [also] there was in any case a general volatility within the student group and many mainstream students felt that the course needed to change. . . .
>
> Looking back, the conflict at LSE was really a microcosm of the wider debate around social work at the time. Social work was, it was argued, about rights and resources that would enable powerless people to gain control over their lives. Housing, employment and welfare rights were more important than psychological adjustment. Remember also that this was not long after the great student revolt at LSE; there had been serious street disturbances [across the nation]. . . . At the same time, the validity of Freudian theories was beginning to be seriously challenged. . . . It was a time of antiprofessionalism. . . . "Professionals" as oppressors were part of the problem not part of the solution. It all seems a long time ago, but I can see that the traditionalists among LSE staff, holding to a narrow definition of social work as a psychodynamic therapeutic process, must have been totally bewildered by the maelstrom around them. . . . In the end, of course, they lost and the term "social worker" became in the U.K. a functional job title rather than a profession and runs the risk of disappearing altogether. . . .
>
> . . . where Clare Winnicott fitted in to all this I have difficulty in saying. It was apparent that she was very unhappy and it was, of course, not long after her husband's death. She certainly spoke of continuing to grieve. From my perspective, she appeared ineffectual as a manager and at responding to pressure for change . . . and was unable to channel the ferment of ideas and idealism in positive directions. Nor did she appear able to control the more authoritarian members of staff whose resistance to change and attempts at repression provoked only damaging confrontation."[110]

Another student with psychoanalytic interests outlined a similar picture:

> Her husband was not long dead, and I think in the eyes of many he was the "name", and she was the "poor widow". Her own background, if I remember well, was children in care. . . . I have clear

memories of her "interest" being a bore to a lot of people—that this
fed much of the dissatisfaction with her leadership. [Among the
competing ideologies, child care] had low priority for a lot of people,
and she "wasn't taken seriously". . . . I forget whom she followed as
Coordinator . . . whoever it was, was a "hard act to follow", and
Clare was never a very charismatic leader.

. . . there had been a tradition in social work that the word of the
supervisor/tutor was holy writ. Maybe, after the turbulent 60s;
maybe because of changes in social work practice . . . or the development of local authority work . . . for all these reasons. . . . Clare found
it hard to be a friend to her students; to come off some imagined
pedestal maybe? . . . I have to confess that I was never close to her . . .
and I remember trying in some way.[111]

The experience of Clare by these students certainly seems a testament
to both the level of professional conflict and the depth of her grief
reaction; their observations—ineffectual, unpleasant, boring, uncharis-
matic, even pitiful—are in contrast to Clare's behaviour and persona
throughout her career.

Clare found this year trying as well. Angered at being viewed as a
reactionary, she reported telling her rebellious students: "Don't talk to
me about changing the system. You don't change the system by over-
throwing it. You can change the system from within and it's much
more effective if you do that. And I've taken part in changing the
system".[112]

At the same time, other students were becoming more interested in
practicing psychotherapy than social work. She recalls former students
complaining about the limitations of agency work:

They'd been in their jobs for a year; they were all very hopeless and
said: "We can't do casework. Casework's not possible to do in our
jobs." I remember saying to one of them who was a medical social
worker, "Well come on, why can't you do casework? What's stopping you?" "Well, here I sit with a client in my room and I'm getting
on, we're having an interesting interview, and they keep knocking at
the door." So I said, "What are they knocking on the door for?" "Oh
somebody wants an ambulance or somebody else wants some arrangement made for convalescent home or . . ." I said, "Is that your
job or not?" "Well I suppose it's my job but it means I can't do any
social work." So I said "Isn't this social work?"

Then I remember making the point that some of the most profound things we do to touch the lives of other people are in terms of
the provisions we make for them, not in anything we say. I really

believe that, very strongly. . . . Students were always wanting to do "deep casework". So I said "the deepest casework you'll ever do is making good provision for somebody. That's caring. Basic fundamental caring without which life isn't possible." I feel very strongly about all this."[113]

Clare's inability to contain these diverging foci within social work— the personal and the environmental—may have contributed to her departure from the professional world of social work after this disappointing tenure at the LSE. She contributed to the profession in a few small ways in her last years, writing several commentaries for social work journals (C. Winnicott, 1972a, 1972b) and giving an eloquent paper at a social work conference in 1977 (chapter 9 herein).

In 1974, Clare testified at the governmental inquiry into the death of Maria Colwell, a 7-year-old girl who was beaten to death in 1973 by her stepfather after being returned to her birth mother from a foster home. This case was a national scandal in Britain and focused attention on the child care system and the social work profession (Holman, 2001).

While she actively maintained her friendships with social workers and supported them in their professional endeavours, Clare never again played a significant role in the social work profession. John Sutherland, Medical Director of the Tavistock Clinic and Editor of the *International Journal of Psycho-Analysis*, wrote that he wished: "she had become less involved in analysis and become more of a crusader for [a personal social casework]. Of course, she actually did a great deal, but becoming even a part-time analyst can be misinterpreted as feeling dissatisfied with the less intensive work."[114]

Clare's social work friends and colleagues never viewed her as turning away from social work; her profession remained important to her until her death.[115] However, after first losing her organizational and governmental positions, then Donald's death and the LSE experience, she lost her desire to fight a battle for the soul of a rapidly changing social work profession.

Her friend, the late Baroness Lucy Faithfull, a former Children's Officer in Oxford who became a member of the House of Lords, recalled Clare's despair about British social work in the last weeks before her death. Sadly, Clare felt that her approach to casework was no longer the "Golden Rule" in social services departments and that professional training was no longer valued. Familiar with the overall status of social welfare programmes across Britain, Faithfull could not disagree.[116]

Preserving Donald's legacy

After leaving the LSE, Clare focused on three activities in her last twelve years: editing and disseminating Donald's writings and ideas, conducting a private psychoanalytic practice, and continuing her relationships with a wide array of friends and family.

In his will, Donald essentially bequeathed Clare all of his property. This estate implicitly left Clare as Donald's literary executor, a role she fulfilled until her death (Kahr, 1996). This decision was devastating to M. Masud Khan, an analyst and former patient of Donald's who had been instrumental in editing and publishing Donald's writings since the early 1950s (Cooper, 1993). Literally working with Donald on his papers until the day before he died, Khan had assumed that he would continue to play a central role in editing these voluminous writings after Donald's death.

However, Clare deliberately excluded Khan from this process. As Khan's professional work with Donald's material was highly regarded, it seems likely that this exclusion was primarily personal. Khan reported that she was never hospitable to him:

> I went every Sunday at 7 o'clock to write, would come back at 10. Worked with Winnicott on his manuscripts. That's all Winnicott, is edited by me, since 1950. His wife would ring: "Donald". He said, "yes". We were working in the basement. In fifteen years, she never asked me up for lunch. We used to have a cup of tea downstairs. I would leave."[117]

Pearl King recalls that Clare was insistent that Khan leave their home by Sunday at noon; Clare wanted her private time with Donald.[118] In general, few of Donald's analytic colleagues were personal friends of Clare's, but it is not difficult to imagine that she had a specific antipathy to Khan's narcissism and other problematic characteristics (Cooper, 1993, Hopkins, 1998). Soon after Donald's death, Khan's behaviour began a gradual deterioration into alcoholism and perhaps psychosis; Cooper (1993) suggests that losing his role in the publication of Winnicott's papers was a key precipitant of his psychic demise.[119]

Instead of working with Khan, Clare gathered three colleagues—Madeleine Davis, Robert Tod, and Ray Shepherd—and began an informal "publications committee" to edit Donald's many unpublished papers. Madeleine Davis had been a neighbour and friend of the Winnicotts'; her husband, John Davis, was a paediatrician and had worked with Donald at Paddington Green Hospital. Robert Tod was a social worker who had worked with Clare at the Home Office; he had also edited a volume (Tod, 1968) about child care that included a foreword by Donald and a chapter by Clare (chapter 8, herein). Ray Shepherd was the only psychoanalyst in this group.

Not long after Donald's death, Clare visited Harry Karnac, a seller and publisher of psychoanalytic books, who had been a close friend of Donald's. She asked his opinion on the feasibility of publishing a standard edition of Donald's works. To Clare's dismay, he quickly dismissed this idea, noting that Donald's works were still in print with a variety of publishers who would be unlikely to surrender their publication rights.[120]

The committee met regularly on Saturdays several times each month until Clare's death. Their first project was to publish *The Piggle* (1978), an account of Donald's treatment of a troubled girl; Clare wrote the introduction, and her sister, Elizabeth, contributed a drawing of Donald's consulting-room. Next, they published *Deprivation and Delinquency* (1984), a collection that began with the papers about the evacuation scheme; this collection included an important introductory essay (chapter 3 herein), in which Clare traced the emergence of many of Donald's central ideas to their wartime work in Oxfordshire.

Although published after her death, Clare was also involved in the editing of several other collections of Donald's papers, including *Home is Where We Start From* (1986), *Babies and Their Mothers* (1987), and, to a lesser extent, *Psycho-Analytic Explorations* (1989).

As she neared death, Clare recognized that a more formal institution would be needed to continue the publication of Donald's works. Also, as she and Donald had no direct descendants, Clare wanted to ensure that the royalties from Donald's writings would contribute to the development and dissemination of his ideas. Thus, on 15 March 1984, exactly one month before her death, she signed papers formally establishing "The Winnicott Trust". The stated object of the Trust was to: "advance the education of the public by promoting the training and research in the field of psychoanalysis and child health of Paediatricians, Child Psychologists and other professional persons and more particularly to promote the study of the work of Doctor D. W. Winnicott and to disseminate the results thereof." The Trust Deed appointed a Board of Directors—Stella Ambache, Martin James, and Jonathan Pedder, all psychoanalysts—to administer the Trust: Their main function was to manage the finances of the Trust and to provide: "financial assistance whether by way of grant or periodic payment to assist

Paediatricians, Child Psychiatrists and other professional persons working in the field of child health in the study of psychoanalysis to study the work of Doctor Winnicott."

The Trust Deed also appointed three editors to continue the publication of Donald's writings: Ray Shepherd, Madeleine Davis, and, as Robert Tod had died, Christopher Bollas, a social worker who had become a psychoanalyst. Interestingly, this group was empowered to select other editors when replacements or additional editors were needed; the only requirement was that future editors be psychoanalysts.

In addition to the royalties from Donald's writings, Clare's will, signed on the same date, 15 March 1984, left half of her estate to the Winnicott Trust. The will also left all proceeds from her writings to the Trust. However, the Trust Deed made no mention of her written work, and the Editors had no idea of the extent of Clare's this.[121]

The Trust continues its work to the present day and has published a number of other collections of Donald's work, including *Human Nature* (1988), *Talking to Parents* (1993), *Thinking about Children* (1996), and *Winnicott on the Child* (2002). Much of the Trust's funds have gone to support the work of Dr. Lynne Murray, a child psychologist, and the work of her Winnicott Research Unit at Cambridge University which conducts developmental research on infants and mothers (Jacobs, 1995).

Clare also worked in other ways to disseminate Donald's ideas. She collaborated with Simon Grolnick in publishing a collection of professional papers on transitional objects and phenomena (Grolnick & Barkin, 1978) and contributed an eloquent essay on Donald to that volume (chapter 13 herein). This collaboration with Simon Grolnick, one of Winnicott's leading supporters in the United States (Grolnick, 1990), led to Clare's decision to house Donald's papers and letters with the Archives of Psychiatry at the New York Hospital–Cornell Medical Center in New York City. Although Donald's analytic colleagues were upset that these papers would be crossing the Atlantic, Clare believed that this library would offer the most secure repository. She also allowed F. Robert Rodman, an American psychoanalyst, to have access to Donald's correspondence. He published an edited collection of these letters (Rodman, 1989) and included much of this correspondence in his Winnicott biography (Rodman, 2003).

Clare engaged in other activities to commemorate Donald's name and work. In 1978 she attended the opening of the Donald Winnicott Centre at the Queen Elizabeth Hospital for Children in London, a treatment unit for physically and mentally handicapped children (Kahr, 1996). She also opened the Winnicott House for the Messenger Trust, a home for young single mothers, and bequeathed this project a generous sum.[122]

Sadly, in January 1974 Clare was diagnosed with a melanoma on her foot.[123] It was removed surgically but recurred repeatedly and required over thirty-five operations.[124] Some physicians recommended that her foot be amputated, but Clare adamantly refused to allow this. As the illness progressed, her foot was often bandaged continuously and was raised on a footstool during her analytic sessions. Yet, in the intervals between her operations, Clare continued to live her life as normally as possible, often travelling within Britain and abroad.

Psychoanalytic practice

Not long after leaving the London School of Economics, Clare began a private psychoanalytic practice in her Chester Square home. She did not use Donald's consulting-room, renting that instead to Dr Max Goldberg, a South African analyst affiliated with the Anna Freud Clinic. Her first consulting-room was a large drawing-room, with a piano and bookshelves filled with literature. Only after Goldberg's death in 1976 did she move down into Donald's consulting-room, which had been left essentially as Donald had furnished it, with book-shelves of psychoanalytic books. Clare indicated to an analysand that she had sufficiently resolved her grief, enabling her to work in this room.[125]

Many of Clare's analytic patients were trainees in psychoanalytic psychotherapy. Some were trainees in child psychotherapy at the Tavistock Clinic, and others were in training at the British Association of Psychotherapists (BAP). Martha Harris, a Kleinian who was married to Donald Meltzer, referred several analysands. She was the director of Tavistock's child therapy programme and had been a classmate of Clare's in her analytic training. Another analysand was referred by Enid Balint, a social worker and psychoanalyst who was married to Michael Balint. At least three of these analysands had done graduate training in social work, and a fourth had been working in a social work position. The referral sources often indicated that these common professional backgrounds were a reason for their referral.

At the time of Dr Goldberg's death in early 1976, Clare had a full practice and was turning away patients.[126] In a 1977 paper (chapter 9 herein) she reported that she was seeing twelve patients in analysis or psychoanalytic therapy[127] Early on, Clare also began an affiliation with the British Association of Psychotherapists, a training centre in psychoanalytic psychotherapy. She was a popular supervisor and also taught a class on Donald's work.

Clare also continued an affiliation with the British Psychoanalytical Society, occasionally attending meetings or seminars. She presented her paper "Fear of Breakdown: A Clinical Example" (chapter 17 herein) to this group before giving it at the 1979 New York Congress of the International Psychoanalytic Association.

Over the years, Clare's analytic practice evolved, moving from a more classical Kleinian technique, with a focus on transference interpretation, to a more personal and conversational style. With Ms A, a therapist trainee who entered analysis with Clare in the summer of 1972 and was one of her first patients, Clare's technique was "fairly rigorous" and relied heavily on interpretation. Clare would interpret Ms A's interest in a social life as a defence against a transferential attachment and would carefully examine the Ms A's experience of the analyst when treatment was interrupted because of holidays or illness. As she did with all of her patients, Clare explored childhood trauma and separations, focusing on the client's unhappy experience as a six-year-old at summer camp.[128] Less than two years into this analysis, Clare had her first surgery for melanoma. It was apparent that she was uncomfortable, but this was not addressed in detail.

Ms B, another trainee at the Tavistock who identifies herself as a "Kleinian", viewed Clare as having unique clinical skills. She saw Clare as being able to apply many of the central elements of Kleinian technique without exacerbating persecutory anxieties. In her view, Clare would "hold" Ms B's projections without rushing in with interpretations. When Ms B discussed material from her training programmes with transferential implications, Clare was judicious in her interpretations—allowing this displaced material to remain "out there".

At the beginning of one session, Ms B indicated that she was suffering from a migraine headache. Clare quickly got her some aspirins and a glass of water. When Ms B expressed her anger at Clare for acting in what Ms B viewed as a non-analytic manner, Clare calmly suggested that the distress needed to be relieved before analytic work could proceed.[129]

Mr C began his analysis with Clare around 1975 while pursuing analytic training. He viewed her as a very helpful "therapist" but less useful as an "analyst". In his situation, Clare rarely addressed or interpreted the positive transference. Unlike most of Clare's other patients,

Mr C had a rather unremarkable middle-class upbringing, with no painful traumas, separations, or neglect.[130] With similar patients with relatively intact egos, Clare advised supervisees to quietly allow their patients to mobilize their own resources with a minimum of interpretive intrusions.[131]

Mr C experienced his treatment at times as hardly like an analysis and more like a conversation. He viewed Clare as "extraordinary" in her ordinariness and authenticity. As he had extra-analytic contact with her in a training seminar, he was impressed that there was not one persona as the "analyst" and another as the "teacher"—only one "Clare Winnicott".

Mr C's analysis continued until Clare's death in 1984. He observed her progressive illness and experienced repeated disruptions in the analysis as she would require further treatment. While generally impressed with her energy and robustness, one day Mr C noted that Clare exhibited an unusual pallor. She asked for his associations, then paused and acknowledged that she had just received a call from her oncologist. Although Clare rarely burdened Mr C or other patients with information about her illness, he appreciated her candour and unwillingness to imply that the patient's anxiety was only transferential. However, Mr C acknowledges that his awareness of Clare's illness may have inhibited him from developing and exploring more negative transferential responses.

A fourth analysand in professional training, Ms E began her treatment with Clare in 1981 or 1982. Although Ms E knew that Clare had been ill and saw her bandaged leg, she saw no signs of frailty, only "someone who was extremely alive". Ms E felt that Clare's vitality and spontaneity "in the face of illness" was "one of the most powerful things" she conveyed to her.[132]

Clare's spontaneity and authenticity impressed Ms E from their initial telephone call. When she asked Clare if they should have an initial consultation before beginning analysis, Clare playfully replied "Yes, we might not like each other." Again, like Mr C, Ms E experienced Clare as trying "very much to let me find my way". She felt very "contained" by Clare but also found her more conversational than her earlier patients had done. Her interpretations were evocative, even passionate; in one instance, Clare playfully told Ms D that she'd like to "murder" her superego. On occasion, Clare would quote poetry as a sort of empathic gesture; Ms B also recalled Clare's literary passion.

Clare's sole published analytic paper, "Fear of Breakdown: A Clinical Example" (chapter 17 herein), offers a more complete view of her analytic technique. In her case report of Miss K, a more troubled patient than the aforementioned analysands, Clare responded to the patient's claim of self-sufficiency with the remark that "one thing that you can't do is to *be the other person*" (Clare's emphasis). This interpretive comment reflects Clare's skill at simultaneously being a "real person" while making herself available as a transferential object.

In this case, Clare explored Miss K's actual childhood trauma. When her family photo album revealed painful childhood experiences, Clare worked with Miss K to reconstruct these years against the backdrop of wartime chaos. Inner and outer "reality" could not be addressed separately. For Clare, understanding one "reality" only contributed to understanding the other.

Another area of technique that emerges in this case report was the therapeutic use of transitional objects and phenomena. When Miss K's allowed herself to experience Clare as a transferential mother through an evocative dream, she then became aware of a deep longing for her "Teddy". Miss K then actually went to her parents' home, collected this "much-used, much-battered object", and brought it to her next analytic session. This enabled her to re-experience early positive experiences with her mother.

In addition to her skills as an analyst, Clare was also a talented clinical supervisor. Jill Curtis, one of her first supervisees at the British Association of Psychotherapists, particularly recalls Clare's warmth and supportiveness. She recalls Clare's "lightness of touch": "she would say something, but it would not be a heavy-handed interpretation with a capital I. She would say something that might well sound like a comment, but actually she would have her finger right on it."[133]

Jane Petit, another BAP supervisee, remembered a similar quality. Her training case was a 25-year-old woman whose mother had died when she was around 2 years old. Although the patient was functioning well, she was disturbed by the emerging grief around this early loss. The patient was often very quiet as she re-experienced this grief. Clare's supervision focused on helping Petit "hold" the patient with a minimum of intrusiveness as she completed the mourning process, avoiding the temptation to impress her supervisee with imaginative interpretations.[134]

Curtis also remembered Clare's "tremendous sense of humour". She laughingly told Curtis the story of how she had walked out of her analysis with Klein and how Donald had had to "ring Klein" to take Clare back. Of course, Klein's long-winded interpretation was used as an example of "what not to do in the consulting-room".[135]

Friends and family

Throughout her last years, even though they were marked by a painful illness, Clare's energy and vitality impressed all who knew her. She remained involved with a wide array of friends and relatives, yet she often said how much she missed Donald. For most of her last years, she shared her home with live-in companions.

First, several years after Donald's death, her sister Liz and her niece Alison Britton, then an art student (and later a renowned potter, who, like Clare, was also awarded the Order of the British Empire), moved in with Clare. Liz moved into a basement apartment, while Alison lived in an attic room. As a young person influenced by the "sixties" counterculture, Alison had a very different experience of Clare from the LSE students who rejected her during that same era. She found her approachable, easy to talk to, and young in spirit.[136]

Around 1977, after Alison had moved on, Clare decided to sell the large Chester Square home and move to a more manageable one on Lower Belgrave, just around the corner. Her youngest sibling, Liz, moved with her, but this arrangement was suddenly ended in 1979, when Liz died, having been struck by a car. This was a major blow to Clare, who had been looking forward to her sister's companionship for many years.

Two years later, in 1981, Clare rented a basement flat in her home to Margaret Fosbrook, a young social worker. Like Alison, Fosbrook developed a close friendship with Clare, which continued until the latter's death. Clare would often reminisce with Fosbrook, often about Donald, but about other aspects of her life as well. She also took an interest in Fosbrook's career as a social worker in a community agency. Fosbrook particularly recalls their love of poetry. Clare had eclectic tastes, which included Shakespeare, T. S. Eliot, Rilke, and Dylan Thomas, among others; she could recite many of her favourite poems from memory.[137]

In addition to her relationships with her living companions, Clare remained actively involvement with a wide array of friends, frequently dining out and attending concerts or the theatre in London. She would often travel away from London for weekends in the country, visiting George and Janie Thomas in Brighton, Joan Cooper in Lewes, and Pamela Mann and Juliet Berry in Derbyshire. In 1979 she travelled to the New York to attend the Congress of the International Psychoanalytic Association and deliver a version of her only published analytic paper, "Fear of Breakdown: A Clinical Example" (chapter 17 herein).

In August 1981, Clare travelled to Finland to visit Pati Auterinen, a former LSE student who had married a Finn; she had visited there previously with Donald, who was invited to consult. Her guestbook entry conveys her love of nature and simple pleasures:

> The last day of an unforgettable four days of summer in this lovely house in the Finnish countryside. I shall always remember the tall trees—the changing colour of the sea and the sky—the birds and the flowers. I have also enjoyed the large family room where everything happens at once. Going to bed early and sleeping late. The smell of the sauna and the log fire early and late. Patty's cabbage pie and lovely food always ready just when wanted. The boat rides into the distance giving a new perspective. So much and so much . . . thank you for sharing it all![138]

Her colleague from the Home Office, George Thomas, shared the following recollection about Clare's life in her last years and her friendship with George and his wife, Janie, a former student of Clare's at the LSE:

> The kitchens in Chester Square and later in the Beagle Place were places where much sharing and feeding took place. Clare had always fed people intellectually and emotionally, but food itself was given with care in an atmosphere which enabled one to feel at home with her and with oneself. . . .
>
> [The loss of her sister Liz] tested Clare again—and again, [Clare] was an example of how to manage life and its odds and to overcome them even in the face of the cruellest and most hurtful of blows. In everything, she displayed the kind of courage which most of us can only see after, this courage was amply demonstrated during the many years of her illness which she tackled head on. Like Donald, she was determined to be alive when she died and this was made possible, amongst other things, by her ability to talk about death and of the need to care and be cared for.
>
> Reflecting on friendship with Clare has clarified for me that what was special was its wholeness. Often, one's friends satisfy a particular facet of life—a particular interest or mood. With Clare, all of life was there. One could be serious, discussing deeply professional, social or personal matters, or mutually shared negative and positive feelings—and also be frivolous and enjoy the fun of being together as an end in itself.
>
> This might have meant listening to music or a sing song around the piano, but part of the frivolity was related to Clare's love of clothes—an important source of pleasure to her. She and Janie egged each other along shamelessly in this respect and after shopping

sprees, I would provide a one-man audience for impromptu fashion shows. I think this was another example of Clare's healthy caring for herself which enabled her to care for others. Some of the happy times included visits to Violet, Donald's sister; Clare's unfailing loving response to her and enjoyment of her were examples of mutual caring which one was privileged to share.

Looking back, it's not surprising that friendship with Clare was such a total experience, for she herself was a total person. Apart from the stress and distress at being with her at times of illness and particularly during the bad summer of 1983, there was never a time when we did not feel better for her company. Even at bad times, she gave by seeking and accepting dependency, thus acknowledging reciprocity of friendship."[139]

This eloquent statement mirrors the views of many other friends who knew Clare in her last years. Madeleine Davis, her former neighbour and an editor of Donald's works, recalled the following story from Clare's last days:

The last time we worked together [Clare] was in bed under strict orders . . . she could eat very little . . . [later at] home that evening, I remembered that I had forgotten to ask Clare where to find a certain reference. I rang her number and there was no answer. This I did several times, becoming more and more anxious. Then I obtained a phone number of Margaret Fosbrook [her roomer] with a view toward raising an alarm. I decided to track her once more—at last with success. "Where the devil have you been", I said. A voice that was at once weak and triumphant answered, "I have been to a party; it is such a waste of one's life spending it in bed; isn't it?[140]

Soon after this, on 15 April 1984, Clare died after several months of infirmity. A Cremation Service was held on 25 April 1984 and was attended by a large group of relatives, friends, and colleagues. Some months later, on 3 November 1984, a memorial service was held at the London School of Economics, where a string quartet performed Schubert and reminiscences and poetry were shared by friends, colleagues, and her brother Jimmy. The programme was concluded as Margaret Fosbrook read "East Coker" from T. S. Eliot's "Four Quartets", one of Clare's favourite poems.[141]

The legacy

Undoubtedly, Clare's legacy involves both her profound professional impact on British child care and social work as well as her personal influence on scores of social workers, psychotherapists, and friends. Her teaching at the LSE influenced a generation of leaders in the emergent post-war child care service throughout Britain, and, as noted, she played a seminal role in the founding of the Association of Child Care Officers. Similarly, her testimony to the Curtis Committee, her leadership while at the LSE, and her tenure in the Children's Department of the Home Office had an ongoing impact on British child care policy between 1946 and 1971.

Clare's ideas on working with children seeped into the collective consciousness of social workers across Britain, reminding them to pay attention to the inner world of the child as well as their external circumstances (Holman, 2001). Yet, for several reasons, her contributions to professional practice have been largely forgotten today.

First, Clare expressed herself in direct, plain English, inventing no catchy phrases or memorable jargon. Her teachings and writings have a clarity that can, unfortunately, be dismissed as "common sense". Largely focused on the immediate needs of her students and professional audiences, she never attempted to organize her ideas into any sort of theoretical schema that could be more easily transmitted.

Second, her written work has not been easily available to recent generations of social workers. Her only collection of papers was published by a small press with limited distribution and has been out of print for many years (C. Winnicott, 1964). Similarly, although several of her papers have been republished since her death, her articles were mostly published in obscure social work journals that are largely unobtainable. After she wrote her papers for a professional occasion, Clare appeared uninterested in disseminating them more widely. She took a very different approach towards Donald's ideas, successfully investing much energy to bring his concepts and observations to an international audience.

Third, professional social work in Britain has evolved in a very different direction from Clare's work. Psychoanalytic theory is eschewed in most social work institutions, and social work practice in the public sector has become less personal and increasingly bureaucratic. Also, the professional organizations and journals, governmental departments and training programmes that focused on working with children have largely been subsumed into more generic institutions.

At the same time, social workers interested in more personal involvements with clients have become psychotherapists, both in agency and private practice. Both in Britain and in the United States, the sort of personal "casework" that Clare exemplified has been largely neglected in social work institutions, organizations, and journals.

Sadly, Clare had few colleagues who shared both her social work and psychoanalytic interests. With the exception of Juliet Berry and Pamela Mann, both experienced child care workers who later practiced as psychoanalytic psychotherapists, Clare's friends and colleagues tended to identify themselves either as social workers or as psychotherapists or analysts. Perhaps when she lost Donald, a partner who traversed these professional worlds with her, Clare decided to remain on the analytic side of the professional divide. In doing so, she shared almost none of her ideas from her social work background with even her closest analytic colleagues.[142]

Finally, over time, Clare's public identity became subsumed into Donald's. Among psychotherapists in Britain and elsewhere, Clare is known, if at all, only as Donald's wife and editor. Even at the British Association of Psychotherapists, where she supervised and taught for ten years, few therapists are aware of her extensive writings from her social work career. And even her one analytic paper, "Fear of Breakdown: A Clinical Example" (chapter 17 herein), could be viewed merely as a "clinical example" of Donald's concepts.

Yet, regardless of these impediments, Clare's work and thinking deserves more careful scrutiny for a variety of reasons, including her impact on Donald's conceptualizations, her ideas about communicating with children, and her profound observations about helping relationships of all kind. As Elizabeth Irvine (1966) commented in a review of *Child Care and Social Work* (C. Winnicott, 1964), her writing possesses:

> a kind of luminosity based on the palpable fact that her thinking is always a verbalisation and generalisation of deep and vivid experience, with no trace of any juggling with abstractions. [Irvine, 1966, p. 23]

Irvine went on to describe Clare as:

> one of the rare psychiatric social workers who has become a psychoanalyst without turning her back on social work. Her analytic training has not only enriched her understanding, it has freed her from any trace of envy of the analyst which so often drives the caseworker to injudicious imitation of analytic method. . . . Moreover, the child care service . . . inevitably involves so much responsibility for practical arrangements, for creating and maintaining the child's real envi-

ronment, that she has of necessity concerned herself with the casework process as a total interaction, in which works and deeds form
the warp and woof. [ibid., p. 23]

Clare's writings illuminate six general topics:

1. the ideas of Donald Winnicott;
2. understanding the intrapsychic experiences of children;
3. techniques for communicating with children;
4. the role of the social worker as a "transitional participant" in the
    lives of clients;
5. engaging significant others in the therapeutic process;
6. countertransference responses in helping relationships.

Each of these topics is explored in the final sections of this introduction.

Impact on Donald Winnicott

Teasing out Clare and Donald's contributions to one another is an
impossible task. Kay McDougall, a social work colleague at the LSE,
and Pearl King, an analyst colleague at the British Psychoanalytical
Society, used exactly the same phrase to describe their interaction:
"they sparked each other off".[143] Similarly, John (Jock) Sutherland, the
Medical Director of the Tavistock Clinic, wrote that Clare "had a great
natural empathy which filled in with [Donald's] and they did a great
deal for each other". Marion Milner (1985), a supervisee and friend of
Donald's, wrote that Clare's "gifts of liveliness, sense of fun, even
mischievousness, combined with a deep seriousness, met the same in
Donald Winnicott and she undoubtedly had a great influence on his
work" (p. 4).

As noted earlier, Donald himself wrote to Clare in 1946 that his
"work is really quite a lot associated with you" (chapter 13 herein).
Years later, he told his students at the LSE that "some of my best ideas
are Clare's".[144]

Throughout Clare's writings, themes and language commonly associated with Donald's work emerge repeatedly. In some instances,
her references to certain ideas clearly preceded his discussion of similar concepts.

A notable example of this are Clare's observations of transitional
objects. During the war, Clare travelled to London to seek out the

parents of the children in the hostels. When she found them, she asked them to prepare a note or "give me something to take to them" (chapter 5 herein).

In the case vignette of Jane, an evacuee in her care, Clare specifically notes the significance of a gift of grapes from Jane's abusive mother. Also, after Jane steals a valued ring from a hostel parent, Clare asks her to lend Jane her ring on Sundays—to tell Jane, "it's very precious to me but you could have it one day a week" (chapter 5 herein).

Similarly, Clare's case notes from 1946–47 describe a 2-year-old child's use of a toy duck in making the transition from a foster placement to an adoptive home.[145]

Several years later, Clare described this phenomenon in evocative detail:

> The moment of uprooting is just when a skilled child-care officer is needed to see that what a child clings to in the past is brought with him and accepted in the new environment. . . . there are many stories, which now, it is hoped, belong to another era, of children clinging to their own clothes and being given an anaesthetic to enable the clothes to be removed, or favourite but filthy teddy-bears and other possessions being taken away and burned, but these did not belong to the past, and something became damaged and lost when the familiar things were taken away. These possessions stood for everything the child brought with him from the past and he could not afford to lose so much. [C. Britton, 1950, pp. 173–174]

The following year, in May 1951, Donald presented his classic paper "Transitional Objects and Transitional Phenomena" to the BPS (D. W. Winnicott, 1953); but in her teaching, Clare preferred to use the evocative phrase "the first treasured possession".[146]

In the aforementioned 1950 paper, Clare also discussed many of the core ideas about delinquency that Donald articulates more fully in his 1956 paper, "The Antisocial Tendency":

> As the child-care officer comes into the lives of these children, she must first be able to sort out the whole situation carefully until she finds the alive bit from which new growth can come. For the alive bit is the thing the child is clinging to as the focus of his feelings. It may be hidden in a memory, or a fantasy, or a habit. It will certainly be at the point of tension. The delinquent act is in many cases an unconscious effort to deal with loss. . . . The depression and grief of a child who has lost a loved parent shows that he is alive and dealing with his loss, and that with help recovery is possible. Perhaps the most

difficult children to help are those with nothing alive about them. Here the only thing is to wait and watch for signs of life—encouraging the slightest effort, which may be made perhaps towards the possession of something, or a sudden desire to sit next to somebody special. [C. Britton, 1950, p. 174]

As Donald himself noted, he "avoided the immensely exacting organised antisocial case during the early stages of my career, but in the war became forced to consider this type of disorder through the work I was privileged to do with evacuated children in Oxfordshire" (D. W. Winnicott, 1988, p. 2).

Clare's first solely authored paper, "Children Who Cannot Play", written and published in 1945, presages Donald's classic 1971 volume, *Playing and Reality*, which discussed the significance of play inhibitions many years later.

Finally, Clare emphasizes the concept of "holding" in her 1954 paper "Casework Techniques in the Child Care Services", saying that social workers provide

a reliable medium within which people can find themselves or that part of themselves about which they are uncertain. We become, so to speak, a reliable environment, which is what they so much need— reliable in time and place; and we take great trouble to be where we have said we would be at the right time. . . . we take deliberate trouble to remember all the details about the client's life and not to confuse him with other clients. We can "hold" the idea of him in our relationship so that when he sees us he can find that bit of himself again which he has given us. This is conveyed by the way in which we remember details and know exactly were we left him in the last interview. Not only do we *hold* a consistent idea of the client as a person, but we *hold* the difficult situation which brought him to us by tolerating it until he either finds a way through it or tolerates it himself. If we can *hold* the painful experience, recognizing its importance and not turning aside from it as the client relives it with us . . . we help him to have the courage to feel its full impact; only as he can do that will his own natural healing processes be liberated.

I have deliberately used the word "hold" in what I have been saying, because, while it obviously includes "acceptance" of the client and what he gives us, it also includes what we do with what we accept. [chapter 6 herein]

Although the "authorship" of this concept cannot be established, Donald specifically footnotes this 1954 paper in his 1960 article "The Theory of the Parent–Infant Relationship", which first highlights the concept of "holding". Interestingly, one of Clare's analysands, Mr C, clearly recalls her telling him that the concept of "holding" was her creation.[147] As Clare rarely sought credit for any idea or concept—and was preoccupied with preserving Donald's legacy—this comment has special significance.[148]

Of course, one could argue that Clare's whole perspective on children and helping relationships was shaped by Donald's influence; that if ideas appeared in her papers before Donald's, it was because she had gleaned these ideas from him. Yet her accounts of her work in Oxfordshire convey a creative spirit and independence of mind that render this hypothesis improbable. As discussed earlier, at their initial meeting Clare cautioned this renowned paediatrician about the children's butter rations. And, as the Oxfordshire project continued, Clare ran the day-to-day operations while Donald only visited on Fridays.

Milner addressed this issue in her remembrance of Clare: "The fact that she could actually say to him—and also tell us, who were their friends—what she had told him: that is, that he suffered from 'delusions of beneficence', does, I think, give a vivid glimpse of the creativeness of their relationship and the area of fun and honesty in it" (Milner, 1985, p. 5).[149]

Yet, Clare was also an effective interpreter of Donald's ideas. Her introductions to various collections of his writings succinctly highlight central elements of his thinking and practice (see chapter 6 in C. Winnicott, 1978) and her analytic paper, "Fear of Breakdown: A Clinical Example" (chapter 17 herein) provides an evocative illustration of his important concepts.

At the same time, Donald was undoubtedly influenced by Clare and her social work profession. Perhaps uniquely in the world of psychoanalysis, Donald was actively engaged with the social work profession, delivering hundreds of lectures at the LSE, speaking at dozens of social work conferences, and regularly publishing in social work journals (D. W. Winnicott, 1954, 1955, 1959, 1961, 1963, 1964, 1970).

Irvine (1973) described Donald's unique

> two-way involvement with the fields of social work and residential care which Clare Winnicott has done so much to bring together in mutual identification . . . because he devoted so much time to communicating with these professions, in terms of a real exchange of views and experience, [Donald] gained such deep understanding and empathy for them (analogous to his empathic understanding of

parents). He became an outstanding communicator, but much more than that; in a very real, though symbolic sense he nurtured the nurturing professions, feeding them with a continual flow of wisdom, insight, experience and support. [ibid., p. 390]

Donald's identification with social work is perhaps best expressed in the following passage in the final issue of the social work journal *Case Conference*:

I would like to use this last chance to appear in *Case Conference* to give the bare bones of a sort of belief which I believe is a common denominator among social workers and psychotherapists.

Whatever we do in social work is related to quite natural things that get done in child care and in baby care. The difference is that in a professional setting, which carries its own limitations and allows its own freedom within the framework, we do the same things that are done in child care and we do nothing else. . . .

The essential part of the theory of the emotional development of the human individual has to do with the earliest stages when dependence is very much a fact and adaptation to need is the main environmental function. In personal or in social illness, these early phenomena tend to reappear and demand new enactment in a professional setting. . . .

When the social worker is not able to see his work in terms of the natural evolution of the maturing child in the environment that has its own evolution relative to a child's personal growth, then the social worker has stepped outside his or her social work job. There may be friendship, teaching, authoritarian indoctrination, charity, vindictiveness, religious conversion, political transmutation, or pharmacological modification of a client's neuro-physical apparatus. None of these things, however, is social work, which by definition is derived by direct route from an understanding of the emotional development of the human individual in the long steady climb out of absolute dependence and toward independence.

I suppose this is a kind of faith. Faith in human nature. It seems to me to have value as a basic social work principle. I think *Case Conference* has illustrated this principle. [D. W. Winnicott, 1970, pp. 504–505]

With the exception of Jacobs (1995), psychoanalytic scholars of Winnicott (Fromm & Smith, 1989; Giovacchini, 1989; Goldman, 1993; Grolnick, 1990; Phillips, 1988; Rodman, 2003) have rarely acknowledged his active participation in and identification with the social work profession even though he explicitly acknowledges this in dozens of papers (Kanter, 1990). Apart from enhancing his appreciation of such clinical phenomena as adolescence, delinquency, holding environments, management and transitional objects, Donald's engagement with social work—largely facilitated by Clare—had a major impact on his ideas about clinical interventions (Kanter, 2000a).

After intensive pre-war experience in child psychoanalysis, after the war Donald rarely treated child patients in psychoanalysis (Kahr, 1996). Instead, he largely embraced a consultative approach with parents and other caregivers (D. W. Winnicott, 1971b), a method outlined in his 1955 paper, "A Case Managed at Home". This paper was first published in a social work journal but was also included in Donald's first collection of analytic papers (D. W. Winnicott, 1958).

As Susanna Isaacs Elmhirst, a paediatrician and psychoanalyst who worked closely with Donald at Paddington Green Children's Hospital, recently noted:

> between (Donald and Clare), they developed (in Oxfordshire) unique experience and skill in devising and supporting environmental changes which nourished the emotional and physical growth of children. Out of this lively mutual co-operation, involving various non-medical and often non-parent, adults, gradually developed Winnicott's "Monday afternoons" at the Green. [Kahr, 1996, pp. xviii–xix]

These paediatric consultations at Paddington Green attracted visitors from around the world and became a model for interdisciplinary collaboration.

Often using the term "management", Donald repeatedly identified the advantages of social work interventions in working with severely troubled children and adults (Kanter, 1990). In a characteristic passage, he noted that the psychoanalyst is relatively impotent with severely disturbed patients unless "he steps outside his role at appropriate moments and himself becomes a social worker" (D. W. Winnicott, 1963, p. 219). He added that "psychiatrists and psychoanalysts constantly hand over [psychotic patients] to the care of the psychiatric social worker [because] they can do nothing themselves" (D. W. Winnicott, 1963, p. 227).

In a 1970 talk to a group of child psychologists and psychiatrists, Donald made a similar point about working with children: "Social workers have been carrying the burden of the practice of child psychiatry all these years, and it is to social work that we must look for an extension of psychiatric practice to cover all types of case and to engage in preventative work" (D. W. Winnicott, 1996, p. 281).

Looking back, Donald became part of Clare's world in social work while Clare became part of Donald's world in psychoanalysis; in doing so, both enriched their respective professional domains. No similar collaboration between leaders in these professions has occurred since the inception of these professions.

Understanding the inner world of children

One of Clare's most important contributions to social work and related professions is her appreciation of the inner life of children in need, especially those who have suffered from loss, separation, and transitions. In many respects, this is different from child psychiatry, which often examines childhood disorders apart from environmental trauma. The Oxfordshire experience presented a unique historical opportunity to learn about such reactions; perhaps never before had an organized government plan separated so many children from their families. In understanding the responses of children to the evacuation, Clare was influenced by the ideas of Melanie Klein, using her object-relations perspective to appreciate their inner suffering. This Kleinian perspective was evident in her 1945 paper "Children Who Cannot Play":

> The mother, however, must do more than give to the child; she must be able to accept his love in return, thereby proving to him his own goodness and loveableness. Her acceptance of his love also helps him to feel secure through his own bad moments of feeling angry and destructive. . . .
> . . . the child finds that not all the desirable things in his world are for him. His mother's love, for instance, has to be shared with the other members of the family. This discovery may give rise to anger, hatred, fear, and the wish to destroy; and these are feelings which in their turn cause guilt and anxiety. [chapter 3 herein]

Even after her difficult experience with Klein, Clare continued to eloquently articulate a Kleinian metapsychology in a 1964 paper:

> anxiety . . . arises from our instinctual drives, which are ruthless and aggressive as well as loving and constructive toward other people. The pain caused by this situation is obvious. It is that arising from the fundamental fear that we shall destroy that which we love. The complex defences which can be constructed against this anxiety cannot be enumerated now. An important one can be the inhibition of all instinct, all impulse, but I suppose the most common one, and one which I think each of us can recognise in ourselves is that we tend to divide the world into good and bad people. The good we preserve,

and the bad we destroy over and over again and feel justified in doing so. Most of us find that we can manage life perfectly well so long as there are certain people or categories of people or things which we do not like. For example we may not like the people who go fox-hunting, or the "other" religion, or those in authority—or simply people with red hair, etc. In this way, although our view of the world may be distorted, we can save ourselves a lot of pain. [chapter 12 herein]

Yet, unlike Klein, Clare believed that it was essential to understand and acknowledge the objective reality of children's losses and traumas in order to help them to achieve the goal of successful maturation:

> our real aim is to keep children alive. . . . By keeping children alive I am of course referring to maintaining their capacity to feel. If there are no feelings, there is no life, there is merely existence. All children who come our way have been through painful experiences of one kind or another, and this has led many to of them to clamp down on feelings and others of them to feel angry and hostile, because this is more tolerable than to feel loss and isolation.
>
> Our work, therefore, is not easy because it will lead us to seek contact with the suffering part of each child, because locked up in the suffering is each one's potential for living and for feeling love as well as feeling hate and anger. To feel a sense of loss implies that something of value, something loved, is lost, otherwise there would be no loss. Awareness of loss therefore restores the value of that which is lost, and can lead in time to a reinstatement of the lost person and loving feelings in the inner life of the child. When this happens, real memories, as opposed to fantasies, of good past experiences can come flooding back and can be used to counteract the disappointments and frustrations which are also part of the past. In this way, the past can become meaningful again. [chapter 8 herein]

In this regard, Clare's simple intervention during the war of seeking out the parents of evacuated children (see chapter 5 herein) had important ramifications. Instead of encouraging children to forget about their "lost" parents, Clare supported the efforts of evacuees to keep these internal representations "alive". Similarly, her 1954 paper "Casework Techniques in the Child Care Services" (chapter 6 herein) highlights a case vignette where children in care were kept apprised of the status of their ill mother.

Elizabeth Mapstone, a leading scholar in the child care field in Scotland, viewed Clare's recognition of the importance of the child's internal relationship with the lost parental figures as one of her central contributions to British social work.[150] Too often, when children have to be removed from their home—or even when their parents divorce—their attempts to keep their absent parental figures "alive" are either ignored or actively opposed.

Communicating with children

Using this understanding of the inner world of children in need, Clare elucidated specific techniques for communicating with them. Although these techniques can be applied to child psychotherapy, they emerge from the everyday interactions of social work practice. In these encounters, the contact with the child may be in the home or in the community; it may be relatively brief or involve a great portion of a day. These contacts are often intermittent, but most frequently they occur at times of crisis or transition.

Understanding the difference between these social work interventions and child analytic practice, Clare emphasized the need for an indirect approach where the social worker gets "alongside rather than face to face with children" (chapter 9 herein). She elaborated on this approach in greater detail:

> I now want to turn to the question of how we set about trying to get into touch with a child's real feelings. We find that usually it is no good if we set about this task in a deliberate way by trying to delve into the child's inner world because we shall be resisted if we do . . . in our work with children, we therefore find that we spend a good deal of time creating the conditions which make communication possible. We try to establish between ourselves and the children a neutral area in which communication is indirect. In other words, we participate in shared experiences, about which both we and the children feel something about something else, a third thing, which unites us, but which at the same time keeps us safely apart because it does not involve direct exchange between us. [chapter 8 herein]

Clare offered specific examples of how social workers could begin to discover this "third thing" or "third object"—an area of shared experience in which communication could emerge:

> If we ask questions, we either do not get answers, or get fictitious ones that spring from the child's imagination. . . . So we have long since given up this approach. Then we remember to start up the conversation by talking about something else—not about the child himself directly. I remember a terrified child being greeted by the words: "Hello, Linda, how nice of you to come and see me in your red shoes." The response was immediate "And my red gloves, and

my red scarf" which she proceeded to display. But the ice was broken and the child was willing to go on co-operating. The idea is to pick on something to talk about at the beginning that the child might be, or already is, showing interest in. The social worker might say, for example "Has Teddy got a name?" or "That looks a nice game, shall we see if it is?"

> . . . my second point . . . concerns the whole area of shared experiences, which is such an important part of life, and of relating and of being related to. The ride in the car, or the game being played together, or the TV programme watched, or even the visit to a clinic or hospital, all give opportunities for shared experience, and this perhaps the most non-threatening form of communication there is. It can build up confidence and mutual trust and provide neutral safe area within which direct communication is possible when needed. [chapter 9 herein]

> we shall find that there evolves between us and the child a language for talking in, which is quite special to each child because it contains his or her own words and way of remembering, and imagery, which we take the trouble to learn and use. [chapter 8 herein]

However, the purpose of this seemingly casual approach to communicating with children was not only to facilitate rapport with the social worker; Clare believed that such interactions could have a profound psychotherapeutic impact:

> Moreover, shared experiences can be talked about, and relived over again, thus enriching the inner life of the individual and at the same time building up his/her personal history which can be validated by the person who shared it. An experience shared can be a complete experience and a permanent possession. If social workers are to know . . . children . . . they will seek to create an area of shared experience. . . . Once established, this area can be widened out to include other people and new experiences which will, hopefully, outlast the social worker's (time-limited) responsibility. [chapter 8 herein]

Clare also noted that "social workers [often] are in the position of having factual knowledge of a devastating nature about the lives, or the death of a parent" (chapter 9 herein). She discussed how this "painful and damaging information" could be imparted over time:

> much hard work has to be done to build up the child's confidence, and trust . . . sooner or later questions about the past will be raised, tentatively at first, and then bit by bit the details will be filled in as the child becomes strong enough for the next part of the story. If the first question can be answered briefly and factually without anything added or commented on that is not implied in the question, then the

process of finding out is likely to progress at the child's pace. [chapter 9 herein]

In order to accomplish this task, Clare had to spend "much time tracing parents, and brothers and sisters and other relatives, and in giving the child as true a picture as I could of the family set-up and the whereabouts of its members" (C. Britton, 1946.)

While seemingly straightforward, these methods for communicating with children are rarely taught to social workers today on either side of the Atlantic. Only social workers and other professionals specializing in psychotherapy with children receive adequate training in establishing a dialogue with children. However, while Clare's approach with children has many of the same objectives as child psychotherapy, it enables workers to contact the child's inner experience without the use of interpretations or play techniques like Donald's squiggle game. Perhaps it can be considered a form of play therapy where the "play" occurs in seemingly ordinary conversation and in shared experience. A similar approach can be seen in the work of August Aichhorn (1925) and in Selma Fraiberg's 1952 paper "Some Aspects of Casework with Children: Understanding the Child Client".[151]

The overlap between Clare's approach to casework with children and child psychotherapy becomes evident in the following vignette:

A [social worker] found that the only way that she could feel in touch with an unhappy 4-yr-old was to sit quietly beside him watching his favourite TV programme. This was not a waste of time because the programme brought them together and united them in a way which was tolerable for the child. When this had happened a few times, the child was able to sit nearer to the [social worker] so that she could quite naturally put her arm round him . . . once having established communication by means of her arm round him, he then on a later occasion was able to throw himself into her arms and cry for his mother who was in hospital. The intensity of his love and longing for his mother was felt in these moments, and this in a sense restored her again for him, and made the mother more real. He could not have reached this point alone. [chapter 8 herein]

The "transitional participant"

This vignette illustrates perhaps Clare's most original and important concept: how social workers and others can serve as what I will call "transitional participants" in the lives of children. Through the reality of their contact with significant persons and experiences in the child's life, the social worker can help the child to maintain contact with positive life experiences that can enhance ongoing intrapsychic and interpersonal relationships (Kanter, 2000b).

As Donald outlined in his paper "Transitional Objects and Transitional Phenomena":

> there is a third part of the life of a human being, a part that we cannot ignore, an intermediate area of experiencing, to which inner reality and external life both contribute . . . it shall exist as a resting-place for the individual engaged in the perpetual human task of keeping inner and outer reality separate yet inter-related. [D. W. Winnicott, 1958, p. 230]

However, his discussion focused on what he identified as the "first not-me possession": inanimate objects, such as teddy-bears or baby blankets.

Early in her career, Clare identifies how social workers themselves play a similar role in the lives of children. She recalled how, during the war, she went to London to search out the parents of evacuated children:

> So what I did there was try and make a link between the children and their parents and actually I got such a name for it that every time I appeared into a hostel they would rush up and say, "Miss, have you seen my mum? When did you see my mum last?" And it was quite hard for them when I had to say, "I can't see your mum every week." . . . But it did awaken some parents to their own responsibilities. . . . Because I could say, "Look he's missing you terribly. What about a note? Give me something to take to him." So I did work very hard to make links between home. And I think that was very much encouraged by Dr Winnicott. [chapter 5 herein]

By 1944, Clare and Donald specifically articulated this role in a jointly authored paper:

> The function of the psychiatric social worker as far as the children are concerned is to give them a sense of continuity throughout the changes to which they are subjected. She is the only person who knows each child at every stage. It is she who first comes to his rescue in the billet in which he is causing a disturbance. She sees him in his school and billet, and then in the hostel, and possibly in more than one hostel. If there is a change in hostel wardens, it is the psychiatric social worker who gives some feeling of stability during the period of change. It is the psychiatric social worker who re-billets the child if and when the time comes. She is also in contact with the child's home, visiting the parents whenever possible. She is thus able in

some degree to gather together the separate threads of the child's life and to give him the opportunity of preserving something important to him from each stage of his experience. [chapter 2 herein]

However, while Donald's focus shifted towards the intrapsychic function of inanimate possessions, Clare continued to elaborate on this concept of social workers as "transitional participants" in their clients' lives:

In considering work with children, it seems to me that a very simple and clear distinction can be made between psychotherapy and social work. . . . The psychotherapist starts from the inside and is concerned with inner conflicts which hamper social development. He or she remains, usually until the very end of treatment, a subjective figure in the child's world. The effectiveness of treatment depends on the degree of subjectivity that can be maintained.

The social worker, on the other hand, starts off as a real person concerned with the external events and people in the child's life. In the course of her work with him, she will attempt to bridge the gap between the external world and his feelings about it and in doing so will enter his inner world too.

As a person who can move from one world to another, the social worker can have a special value all her own for the child, and a special kind of relationship to him which is quite different in kind from the value and relationship that a psychotherapist has. [The social worker] can never become entirely the subjective object which the psychotherapist becomes; she is bound to external reality because she is part and parcel of the child's real world, and often is responsible for maintaining that world. The social worker with children is therefore in a strategic position in their lives because she is in touch with a total situation representing a totality of experience.

Undoubtedly, a very valuable part of our relationship with children lies in their knowledge that we are also in direct touch with their parents and others who are important to them. Of a time, perhaps, our relationship is the only integrating factor in their world, and we take on a significance which is beyond what we do or say. We make links between places and events and bridge gaps between people which they are unable to bridge for themselves. As we talk about real people and real happenings, feelings about them soon become evident and before we know where we are we have entered the inner world of the individual, and so we bridge another gap, that between fact and fantasy.

I remember very clearly in my own experience as a social worker this awareness I so often had that I was bridging gaps between people. It struck me first one day when a mother said to me with incredulity on her face: "You saw Brian yesterday—it doesn't seem possible." To her, Brian was more than a matter of miles away—he almost didn't exist anymore. But as I told her about him, ordinary things, that he was learning to swim, and had lost some more teeth since she'd seen him, gradually her feelings came to life and he existed once more in her inner world. But this could not have happened if I had not really known her child. [chapter 7 herein]

Apart from focusing on how the social worker can be used by children—and parents—to keep alive positive internal representations of significant others, Clare also described how the worker's ongoing presence in the child's life can help to facilitate psychic integration across time and space:

> [We would] go over the same ground again and again. It might begin with "Do you remember the day you brought me here in your car?" And we would retrace our steps, going over the events and explanations once more. This was no mere reminiscing, but a desperate effort to add life up, to overcome fears and anxieties, and to achieve a personal integration. In my experience, feelings about home and other important places cluster round the caseworker, so that when the children see her they are not only reminded of home but can be in touch with that part of themselves which has roots in the past and the (outside) world. [C. Winnicott, 1962, p. 9]

Any parent will immediately recall the "remember when" game that is such a significant component in parent–child interactions. Beyond their fascination with photo albums or home videos—especially when shared by significant others—children—and adults—take great satisfaction in the mutual recollection of memorable shared experiences: holidays, the death of a first pet, birthday parties, or even a burnt dinner.

Unlike Donald's concept of the "transitional object", Clare's "transitional participant" is not a passive recipient of the child's projections; the social worker actively positions him or herself in the child's life, making direct contact with an array of significant others and informing all parties of this array of contacts. With the knowledge of this participation, the child is then able to internalize the social worker as an embodiment of this life experience.

However, this participation in the actual lives of children enables social workers to do more than make themselves available as object for internalization. Clare describes how the social worker's actual knowledge of the child's situation can enhance the child's capacity to cope with complex situations, saying that children

> need explanations in words they can understand about what is happening to them and their families, and about past and future happenings and plans. A great deal needs to be discussed and sorted out about real things that have happened, so that children can build up a realistic picture of themselves and what goes on around them. . . . A nine-year-old fatherless boy living in a children's home with his younger cousin John asked "If my Uncle Peter dies, will I be John's father?" This was a genuine question. What a puzzling world it is when you have so little experience to call on in order to sort out its complexities. [chapter 9 herein]

This phenomenon of the "transitional participant" has implications for understanding a wide array of human experience beyond social work with children. Consider, for example, the profound psychic impact of a visit after many years from a long-lost relative or an evening at a school reunion or family gathering. The actual presence of such "participants" in one's life has an emotional resonance that hundreds of hours in psychotherapy can never replicate.

Although Clare did not discuss this phenomenon in her few papers on psychotherapy with adult patients, this concept of the "transitional participant" can easily be applied to work with severely disturbed adults, especially when a social work or "case management" model is used (Kanter, 1988, 1989, 1990, 1995, 1996, 2000b). As with children, the social worker's contacts with an array of caregivers and significant others can be shared with patients, helping them to re-experience fragmented parts of their self-experience as they internalize this "transitional participant".

Engaging significant others

Perhaps Clare's most important contribution was her skill in engaging significant others in the therapeutic process. In her first contact with Donald, she noted that her "first task (was) trying to evolve a method of working so that all of us, including Winnicott, could make the best possible use of his weekly visits" (chapter 5 herein). In subsequent years she visited the parents of evacuees in London, consulted with the staff of a day nursery, and supported the hostel staff in coping with a wide range of difficult behaviours.

Reflecting on the Oxfordshire experience, Clare noted that

for a few children there was individual psychotherapy, but for the rest treatment was not possible, the Psychiatrist having to choose between using his weekly visit to take on a few more of them individually, or to use the time discussing problems with the Wardens, and helping them to deal with the children's difficulties. . . . We felt that in no way should the function of the hostel be thought of as limited simply to housing children who are having psychological treatment. [C. Britton, 1946, p. 30]

Throughout her career, Clare repeatedly explored the question of how caregivers without professional training could establish environments—to use Donald's phrase—that facilitate "maturational processes" (D. W. Winnicott, 1965). These caregivers included the hostel staff, foster parents, residential care staff, and the array of individuals functioning as "child care officers" in the 1960s.

In her classic paper on "Casework Techniques in the Child Care Services" (chapter 6 herein), Clare explicitly identifies the three aspects of social work with children in foster care:

1.   work with the child directly;
2.   work with the foster parents;
3.   work with the biological parents.

In this schema, there was little room for blaming parents or examining the unconscious motives of foster parents. She understood that a wide array of personality types could be "good enough" and explored the many ways that caregivers could be helpful to children in need (C. Winnicott, 1959a).

Throughout her career, Clare displayed an acute capacity for observing care-giving environments, a capacity akin in many respects to Donald's talent for observing mother–infant interactions. In one example, she reported that in Oxfordshire:

we found that the children benefited from some central project or activity being carried on by the staff independently of whether or not they took part in it. We discovered this by accident one day when the children had an unexpected holiday. The Hostel Warden and his Assistant had planned to cut a tree down and saw it up for the fires— and they carried on with their plan while the children played round them in the garden. Sometimes the children stood and watched, or helped a bit—then they ran off on their own pursuits—and returned later—and so on. At the end of the day the job was done, and the children enjoyed it, although they took almost no part in it. They were unusually contented and happy that evening. . . .

It was this same group of children who, earlier in the hostel's life had asked anxiously each night "who's going to look after us to-night?" or "who's going to play with us?" The emphasis had entirely changed, and they found far greater satisfaction in fitting in round the adults, and letting the grown-up world exist in the middle of them—than they had when the grown-ups tried to fit in round them, and create a childish world for them. We found them increasingly capable of creating their own world, when they had become quite sure about the reality of the grown-up world. [C. Britton, 1946, p. 33]

Similarly, Clare carefully observed the interactions in the therapeutic milieu, noting, for example, that

the relationships between the wardens and the other members of staff can be difficult, and need constant sorting out. The jealousy that arises in the children towards the warden's children is something that has to be reckoned with all the time. But the thing can be managed, with help from the psychiatric team, and it is well worth the effort. [ibid., p. 33]

Clare viewed these interpersonal tensions as ubiquitous characteristics of helping environments. Successful caregivers inevitably identify with the persons in their care. She noted that

if there is no tension, there has been no real identification, no real giving, and [the client] will remain fundamentally unhelped although he may have been adequately housed and fed. [C. Winnicott, 1962, p. 13]

Working in these complex social systems, the social worker's task involves (1) understanding the child's needs, (2) interpreting these needs to other caregivers, (3) helping caregivers acknowledge and use their own personal reactions in the helping process and (4) understanding the group dynamics in the care-giving systems. Undoubtedly, Clare's appreciation of these dynamics had an immense impact on Donald's therapeutic interventions as he largely replaced his practice of child psychoanalysis with a therapeutic consultative approach (D. W. Winnicott, 1971b).

Countertransference

Throughout her professional papers, Clare attends to the internal experiences of the social worker, psychotherapist, and other caregivers.

Although she never uses the term "countertransference", her ideas on this topic complement Donald's 1947 paper "Hate in the Countertransference" (D. W. Winnicott, 1949). In this paper, Donald discusses the ubiquitous response of "hate" among an array of caregivers—hospital psychiatrists, foster parents, psychoanalysts, and "good-enough" mothers—arguing that this response does the most damage when maintained outside consciousness.

In her work, Clare explores a different response that is also ubiquitous with caregivers with different roles and backgrounds: helplessness. Recollecting her work in Oxfordshire, she describes her anxiety when asked to consult with a nursery where all the children were bedwetting:

> I remember being driven there and I was absolutely panic stricken. When it stopped at the traffic light I wanted to get out and run, but we got there. And I just had to think to myself, "Look you don't have to know the answer to this lot. All you have to do is to sit and find out what's going on and relax." So in fact this is what I did. I took out my notepad and really wrote down. I said to the matron, "tell me what happens in the nursery from the time you wake the kids up in the morning. Who does it, and what happens all through the day?" And I wrote it down hour by hour by hour. . . .

As the interview progressed, the matron recognized herself that the children were being excessively confined and Clare "did not press it home". Weeks later, when Clare rang a physician involved with the nursery to follow-up, she was told that "the bedwetting cleared up and none of us can think how you did it" (chapter 5 herein).

In this vignette, Clare fortuitously discovered that her conscious acknowledgment and containment of her feelings of helplessness appeared to facilitate reflection and growth in the nursery staff. She describes a similar process with her work with Jane, an abused evacuee. After repeated crises, Jane's mother had died in a "pub brawl", and Jane experienced a dramatic regression that included falling asleep sucking a milk-filled baby's bottle. Clare notes that the hostel staff "let her do it. They were frightened stiff doing it, but they did let her do it. That didn't last long . . ." (chapter 5 herein).

Reflecting on these experiences years later, Clare recalls that:

> The staff living in the hostels were taking the full impact of the children's confusion and despair and the resulting behaviour problems. The staff were demanding to be told what to do and were often desperate for help in the form of instructions, and it took time for

them to accept that Winnicott would not, and in fact could not, take on that role, because he was not available and involved in the day-to-day living situation. . . . As it turned out, I became the one who held the job together because I was able to be in daily contact with the staff and children in the hostels. [chapter 4 herein]

Because of their daily exposure to vulnerable and abused children in a role that permits and even demands "action", social workers in child care are subject to powerful emotional forces. Clare argued that the social worker's helplessness had to be contained and that the "rescue motive" be "avoided":

What I am suggesting is that the quality of love should be akin to that of parents for their children, and we know that parents help their children and go on loving them throughout good times and bad, through distress and difficulties of many kinds as the children come to grips with the essential problems of life and find their way through them. This is often difficult for parents and many long to rescue their children from the difficult things, but by doing so they would deny to their children the right to live their own lives and to discover their own potentialities to overcome difficulties.

As I see it, the social worker of today has to be able to tolerate and help her clients to work through the difficulties and conflicts which disturb their lives. The social worker has to be able to contain in herself and her relationship to the client both the good and the bad in a situation and in the individual. If she cannot bear the conflict herself and seeks to end it by rescuing the client from what she considers to be the bad influences in his life, she is only doing half her job, and, moreover, she is denying to the client the possibility of discovering the strength which comes through finding his own personal solution to his problem. The rescuer will feel better for the act of rescue, but the social worker who encompasses the total situation will feel worse, because she has to stand the conflict of good and evil which the rescuer avoids.

That there are situations from which the social worker of today may have to rescue a client because all other methods have failed in spite of the help given, I would agree. But that is quite different from being motivated to rescue. Furthermore, the social worker is aware that the problem is not solved by the act of rescue. It is transferred from one place to another and it has to go on being solved in the new setting. [chapter 10 herein]

In an unpublished lecture to a group of psychotherapists entitled "I Had to Fail",[152] Clare continued to explore this theme, describing the patient's need to induce the analyst to experience a state of abject helplessness or failure. Again, as in her wartime experience with the nursery, Clare was challenged to contain these painful affects:

I felt as if she could easily slip away from me at that moment. What had been built up was threatened by this disappointment—her depression about it. She was extremely hard to tolerate at this time . . . she was so depressed. She was again completely silent for a long time. I dreaded her sessions. When the bell rang, I went: "Oh God! How am I going to tolerate this another day?" It made me feel a complete failure. I thought I'd lost her.

Then I kept thinking to myself: "What is she doing to me?" I didn't know. I went on feeling an absolute failure. I would say things, but with no response. It was just deep despair. Then one day, I very much got in mind I must work out what she is doing to me, because I felt a failure myself. Took me a long time to think: "Look here, she's doing this to me. It's not just me failing." Then one day she said: "I don't know why you bother to talk." I was doing my usual patter like: "I'm still here" . . . you know, whatever. "Don't know why you bother to talk, I cut your words off as you say them." So I said . . . "Yes." She said: "You must know this; I cut them off." So I said: "Yes, I do know. I suppose I only talk to let you know I'm here." Oh, yes, I know what I did say that's important. I said: "I suppose I only talk in case one day you will hear."

Another day, she said: "You're too dumb to know what's going on." And I felt it. I felt it. By this time, I was almost on my knees. I really felt dumb. I felt stupid. Then I thought: "Come on, get yourself out of this. It's not you. She's doing this to you. What is she doing to you?" So I thought to myself: "Yes, she's making me fail. And why haven't I seen this before? I've got to get to the failure. I've got to fail." So I put this into words for her. That I thought she had to make me fail.

I thought it was to do with her early failure, her mother who went away when she was (an infant). The link had never been made with her mother again. I thought it had to do with the early failure with her mother—only this time with me. She had taken control and she'd made me fail. So that she was in control of the situation.

I left out a point. She had given me a hint after she'd said these two things to me, like: "I don't know why you bother to speak", and "You're too dumb." She came back the next day and said: "How terrible of me to say that to you yesterday. But, I've been longing to say that for months. But you see, I was afraid to say it in case you would stop." So I noted that. I knew that when I came to the crunch point—which was the failure point—that I've got to not stop. So I said: "Look, let's face it. I have failed completely, as your mother failed you. But this time you have caused the failure. You have brought on the failure. And you are in control of the situation. This is your thing you have done to me. You had to make me fail." I added very quickly: "But I'm not giving up." In a flat voice . . . I tried to make it flat.

Well, from that minute on, a lot of things happened. We went over this again. You know—that my failure was her triumph. She triumphed over the whole situation. And I think . . . I felt I knew what it was about. If she could feel in control of the situation— omnipotent control—of me and everything, at least she could, per- haps, incorporate the failure into herself so that it's not a permanent threat to her forever. That was what I hoped would happen. And it really, in a way, did happen. . . . I said things like she "had been responsible for destroying the analysis." And I felt destroyed.[153]

This experience marked the turning point in the analysis, and the painful impasse was eventually overcome. Clare's awareness of mean- ing in the countertransference—of its significance as a marker of pro- jective identification, a term she never used in her writing—is apparent here. However, as Donald argued in his paper on "hate" (D. W. Winnicott, 1949), not all countertransference affects are induced by the patient's projections; some are an explicit response to the objective realities of care-giving relationships. This is perhaps more common in social work than in psychotherapy as the difficulties of social work clients are often precipitated by environmental realities.

In a remarkable passage in her paper on "self-awareness" in social work, Clare moves beyond the usual focus on the toxic elements in the countertransference and discusses the therapeutic possibilities inher- ent in social work practice:

To find out about other people in order to help them to solve their own problems seems to be a more constructive and socially useful way of finding out about oneself and solving one's own problems than to sit down with one's own problems and to try to solve them in isolation. . . . As I see it a benign circle is established when social workers, in understanding their clients and enabling them to solve some at least of their problems, also at the same time gain under- standing of themselves and solve some of their own problems. . . .

The danger in social work is not that social workers by helping their clients help themselves, but that they should fail to help them- selves and to develop through their work. Then indeed a vicious circle would be produced. [chapter 12 herein]

In this paper, Clare straightforwardly acknowledges the personal re- wards that social workers gain from their work, suggesting that a reciprocal exchange is a necessary component of successful helping relationships.[154]

Interestingly, Clare did not advocate psychoanalysis as a necessary ingredient in the social worker's self-awareness. She acknowledged that

> some may need and want this kind of professional help, but that is an entirely personal affair. What I am saying, however, is that we can, if we want to do so, use every means available to enable ourselves to grow up and to further our development into mature human beings. To grow up means learning to live with ourselves and putting up with ourselves the way we are.
>
> We have to be able to tolerate sometimes feeling awful or confused or ignorant and at other times feeling good or clever or lucky. If we cannot tolerate the whole range of feelings of which we are capable, we can easily become rigid and seek to make everyone else, including our clients, fit in with our patterns and our time. This is the easy way out. . . . In social work "time not our time rings the bell" and we find that we have to be prepared to wait and perhaps carry the case through long periods of doubt and uncertainty in which we do not know yet what the outcome will be. [chapter 12 herein]

Clare's writings reflect a consonance between her personal and professional identities; growth in both the personal and professional domains involved a deliberate engagement with the vicissitudes of everyday life:

> Friendships, reading, and cultural activities of all kinds, and holidays, all enrich our lives and our knowledge of the world and of ourselves. We know that every situation in which we can be ourselves, and enjoy ourselves, not only adds another dimension to life, but liberates us for further experiences. Our personal life is the base from which we operate, and to which we return. The firmer the base, the freer we are to make excursions into the unknown. [chapter 12 herein]

Final thoughts

In her life and work, Clare left behind a rich legacy of personal experiences, professional accomplishments, and provocative ideas. In the case of social workers, she reminds us of the importance of the inner life of children and of the creative possibilities of social work interventions. Although her personal approach to children and other persons in need is in conflict with the increasing bureaucratization and mechanization of social worker practice, her pragmatic and intuitive capacity to empower and support a care-giving network around each client enabled Clare to serve a wartime caseload of over 80 children. In an era where the bottom line has become increasingly important, her creative interventions offer examples of how less—when informed by a deep understanding of the human psyche and personal relationships—can sometimes be more.

For analysts and psychotherapists, Clare leaves behind a somewhat different legacy. Her experience and ideas in social work challenge psychoanalytic theories about the essential nature of the therapeutic process. Without interpretation or specialized play techniques, Clare organized "holding environments" that facilitated "maturational processes". In this work, her ideas overlapped with her husband's. Yet her work provides those interested in Donald Winnicott's ideas with both a greater appreciation of the origins of his thinking and new ideas about its creative application in clinical work. Similarly, Clare's ideas on what I have termed the "transitional participant" and on counter-transference have continuing resonance for psychoanalytic practice and theory.

Finally, as her friend Gwen Smith observed—as quoted at the beginning of this chapter—Clare "lived every part of life to the full". Her professional creativity, her personal enthusiasm for all the world has to offer, her dynamic engagement with a wide array of friends, relatives, and colleagues, and her courage in the face of illness and death—these qualities were a source of inspiration to all who knew her.

Notes

1. Gwen Smith, speaking at the memorial service for Clare Winnicott, London School of Economics, 3 November 1984.

2. Obituary, London Times, 4 May 1984.

3. Interview with Olive Stevenson, 29 May 1995.

4. Interview with Ray Shepherd, 31 May 1995.

5. Interview with Nora Calton, 30 May 1995.

6. Interviews with Margaret Britton, 7 August and 17 September 1996; personal correspondence, 16 February 1997.

7. Interview with Celia Britton, 1 May 1996.

8. Interview with Nancy Martin, 7 August 1996. A family tale about Clare's mother suggests that she attended a teacher training school with D. H. Lawrence and found him and his subsequent behaviour repugnant. Most probably this was at the Pupil–Teacher Centre in Ilkeston in 1904; their classmates included two of

Lawrence's future lovers, Jessie Chambers and Louisa Burrows. Lawrence's sexual pursuit of Chambers was detailed in *Sons and Lovers,* and he ended his engagement to Burrows because she refused to engage in premarital sex. Three months later he eloped with Frieda Weekly. Apparently Lawrence's escapades became well known in the local community, and Mrs Britton's probable familiarity with his lovers may have intensified her disgust.

9. Interview with Nora Calton, 30 May 1995.

10. Interview with Andrew Britton, 27 May 1995; personal correspondence, 10 September 1996.

11. Interviews with Alison Britton, 14 April 1996, and with Celia Britton, 1 May 1996.

12. Ibid.

13. Interview of Clare Winnicott by Alan Cohen, 27 June 1980.

14. Letters by Jimmy Britton to Anne Wyatt-Brown, 26 September 1991 and 23 January 1992.

15. Ibid.

16. Interview with Andrew Britton, 27 May 1995; personal correspondence, 10 September 1996.

17. Jimmy Britton's poem "For Elizabeth, II" was published in his collection of poetry (J. Britton, 1994). One part of the poem is as follows:

> It can happen, it did happen.
> Be her. Live through that split second
> Which if you do not master it
> Will reverberate through the years.
> Not for her, but for you.
> Go through it, to the moment of impact.
> Rush ordinarily taken, mere sense of "get on with it",
> Be done, and get home. And the uncalculated,
> Appearing from nowhere, a car suddenly there
> Unstoppable, seconds away from the kerb.

18. Comments by Jimmy Britton at the memorial service for Clare Winnicott, London School of Economics, 3 November 1984.

19. Interview with Beti Jones, 18 October 1995.

20. Personal correspondence from F. Marjorie (Green) Jones, 15 August 1995 and 3 February 1996.

21. Betty Joseph, the distinguished Kleinian analyst, was a classmate of Clare's on the Mental Health Course. In an interview dated 23 November 2001 (available at www.melanie-klein-trust.org), she recalls her experience on this Course as follows:

"Susan Isaacs became very important. She was a friend of Sibyl Clement Brown who was the Head of the Mental Health Course, the training for Psychiatric Social Work. We were of course a wartime group and moved around; we spent some time in London as well as in Cambridge and Oxford. We were all over the place. When at one point we found we were being evacuated to Cambridge, a group of us asked, whether we could have some lectures from Susan Isaacs since she was based there. The tutor agreed and managed to arrange it. Much to our horror, however, Susan Isaacs refused to talk about psychoanalysis. She said, "before you talk psychoanalysis, you have to know something about development." So she talked to us about the development of the infant and young child, which in fact was very helpful. So we got to know her a bit. Her books, particularly *Social Development in Young Children* (1933), were prominent on the reading list. I don't know if people still read that—it's a very good book.

I don't remember how long I was in Cambridge. A term, I think. Everything was so chaotic in the war, as you can imagine. They had to find us accommodation—I think we were in Peterhouse College which was unbelievably cold!"

22. Personal correspondence from F. Marjorie (Green) Jones, 15 August 1995 and 3 February 1996.

23. Ibid.

24. See fn. 21.

25. Interview with Juliet Berry and Pamela Mann, 29 October 1996.

26. Interview of Clare Winnicott by Alan Cohen, 27 June 1980.

27. Comments by Irmi Elkan at the memorial service for Clare Winnicott, London School of Economics, 3 November 1984; interview with Irmi Elkan, 26 May 1995.

28. Comments by Gwen Smith at the memorial service for Clare Winnicott, London School of Economics, 3 November 1984.

29. Clare may also have been influenced by a collegial relationship with Eva Rosenfeld, an émigré psychoanalyst who had opened a nursery school in Vienna at the request of Anna Freud. Analysed by both Sigmund Freud and Melanie Klein, Rosenfeld commuted between Oxford and London and, according to Dyer (1983), worked with Clare in some capacity, although the details of this collaboration are unclear.

30. Clare's 1961 *curriculum vitae* submitted to the BPS indicates that she worked in Oxfordshire with children in 1946, before moving to work at the War Office between 1946 and 1947. However, her aforementioned case notes (see chapter 8 herein) are dated from late 1946 through early 1947. Also, her stories about working with severely traumatized British prisoners of war suggests that this took place soon after these men returned home—i.e., most probably in the latter half of 1945.

31. Comments by Irmi Elkan at the memorial service for Clare Winnicott, London School of Economics, 3 November 1984; interview with Irmi Elkan, 26 May 1995.

32. Interview with Ursula Behr, 3 June 1995.

33. Interview with Olive Stevenson, 29 May 1995.

34. Course syllabus, University of London, 1946.

35. Interview with Diana Williamson, 2 February 1997.

36. Interview with Joan Vann, 29 May 1995.

37. Interview with Diana Williamson, 2 February 1997.

38. Interview with Joan Vann, 29 May 1995.

39. Comments by Irmi Elkan at the memorial service for Clare Winnicott, London School of Economics, 3 November 1984; interview with Irmi Elkan, 26 May 1995.

40. Interviews with Norma (Duncan) Campbell, 22 September 1995, and with Ella (Blumenkahl) Marks, 5 September 1996.

41. Personal correspondence with Mary Bromley, 12 November 1995.

42. "Casework Techniques in the Childcare Services" was Clare Winnicott's only paper published in the United States.

43. Charlotte Towle served as a consultant to the London School of Economics in 1955–56, as the Applied Social Studies Course was developed.

44. Interview with Ella (Blumenkahl) Marks, 5 September 1996.

45. Comments by Irmi Elkan at the memorial service for Clare Winnicott, London School of Economics, 3 November 1984; interview with Irmi Elkan, 26 May 1995.

46. Interview with Kay McDougall, 3 June 1995.

47. Clare had Donald hand-copy her letter to Titmuss and sent this undated copy to Kay McDougall soon after New Year's Day, 1958. In an accompanying note to McDougall, Clare wrote that the letter to Titmuss "won't be any use of course, but I wanted him to hear from me on the subject".

48. Interview of Clare Winnicott by Alan Cohen, 27 June 1980.

49. In contrast, other social work groups, notably the Association of Psychiatric Social Workers—to which Clare belonged—required specific social work qualifications for membership.

50. Interview with Joan Cooper, 27 May 1995.

51. Interview with Kay McDougall, 3 June 1995.

52. Interviews with Diana Williamson, 2 February 1997, and Kay McDougall, 3 June 1995.

53. Interview with David Donnison, 10 November 1996.

Clare's usage of first names also reflected different sorts of identity issues. Named "Elsie Clare" by her parents, Clare was known as "Elsie" in her family for much of her life. Her nephew, Andrew Britton, recalls a family saying: "Aunt Elsie from Chelsea; Aunt Clare from Chester Square", suggesting that the family usage of her first name shifted sometime after her 1951 marriage. Yet, she was known as "Clare" during her tenure on the Mental Health Course and in her work in Oxfordshire. Also, the name "Clare" had been passed down through Clare's maternal lineage from an ancestor named Clare Nathan—a Jewish woman born around 1825 and brought up as a Christian. This family tradition continues, as both Clare's niece and grandniece carry the middle name "Clare" (personal correspondence from Margaret Britton, 2 February 1997).

54. Gwen Smith at the memorial service for Clare Winnicott, London School of Economics, 3 November 1984.

55. Irmi Elkan at the memorial service for Clare Winnicott, London School of Economics, 3 November 1984; interview with Irmi Elkan, 26 May 1995

56. Entries from Karl Britton's diary with the cooperation of Andrew Britton.

57. According to Rodman (2003), Donald's wife Alice became involved in 1943 with a severely disturbed woman known as "Susan", whom she took into their home. Donald arranged for "Susan" to be treated by Marion Milner under his supervision—and at his expense. The story of this analysis is reported in Milner's (1969) book *In the Hands of a Living God*. Milner was also in analysis with Donald at some point, but the dates are unclear. Donald's marital separation from Alice was a major blow to "Susan".

58. Personal correspondence with Joan Rubenstein, 12 November 1996.

59. Donald's classic paper "Hate in the Countertransference" was written during this stressful period (in 1947). It addressed how both professionals and lay persons can acknowledge and cope with their rage at mentally ill persons and helpless dependents.

60. Personal correspondence with Joan Rubenstein, 12 November 1996.

61. Entries from Karl Britton's diary, with the cooperation of Andrew Britton.

62. Ibid.

63. Gwen Smith at the memorial service for Clare Winnicott, London School of Economics, 3 November 1984.

64. Although Clare was 45 years old when she married—ten years younger than Donald—her nephew, Andrew Britton, recalls a family story that the Registrar told the youthful bride that he expected to see her back in a year when she registered the birth of her child.

65. Entries from Karl Britton's diary with the cooperation of Andrew Britton.

66. Comments by Pearl King at the memorial service for Clare Winnicott, London School of Economics, 3 November 1984.

67. Letter from Jimmy Britton to Anne Wyatt-Brown, 17 February 1992.

68. Interview with David Donnison, 10 November 1996.

69. Interview with Karen Proner, 30 October 1996.

70. Interview of M. Masud Khan by James Anderson, 3 November 1981.

71. Interview with Harry Karnac, 19 October 1996.

72. Comments by Pearl King at memorial service for Clare Winnicott, London School of Economics, 3 November 1984.

73. Interview with David Donnison, 10 November 1996.

74. Interview with Norma (Duncan) Campbell, 22 September 1995.

75. Interviews with Alison Britton, 14 April 1996, Andrew Britton, 27 May 1995, Celia Britton, 1 May 1996, Margaret Britton, 7 August and 17 September 1996, and Katherine Grey, 19 March 1997.

76. Letter from M. Masud Khan to W. Clifford Scott, 2 April 1984. In this letter, Khan asks Scott for details of his supervisory and analytic contact with Donald. Khan wrote that Donald had told him about this "short period of analysis" and indicated that Marion Milner had also told him about this analytic experience.

77. Interview with Phyllis Grosskurth, 27 June 1995.

78. There is some confusion about the dates of Clare's analyses. Her 1961 *curriculum vitae* submitted to the BPS indicated that she was in analysis with Scott from 1949 to 1952 and with Klein from 1957 to 1960; the latter dates may reflect the dates of her analysis within her period of formal analytic training. This *cv* also contains several other errors concerning dates in Clare's professional life.

The aforementioned letter of 14 January is quoted both by Rodman (2003) in his biography of Donald Winnicott and by Grosskurth (1986) in her biography of Klein; Rodman dates this letter from 1958, while Grosskurth dates the letter from 1954. I have examined a copy of the letter, and there indeed is confusion about Klein's handwriting. While the "4" in "1954" lacks the closed loop of an "8", it could possibly be a poorly written "8".

However, Scott moved to Canada in 1954, and several accounts suggest that Clare's analysis with Klein was precipitated by Scott's move. Also, Clare quite clearly was in analysis with Klein when she became ill with meningitis early in

1956, and her description of her return to her analysis after this illness suggests that she had been in treatment for some time prior to her illness. Finally, Clare began her formal analytic training in the autumn of 1956, during a leave of absence from her teaching post at the London School of Economics. Most certainly, her analysis with Klein began before the beginning of her analytic coursework.

In my view, the preponderance of evidence suggests that the letter from Klein to Donald was written in January 1954, and Clare's analysis began around that date. However, if this letter was indeed written in 1958, then it is certainly possible that it may have been written several years after the beginning of Clare's analysis.

It is worth noting, on another subject, that Klein did not seem equally concerned about "external disturbances" in analysis when she referred her son, Eric, to Donald for analysis some years earlier and requested that Donald allow her to supervise Eric's treatment. Donald refused this request. Yet Klein often communicated with Donald about her son's treatment. On 1 April 1941, Klein wrote to Donald: "I am thankful for your giving me an opportunity to be of some help with Eric's analysis. (In these matters it is difficult to make a rule but I personally in your place would do exactly as you are doing, —I should also deny that your communications with me about him and would feel justified because it does not mean to me what he would interpret it for.)" (Rodman, 2003, p. 122).

79. Personal correspondence from Peter Hildebrand, 16 and 25 February 1996.

80. Ibid.

81. Interview with Hanna Segal, 4 June 1995.

82. Class notes supplied by Norma (Duncan) Campbell.

83. None of Clare's social work colleagues at the LSE—Kay McDougall, Irmi Elkan, or Zofia Butrym—was aware at the time that she was in analysis with Melanie Klein; nor was Peter Hildebrand, a student in her training year at the Institute of Psycho-Analysis.

84. Interview with Phylliss Grosskurth, 27 June 1995.

85. Ibid.

86. Clare's mother died in December 1956.

87. Interview of Marion Milner by James Anderson, 12 October 1981.

88. Interview with Janie Thomas, 3 June and 8 October 1995.

89. See footnote 78.

90. Interview with Hanna Segal, 4 June 1995.

91. Interview with Kay McDougall, 3 June 1995.

92. Interview with Ms A, 20 October 1995.

93. Interview with Phylliss Grosskurth, 27 June 1995.

94. Interview with Hanna Segal, 4 June 1995.

95. Interview of Marion Milner by James Anderson, 12 October 1981.

96. Interview with Ms E, 17 July 1995.

97. Interview of Clare Winnicott by Alan Cohen, 27 June 1980.

98. Interview with Beti Jones, 18 October 1995.

99. Comments by Joan Cooper at the memorial service for Clare Winnicott, London School of Economics, 3 November 1984.

100. Comments by George Thomas at the memorial service for Clare Winnicott, London School of Economics, 3 November 1984.

101. Interview with Barbara Dockar-Drysdale, 4 June 1996.

102. Over thirty years after the incorporation of children's services into generic social services departments, the British government has reversed course and is again creating separate units that will provide services to children (Carvel, 2002).

103. Interview with Karen Proner, 30 October 1996.

104. Undated letter from Clare Winnicott to Joan Vann.

105. Interview with Eric Rayner, 26 May 1995.

106. Like Donald, Lois Munro was a heavy smoker who also suffered from heart disease with visible symptoms. As Paula Heimann (1975, p. 100), a friend and colleague, noted: "she had choking spasms, most distressing to witness, but when she got her breath back, she would apologize and continue with her cigarette".

107. Interview with Alison Britton, 14 April 1996.

108. Interview with Janie Thomas, 3 June and 8 October 1995.

109. Interview with Sharon Genassi, 7 October 1996.

110. Personal correspondence from Robin Hughes, 24 August 1995.

111. Personal correspondence, Gemma Blech, 2 September 1995.

112. Interview of Clare Winnicott by Alan Cohen, 27 June 1980.

113. Ibid.

114. Personal correspondence from John (Jock) Sutherland, 7 March 1989.

115. Interview of Clare Winnicott by Alan Cohen, 27 June 1980.

116. Interview with Baroness Lucy Faithfull, 30 May 1995.

117. Interview of M. Masud Khan by James Anderson, 3 November 1981.

118. Interviews with Pearl King, 3 June and 29 September 1995.

119. On 13 November 1976, Clare wrote to W. Clifford Scott, her former analyst, on behalf of Khan, who was recuperating from major surgery. She shared her "great shock" about Khan's health and discussed various editorial matters of common interest. The tone of letter suggests that a cordial and collaborative relationship with Khan had continued up to that point.

120. Interview with Harry Karnac, 19 October 1996.

121. Interview with Ray Shepherd, 31 May 1995.

122. Interview with Josephine Lomax-Simpson, 6 August 1996.

123. Interview with Ms A, 20 October 1995.

124. Comments by Jimmy Britton at the memorial service for Clare Winnicott, London School of Economics, 3 November 1984.

125. Interview with Ms D, 5 November 1996.

126. Ibid.

127. In a 4 June 1995 interview Hanna Segal reported that Clare never had a very successful practice after Donald died. Her source of this information is unknown, but it seems to bear no resemblance to the best information available about Clare's practice.

128. Interview with Ms A, 20 October 1995.

129. Interview with Ms B, 23 October 1996

130. Interview with Mr C, 26 May 1995.

131. Interview with Jane Petit, 24 June 1995.

132. Interview with Ms E, 17 July 1995.

133. Interviews with Jill Curtis, 9 and 15 September 1995.

134. Interview with Jane Petit, 24 June 1995.

135. Interviews with Jill Curtis, 9 and 15 September 1995.

136. Interview with Alison Britton, 14 April 1996.

137. Interview with Margaret Fosbrook, 14 January 1996.

138. Personal correspondence with Pati Auterinen, 26 April 1996.

139. Comments by George Thomas at the memorial service for Clare Winnicott, London School of Economics, 3 November 1984.

140. Comments by Madeleine Davis at the memorial service for Clare Winnicott, London School of Economics, 3 November 1984.

141. The title of Winnicott's 1986 collection of papers, *Home Is Where We Start From*, is based on the first line of a verse in "East Coker"; the verse appears as an epigraph in the prelims of Winnicott's book.

142. Interview with Olive Stevenson, 29 May 1995.

143. Interview with Kay McDougall, 3 June 1995; interviews with Pearl King, 3 June and 29 September 1995.

144. Interview with Alan Cohen, 30 May 1995.

145. Case notes from 1946–47 used for discussion at the United Nations Exchange Plan Seminar for the Advanced Study of Social Casework, Leicester, 1954. Clare presented her "Casework Techniques" paper (chapter 6 herein) at the same conference.

146. Interview with Ursula Behr, 3 June 1995.

147. Interview with Mr C, 26 May 1995.

148. Recalling Clare's teasing reference to her husband as suffering from "delusions of beneficence", Clare told Emmanuel Lewis, one of Donald's former analytic supervisees, a story about how Donald had written to Charles Schulz, the cartoonist, and asked whether Linus's blanket could have been evoked by his concept of the transitional object. Clare smilingly told Lewis that Donald received a two-sentence reply from Schulz, along these lines: "Dear Dr Winnicott: I have never heard of you or your idea of a transitional object. My drawings of Linus's blanket come from observing children."

Rodman (2003, p. 413) quotes a 1955 letter from Donald to Schulz 1955 where Donald informs the cartoonist of his interest in including a Peanuts cartoon with Linus and the blanket in a collection of his papers to illustrate his theoretical concepts.

However the direct request for acknowledgment (to which Clare referred) most probably came in a 1967 letter to the playwright Arthur Miller, in response to Miller's children's book, *Jane's Blanket*. Donald wondered whether Charles "Schulz with his Peanuts character who had a transitional object had also read what I wrote. Obviously both he and you are inspired by what you observed in the children around just as I was, but it is rather interesting that we have all started drawing attention to these things at the same time." Miller responded that "the central inspiration for *Jane's Blanket* came from observing my own daughter as a child" (Rodman, 2003, p. 316).

149. See fn. 148.

150. Interview with Elizabeth Mapstone, 3 June 1995.

151. In her Foreword to an edited collection entitled *Communicating with*

Children (Holgate, 1972), Clare makes special mention of Fraiberg's paper, which is reproduced in Holgate's volume.

152. Lecture given in Sheffield, England, 3 July 1981.

153. Ibid.

154. A similar observation was advanced by Harold Searles (1975) in his paper "The Patient as Therapist to His Analyst".

PART I

OXFORDSHIRE

CHAPTER TWO

The problem of homeless children

(1944)

D. W. Winnicott and Clare Britton

There have long been orphanages and homes for the destitute child. Some have undoubtedly done good work, but many of them have been content simply to feed and clothe the children and have failed altogether to provide for their emotional needs. It has been found that the institutional child tends to lack something, not only in personal happiness, but also in development of character and in the qualities of citizenship, and there is a growing public awareness of the seriousness of this fact. The war has produced an increasing number of homeless children in Great Britain and still more in the Occupied Countries. All who have a serious interest in the future, therefore, as well as those directly concerned with the welfare of children, must be brought to realize that haphazard methods of dealing with the problem presented by so many homeless children may have serious consequences.

It seems that we are faced with the need to provide "homes" for vast numbers of children at the very moment when we have begun to realize the inadequacies of institutional life. Adoption into normal loving families is probably the happiest solution for the majority, but it is obvious that, in the Occupied countries particularly, a certain proportion of these children will have been so damaged by the unhappi-

---

First published in *The New Era in Home and School* (September–October 1944).

ness they have undergone that they will be unable to take their place in a normal home circle, at least until they have been helped to recover by special care and understanding. Also, the placing of children in the right foster-homes is something that must take time, and it is obvious that the children will have to be gathered into centres from which adoption can be organized and supervised. Presumably, therefore, there will be hostels or "homes" for them.

It must be assumed that the majority of the children will have originally had satisfactory parents and homes of their own, so that although they may seem to be very ill on account of the bitter experiences they have had, they will be likely to be able to make use of an environment, if it can be provided, that reminds them of that which they have once known and trusted. Others, on the other hand, will have had no early experience of home life, or will be found to be so ill that any attempt to give them the idea of what home means will be necessarily a start from scratch. Some, of course, will have to be recognized as permanently damaged by the too-great emotional strain to which they have been subjected.

In some ways evacuation in England provided us with a situation similar to that which will face post-war Europe. One outstanding difference between the two is that the children in Europe may be permanently homeless, whereas evacuation in England is to some extent a temporary measure; also, in Europe probably all the children will need to be gathered into Hostels at first, whereas in England the majority of children went straight into foster-homes, and only those who showed difficulties were eventually placed in hostels.

The setting-up of evacuation hostels for children who could not settle in billets provided us with an opportunity for experiment in the provision of substitute homes. The complete results of these various experiments have yet to be seen but it is felt that the experiences gained so far may, in the meantime, be of some use to those who face the more serious problem of the permanent placement of homeless children.

We should like to point out that in the Oxfordshire scheme, which provides us with our own experience, we cannot aim at the cure of the permanently damaged children, who all need prolonged psychotherapy. We can, however, aim at the proper management of those who come to us with quite severe symptoms, but whose illness is a temporary one, and in the nature of a defence against an adverse environment. On the whole, these children respond well and eventually are able to enter into home life again. The children get consistent and continuous management, and we find that nearly all of them tend to improve, even though they have had no individual psycho-therapy. It cannot be too strongly emphasized that every child that is neglected becomes a burden on society, hardening into an anti-social character or developing some other sort of mental illness.

Organization

In Oxfordshire there has developed a scheme in which several hostels form a group under the direct administration of the County Council. This has made it economical to obtain the services of a psychiatrist, visiting one day a week, and to employ a whole-time trained psychiatric social worker to carry out the routine management of the hostels under the psychiatrist's direction. Both these officers are responsible to a special committee appointed by the County Council.

The grouping of hostels in this way has also made possible a certain amount of classification in the placing of children in the various hostels, although this is limited by the fact that there are only five hostels. Another advantage in the grouping of hostels is that if the need arises children can be changed from one type of hostel to another without losing all sense of continuity. This seems to us to be important.

The responsibility for the appointment of Wardens for each hostel is taken by the Committee, but the advice of the psychiatrist and psychiatric social worker has always been sought. The psychiatric social worker is responsible to the Committee for the appointment of assistants in the hostels, and this is always done in consultation with the Wardens.

All the hostels are in the country and are accommodated in ordinary houses acquired and adapted for the purpose. In order to meet the needs of evacuation, it has been necessary to make two of the hostels larger than the others. The largest can take 25 children, and we feel that this is the absolute maximum that should be allowed, otherwise the hostel becomes an institution rather than a home and so loses most of its value. We think that large hostels are to be avoided whenever possible and find that 12 children seems the ideal number.

In our experience it seems best not to have the hostels placed too near each other. If they are, the children meet and compare notes, and this may create awkward situations for the staff, as no two hostels can be alike. Also, as far as the hostel staff are concerned, it seems that they have more freedom to develop along their own particular lines if they are not constantly comparing their own work with that done in a nearby hostel.

Psychiatrist

The psychiatrist, who is a doctor, takes final responsibility for the work done in the hostels and is consulted by the psychiatric social worker and the hostel staff about all the important problems that arise. He cannot undertake regular individual psycho-therapy with the children owing to lack of time, but he interviews any particular child who seems to be in difficulties and who is giving special trouble. Also, by visits and discussions with the staff, he attempts to help them in their adaptation to each child, thus enabling them to understand and develop their own work.

The fact that the psychiatrist uses the limited amount of time which he can spend in the hostels in this way, rather than in the regular treatment of three or four children, means that his specialized knowledge is at the disposal of the staff in their dealings with the 80 children in the scheme.

The psychiatrist, through the psychiatric social worker, is responsible for the placing of children in the hostels. He knows most of the children personally, and they value him as an outside friend on whom they can rely in the moments of stress which inevitably arise in hostel life.

Psychiatric social worker

In practice, the psychiatric social worker controls the whole of the work except for maintenance and alteration of buildings. There are many reasons why it is important to have one individual at the centre of the scheme. In the first place, the psychiatric social worker has been able to build up a wide experience by being in touch with all that each hostel has gone through, and so is able to pass on the fruits of this experience to the Committee and to new wardens as they are appointed. The psychiatric social worker will be in a position also to know which type of case does best in each hostel and therefore will be able to place new cases referred to the group and to transfer cases from one hostel to another within the group.

The psychiatric social worker, because of her special training and experience, can appreciate the true nature of the work being done and the difficulties inherent in the exacting task of running a hostel. As she is always available, she must be prepared to discuss difficulties with members of the hostel staff at any time. It is not that the staff need special sympathy, but it is important for them that the officer to whom they are immediately responsible should be personally acquainted with all the work done in the hostels. This officer, in turn, must understand the point of view of the administrative body.

The function of the psychiatric social worker, as far as the children are concerned, is to give them a sense of continuity throughout the changes to which they are subjected. She is the only person who knows each child at every stage. It is she who first comes to his rescue in the billet in which he is causing a disturbance. She sees him in his school and billet, and then in the hostel, and possibly in more than one hostel. If there is a change in hostel wardens, it is the psychiatric social worker who gives some feeling of stability during the period of change. It is the psychiatric social worker who re-billets the child, if and when the time comes. She is also in contact with the child's home, visiting the parents whenever possible. She is thus able in some degree to gather together the separate threads of the child's life and to give him the opportunity of preserving something important to him from each stage of his experience.

Hostel wardens and assistants

There is no particular training for hostel wardens, and even if there were, their selection as suitable people for the work would be of more importance than their training. We find it impossible to generalize about the type of person who makes a good warden. Our successful wardens have differed from each other widely in education, previous experience, and interests and have been drawn from various walks of life. The following is a list of the previous occupations of some of them: elementary-school teacher, social worker, trained church worker, commercial artist, instructor and matron in an approved school, master and matron at a remand home, worker in a public assistance institution, prison welfare officer.

We find that the nature of previous training and experience matters little compared with the ability to assimilate experience and to deal in a genuine, spontaneous way with the events and relationships of life. This is of the utmost importance, for only those who are confident enough to be themselves, and to act in a natural way, can act consistently day in and day out. Furthermore, wardens are put to such a severe test by the children coming into hostels that only those who are able to be themselves can stand the strain. We must point out, however, that there will be times when the warden will have to "act naturally" in the sense that an actor acts naturally. This is particularly important with ill children. If a child comes and whines: "I've cut my finger", just when the warden is in the middle of making Income Tax returns or when the cook has given notice, he or she must act as though the child had not come in at such an awkward moment; for these children are often too ill or too anxious to be able to allow for the warden's own personal difficulties as well as their own.

We therefore try to choose as hostel wardens those who possess this ability to be consistently natural in their behaviour, for we regard it as essential to the work. We would count as important also the possession of some skill, such as music, painting, pottery, etc. Above and beyond all these things, however, it is, of course, vital that the wardens possess a genuine love of children, for only this will see them through the inevitable ups and downs of hostel life.

We believe that if a man and wife can be appointed as joint wardens, many deficiencies are avoided, and many difficulties do not arise. In making such an appointment, we assume that some of the wardens have or will have children of their own. This gives a sense of stability to the group.

Another important requirement in hostel wardens is their willingness to stay in the job. A change of warden means casualties among the children every time. Brilliant people who organize one hostel well and pass on to another to do the same there would be better if they had never existed as far as the children are concerned. It is the permanent nature of the home that makes it valuable, even more than the fact that the work is done intelligently.

We do not expect the wardens to carry out any prescribed type of regime, or even to carry out agreed plans. Wardens who have to be told what to do are of no use, because the important things have to be done on the spot in a way that is natural to the individual concerned. Only thus will the warden's relationship become real and therefore of importance to the child. Wardens are encouraged to build up a home and community life to the best of their ability, and it will be found that this is along the line of their own beliefs and way of life. No two hostels will therefore be alike.

We find that there are wardens who like organizing large groups of children, and others who prefer to have intimate personal relationships with a few children. Some prefer abnormal children of one type or another, and some like true mental defectives.

The education of the wardens in the work is important and has been discussed earlier as part of the work of the psychiatrist and of the psychiatric social worker. This education is best done on the job, by the discussion of problems as they arise. It is a great help if wardens are confident enough in themselves to be able to think along psychological lines and discuss problems with other wardens and experienced people.

The staffing of hostels apart from the wardens presents peculiar difficulties, especially where the children are rather anti-social. With normal children the assistants can be young people who are learning the job and practising taking responsibility and acting on their own initiative with a view to becoming wardens themselves at a later date. Where the children are anti-social, however, the management has to be strong and cannot avoid being dictatorial, so that assistants have to be constantly carrying out orders from the warden when they would prefer to be working on their own initiative. They therefore become easily bored, or else they like being told what to do, in which case they are not much good. These problems are inherent in the work.

True nature of home

One thing that has made us realize the inadequacies of large orphanages has been a deeper understanding of what a good home means to a child, and its function in his development.

Briefly, we could perhaps say that a good home is one in which father and mother live together in a stable relationship into which the child can be accepted and welcomed. In such an environment the child gradually learns to trust his parents and to believe in their goodness. But in order to establish this belief, it seems that he must test over and over again their ability to remain good parents in spite of anything he may do to hurt or annoy them. By means of this testing he gradually convinces himself, if the parents do in fact stand the strain. Thus he builds up that belief which is so necessary if his future development is to be satisfactory. If the child's own parents do not exist, or if they do not stand the strain that belongs to the building up of a stable family life, the child must surely always remain unconvinced, and uncertain of himself and of others.

This is, so to speak, the first lesson in social adjustment, for if the parents are proved to be trustworthy, the child has every reason to believe that other people may be the same, so that he can face life in an optimistic way, ready for the new experiences which it brings.

In the actual evacuation experience it has been found that the children who have had a good early experience and whose homes are intact have as a rule been able to stand the transplantation to billets. On the other hand, of the children who have proved difficult to billet and who have gone back to evacuation areas, or who have been admitted to hostels or placed in Approved Schools, a big proportion have never known a good relation to both parents or to their own homes, or else their homes have recently failed them in some striking way.

If it is recognized how intimately a child's sense of security is bound up with his relationship to his parents, it becomes obvious that no other people can give him so much. Every child has the right to his own good home in which to grow, and it is nothing but a misfortune that deprives him of it.

In our hostel work, therefore, we recognize that we cannot give to the children anything so good as their own good home would have been. We can only offer a substitute home.

Each hostel tries to reproduce as nearly as possible a home environment for each child in it. This means first of all the provision of positive things: a building, food, clothing, human love, and understanding; a time-table, schooling; apparatus and ideas leading to rich play and constructive work. The hostel also provides substitute parents and other human relationships. And then, these things being provided, each child, according to the degree of his distrust and according to the degree of his hopelessness about the loss of his own home (and sometimes his recognition of the inadequacies of that home while it lasted), is all the time testing the hostel staff as he would test his own parents. Sometimes he does this directly, but most of the time he is content to let another child do the testing for him. An important thing about this testing is that it is not something that can be achieved and done with. Always somebody has to be a nuisance.

Often one of the staff will say: "We'd be all right if it weren't for Tommy . . .", but in point of fact the others can only afford to be "all right" because Tommy is being a nuisance and is proving to them that the home can stand up to Tommy's testing and could therefore presumably stand up to their own.

The usual response of a child who is placed in a good hostel can be described as having three phases. For the first short phase, the child is extraordinarily normal (it will be a long time before he is so normal again); he has new hope, he scarcely sees people as they are, and the staff and the other children have not yet had any reason to begin to disillusion him. Almost every child goes through a short period of good behaviour when he first comes to a hostel. It is a dangerous stage, because what he sees and responds to in the warden and his staff is his ideal of what a good father and mother would be like. Grown-ups are inclined to think: "This child sees we are nice, and easily trusts us." But he doesn't see they are nice; he doesn't see *them* at all; he just imagines they are nice. It is a symptom of illness to believe that anything can be 100 per cent good, and the child starts off with an ideal which is destined to be shattered.

The child sooner or later enters into the second phase, the breaking-down of his ideal. He sets about this first by testing the building and the people physically. He wants to know what damage he can do and how much he can do with impunity. Then, if he finds that he can be physically managed, that is, that the place and the people in it have nothing to fear from him physically, he starts to test by subtlety, putting one member of the staff against another, trying to make people quarrel, trying to make people give each other away, and doing all he can to get favoured himself. When a hostel is being managed unsatisfactorily, it is this second phase which becomes almost a constant feature.

If the hostel withstands these tests, the child enters on the third phase, settles down with a sigh of relief, and joins in the life of the group as an ordinary member. It should be borne in mind that his first real contacts with the other children will probably be in the shape of a fight or some kind of attack, and we have noticed that often the first child to be attacked by a new child will later become that child's first friend.

In short, the hostels provide positive good things and give opportunities for their value and reality to be tested continuously by the children. Sentimentality has no place in the management of children, and no ultimate good can come from offering children artificial conditions of indulgence; by carefully administered justice they must gradually be brought up against the consequences of their own destructive actions. Each child will be able to stand this in so far as he has been able to get some positive good out of hostel life—that is, in so far as he has found people who are truly reliable and has begun to build up belief in them and in himself.

It must be remembered that the preservation of law and order is necessary to the children and will be a relief to them, for it means that the hostel life and the good things for which the hostel stands will be preserved in spite of all that they can do.

Types of hostel

It has been stated above that children are placed in this or that hostel according to their psychological classification. In actual practice, however, we found that we could not *set out* to run one hostel for depressed children, another for the normal, and another for the anti-social, etc. But by careful experiment and in the course of time we found that one hostel warden was particularly successful with one type of child and another with another type. We therefore try to send each warden the children that suit him best. In this way specialization has come about, not by planning, but by careful observation of the work of each warden and his ability to develop along certain lines.

As far as the child is concerned, it is important that he should go to a hostel in which the children are not too dissimilar from himself in experience and in their reactions to experience and in their need to be strongly managed or allowed freedom.

If it is to be presumed that the majority of children in hostels in post-war Europe will be children who have had a good start in life but who have been hurt by their experiences, they can to some extent be expected to recover, given time and a stable background. In so far as this is the case, the hostel's job will be to provide a firm framework for their lives, a framework of human relationships, and to allow for the natural processes of healing which will take place in the course of months or years. It is surely very important that the main layout of any scheme should be designed primarily for the benefit of these children who can recover.

In our experience the only good method of distinguishing these comparatively normal children from those who, on account of their early experiences and disturbed emotional development, have to start from scratch is by trial and error under hostel conditions. Severity of symptoms is a poor guide. In each group of hostels it will therefore be convenient to plan to have one hostel which we will call Hostel A, to which will be sent children who are considered to be fundamentally healthy. Some of these children will remain here permanently, but the aim would be wherever possible to send them into households very carefully chosen as suitable for adopting a normal child. On the other hand, there would have to be Hostels B, C, and D, for the various types of ill children, some of whom would be directly placed in them according to initial diagnosis, and some of whom would be transferred from Hostel A after being found to be ill.

With regard to the ill children, the first group requiring special management will be the *anti-social children*. This group is bound to contain children with varying types of illness, but a common feature will be that each child in it will be specially active in testing his environment. Even when the environment stands up well to the test, anti-social children cannot believe this fact for more than a short length of time, and they have to be managed in a group in which more or less constant testing is being carried out. In the management of a hostel of this type there will have to be more of a dictatorship than would be desirable for normal children. If the management is successful, the testing will not be so obvious all the time, but any relaxation on the part of the staff will mean that it becomes constant and active again.

Gradually, however, in any one group, individuals can be seen developing a belief in the environment's ability to remain both good and strong.

If in any group there are several hostels for anti-social children, these should be classified as far as possible into (1) those catering for children who have known good homes, but whose homes have been destroyed through the accident of war rather than through parental troubles, and (2) those catering for children who have never known good homes—for instance, illegitimate children and children who have experienced homes of their own which failed to stand the test and which went to pieces quite apart from the physical effects of war.

Anti-social children, although not fully or easily believing in a good environment that can stand the test, nevertheless have not given up hope. Children who have given up hope are ill in some other way, depressed or confused or introverted, and they all tend to pass through the anti-social stage as they recover hope on their way to recovery.

Introverted children, who have defended themselves against adverse external conditions by withdrawing altogether into themselves, form a group quite distinct from the anti-social children. They may be apparently mentally defective and yet are capable of making a complete recovery. Their treatment is particularly interesting to some workers. If the hostel warden can enter into, and really appreciate, the child's inner world and help him to share it with others by expressing it in drawing and painting, etc., he will be doing important therapeutic work. The amount of recovery that children of this type will make in response to appreciative understanding can be very marked.

Depressed children may be passing through a phase, or may be more or less permanently organized into a depressive state. They may have strong suicidal ideas or hypochondriacal fears and all kinds of worries, just like depressed adults. Of all the groups of ill children, this group probably contains the most valuable children, who tend to feel responsible and who, when well, can be trusted with important things. Some of the more healthy children will pass through phases of depression, which can be looked on as periods of sadness or mourning in which the child is unconscious of what is mourned.

Extreme care has to be taken with the staffing of a hostel for such children, and the wardens have to be able to *tolerate* depression. The basis of the management of depressed children is that they are capable of making a spontaneous recovery. There are very special problems associated with the false cure of depressed children by forceful personalities on whom the children become very dependent. But details of these cannot be fully developed here.

Some of the children are distinguished from the others by being *distorted* in one way or another, so that they torture animals, or eat worms out of turnips in the fields, or go round the garden pulling up the carrots and replacing them after cutting them; or else they are curiously suspicious, especially distrusting kindness, or are always trying to put people against each other by exploiting their carefully observed weaknesses, or they are always causing trouble by suggesting nasty things to other children, while remaining outside and detached and uninvolved in what subsequently happens. These children form a heterogeneous group, and the word "insane" could be applied to some of them. They cause great difficulties in the various hostels for other types of children but, of course, to some extent must always be found in any big group. The point is that no amount of skilful management and tolerance can cure these children who need long, personal psycho-therapy, which unfortunately is not usually available. It is certainly no solution of their problem to herd them together into an institution.

For the success of any scheme it is essential to have the *backward children* dealt with on their own. Obviously mental defectives with an intelligence quotient of 70 and under quite easily get recognition, and there is usually some already existing provision for them. We are referring, however, to the backward children with a higher intelligence quotient who really need specialized education and a specialized kind of friendly management which does not aim too high. These same children, who respond well to specialized education, are a constant nuisance in a mixed group, especially as the other children are likely to be excitable, quick-witted, restless children who become impatient of a classroom technique which is too slow for their quickness of uptake.

Re-sorting and re-billeting

Sometimes we find that it is necessary to move a child from one hostel to another within the same group. This may be because he is the wrong type for the hostel into which we have put him, or the hostel at that moment is unable to absorb him. Another reason for transfer would be that a child sometimes grows out of the particular environment which a hostel provides, in which case he is told why he has been removed. In practice we do not make many of these changes, but we regard as important the ability to do so, should need arise. Often one child can hinder the work of a whole hostel, whereas another hostel with another set of children can accommodate him and his difficulties. Often a difficult situation has been saved by the timely transfer of a child in this way.

On the whole, we do not believe in changes for the children, and we find that they do not stand changes at all well. This is not in the least surprising, of course, and it only means that if the child relapses, he has not yet had a long enough time in a constant environment. Possibly in the hostel he appears to be fairly natural and stable—but it must be remembered that this stability may still depend on the hostel—and if he leaves it too soon, he has to begin painfully all over again to build up a belief in his environment. This time it will be more difficult, because every time he fails, he is less likely to have the courage to start again. We have found that given enough time in one environment, children can and do work through to a measure of independence.

In practice we do re-billet some children from hostels in accordance with the policy of the Ministry of Health. If we are fortunate and find a really good billet, the project is often successful. But we do not often say: this child is now billetable; if we find a good billet, we look round for a child who is fit to make good use of it.

In order to preserve the work already done with hostel children, we feel that it is of great importance that the hostel should be able to see a child through adolescence and placed in suitable employment. To cut him adrift at such an important stage in his life is surely unfair, and it may indeed be disastrous.

Some limitations of a war-time experiment

It is a misfortune in evacuation hostels that the work is felt by all concerned to be temporary. In an important, fundamental way this affects the staff as well as the children. As far as the child is concerned, he knows that at the end of the war he will go home—if he has a home to go to. If his home does not exist, or he has had no satisfactory contact with it for years, then he does not know what will become of him. The child may then very well be too anxious to let himself trust the people in the hostel and make use of what they can give him—his fear of being eventually let down and separated from them is too great. In the same way some members of the staff may feel that they cannot give all they would like to give to the children because they realize their contact will only be a temporary one, and, moreover, they themselves may dread separation from the children who come to mean much to them. "Homes" of a more permanent nature would not be built on the knowledge that any outward event (the end of the war) would cause their disintegration.

Another war-time difficulty has been that of finding suitable billets for children who are getting better, and for children who have grown up out of a particular hostel, children whose newly won confidence in life can be easily undermined. War-time conditions make it difficult for foster-parents to give all the time and supervision required by the child. By pressure on hostel accommodation we have often been obliged to billet a child whose stability was not sufficiently established, and we have also been obliged, because of the shortage of billets, to use those of which we felt rather uncertain. In a more permanent scheme placing out would be done only in the case of children who were really ready for it and when really good foster homes had been found.

Another limitation to actual experiment which the war has imposed has been the fact that primarily hostels exist to relieve billeting officers of difficult children. We have never lost sight of this fact, and this has meant that many children who are unsuitable for our hostels have nevertheless had to be admitted. In other words, we exist to deal with a practical social problem and not to carry out an experiment with carefully selected children. We feel that this gives value to our work, but we should like to point out that at the same time it imposes limitations. Obviously the work done in each hostel would be easier and better if cases could be selected every time for suitability rather than accepted from necessity.

In conclusion, we should like to say that in spite of the limitations of a war-time experiment we personally feel that it has been one well worth making. For not only has it demonstrated the difficulties and possibilities of providing substitute homes for children, but it has surely established the fact that in the treatment of children suffering from emotional disturbances, residence in a hostel under specialized management can have definite therapeutic value.

Evacuation hostel schemes have been allowed to develop in the various localities according to local conditions and local needs, with the result that a really big collective experience has been gained. It is hoped that from the increased knowledge of children and their difficulties which has been gained some positive good will have been brought out of a war-time necessity.

CHAPTER THREE

Children who cannot play

(1945)

S ome children cannot play. This sad fact has to be reckoned with by all those who work among them. Their predicament is best understood if we consider what playing means to children who can play.

The importance of play

Like all human activity, play can be regarded as having importance on two levels of experience. There is its personal inner importance to the individual concerned, and there is its importance in relation to the things and people outside the individual. Satisfactory human activity, whether it be called work or play, aims, consciously or unconsciously, at the achievement of harmony between the individual and his environment. Unfortunately, this state of equilibrium is not something which is established once and for all. It has to be constantly maintained and is won and lost over and over again at each stage of development. It can be said, therefore, that the aim of all activity is the satisfaction of inner personal needs within the framework and limits of real life, and that on this achievement well-being and happiness depend.

First published in *Play and Mental Health* (London: New Educational Fellowship, 1945).

The process of coming to terms with reality is an extremely complicated one in which the child has to build up, through experiences, his own conception of reality and his own interpretation of the world—in other words, his own philosophy of life. The emergence of this philosophy is the important thing, for it means that the child is beginning to manage his own life in relation to the world outside him. Quite young children can be seen doing this. But the child's own idea of reality must be constantly revised and tested out in the outside world, and he must, therefore, be provided with ideas and real situations, people, and experiences with which to deal. If he is starved of these, his idea of reality will be distorted. The whole process of the assimilation of experiences may be compared with the process of physical nutrition in which the child takes in food and digests it and eliminates what he cannot use. Thus, to satisfy his inner needs, the child selects objects and experiences from the outside world, which then have meaning and become real for him. The experience which he cannot absorb he has to get rid of in some way, either by repressing it or turning away from it.

It seems, however, that the normal child has a tendency to tackle only the experiences with which he can deal at a given moment and to leave others for a later time. What he needs, therefore, is to be neither over-protected from experiences which the adult may feel are too difficult for him, nor over-burdened with difficulties which should be shouldered by the adult. An example of the first situation is the story of the child brought up in an institution who, at the age of sixteen, was shocked to see a funeral procession. It was her first real experience of death. Many children, on the other hand, are overburdened by having to make decisions for themselves which should be made by their parents, or by becoming too deeply involved in the parents' personal problems. If the child is left free to take for himself what he is ready for, he has the chance of achieving his own adjustment to life in his own time.

The actual process of the absorption of experiences can be seen in the child's ability to use and express them in the activities he undertakes on his own initiative. In this way, we see the meaning of play to the child: it is his method of absorbing into himself and using for how own personal satisfaction what is important to him in his environment—e.g. when a little girl is putting her dolls to bed, she is not merely passing her time agreeably among her own familiar possessions but living the life of a mother and a baby and learning, besides, to understand and to adjust her relationship to her parents and the other members of the family.

Thus, through play, the child is experiencing on two levels. There are his inner personal experiences which satisfy his inner needs, and there is the experience of the activity itself in relation to the environment. If inner experiences do not get used and related to the environment in this way, then the child is in a dangerous position. Either he will concentrate on them and cut himself off from vital effective contact with life around him, or he will concentrate on external activities and become cut off from his own inner life. Obviously, in both these directions lie illness and maladjustment.

If life is to be tolerable, the bridge between the individual and the outside world must be secure, and, as we have already seen, this security is achieved by a "give and take" between the individual and society. Satisfactory activity is not merely the express of this underlying security, but the means of achieving it. It is not enough that the child absorbs from those about him; he must grow on his experiences and then relate them again to real life. In other words, he must give back something for all that he has taken. In doing this, he begins to send out his own roots into life, and from these he can grow eventually into an independent individual.

The adult's responsibility

The child's mother and the other adults who look after him form the most important part of his life, for not only do they control the physical world as he knows it, but they can give him the love which will satisfy his inner needs. The mother, however, must do more than give to the child; she must be able to accept his love in return, thereby proving to him his own goodness and loveableness. Her acceptance to his love also helps him to feel secure through his own bad moments of feeling angry and destructive. Moreover, if he feels anchored to the external world in this way, he will have greater courage and ability to face and work out his inner needs and conflicts.

In all our dealings with children we recognize that much of their play is performed in direct relation to the adults whom they love. If these adults can also understand what is going on, so much the better, but it is not necessary. There are times in play when the child seems aware of and symbolizes what he needs and will come again and again to the adult, bringing toys and drawings to be kept till he asks for them again. Then there are the giving-and-taking games, such as playing ball, and buying and selling, which, at moments, the child needs to play to gain reassurance. These activities are expressing the child's inner need to be accepted and loved, so that he in his turn may accept and love others.

The child's problems and difficulties

This task of bridging the gap between inner needs and outer reality gives rise to many difficulties. I will mention two important kinds of frustration. First, the child finds that not all the desirable things in the world are for him. His mother's love, for instance, has to be shared with the other members of the family. This discovery may give rise to anger, hatred, fear, and the wish to destroy: and these are feelings which in turn cause guilt and anxiety. In such a case the child knows where to find the good he wants but has not yet brought himself to realize that he cannot have it all to himself. The second kind of frustration occurs when a child's environment has really "let him down." That is to say, he never found anyone who gave him, even temporarily, the feeling of being satisfied. Such a child is aware of a need and constantly expects the people nearest him to satisfy that need, but he lacks altogether the confidence from knowing that someone did once give him what he wanted. This frustration, therefore, gives rise to constant anxiety, and the child is not able to take even the good things that are available for him. And as we have already seen, where a child has been able to take from his environment, he is anxious to give back something of his own in exchange.

Every child, therefore, is faced with the task of either preserving or finding the satisfying object. The solution must lie in accepting the world as it is, with all its real possibilities, and in abandoning the impossible. There is no doubt that, in a hundred different ways, play helps the child to carry out this task. For example, the child putting her dolls to bed is surely learning what it means for a mother to have and to love more than one child. In moments of anxiety the child will live in play experiences which have been satisfactory to him in the past. In throwing stones and smashing toys, the child gets rid of his hatred and so preserves the people he loves. In wild-cat jungle games, he impersonates the object of his own fear. Play can also be experimental; the child tries out new objects for his emotions, new ways of satisfying the unsatisfied needs.

But, of course, play is not all compensatory. We have all watched the moments of "pure" play—moments when equilibrium has been achieved and anxiety overcome. The child is in harmony with is environment; the imagination is free, and the activity is new and creative and the unique expression of the total personality. These moments come and go throughout childhood, but as life becomes more complicated and burdened with responsibilities, such freedom is achieved more rarely.

Means of assisting the child in his play

Satisfactory play can be regarded as a real achievement for the child, but adults can help enormously and give him the encouragement which he is sure to need at times. I would suggest the following ways in particular:

(1) By loving the child and giving him the security which he needs in the outside world, so that he may be able to face and deal with his inner world.

(2) By passively accepting and appreciating the child and his play, letting him feel that you are able to enter into it and are part of his world.

(3) By accepting responsibility for the child's environment, and by controlling him in his play, should need arise. This will lessen his anxiety about his own destructiveness and leave him more freedom to develop.

(4) By actually playing with the child at times. By entering into his phantasy life and becoming a lion or an elephant and enjoying with him the creatures of his imagination. Many a child has been helped through a difficult period in this way. If the adult enters his world, it becomes a less frightening place for him, and he can more easily link it real experiences. Also, by playing with a child, the adult can introduce him into the grown-up world by playing out real situations with him, e.g., a mother can let her child "work" with her and for her. This again strengthens the bridge between child and reality and is altogether to his advantage (provided that the adult has the right attitude, and is not patronizing).

(5) By providing ideas and apparatus which will enrich play, and by seeing that the child has time and space to play undisturbed.

(6) By organizing groups of children for communal play and teaching them the traditional games and songs that are their heritage. A child who has found it difficult to play on his own may, through the group, find a new freedom and learn to develop his own play.

(7) By avoiding interference in a great deal of the child's playtime, especially when he is absorbed and getting on happily.

For the child who has special difficulties in playing, there is even more that the adult may do to help him, but I will discuss these questions later in relation to the difficulties.

Inability to play

We can now realize how serious is the predicament of the child who cannot play. He is cut off from the means of solving his own problems. It seems that the breakdown occurs at the point of contact with the environment. The child has not found the security and reassurance that he needs and therefore feels frustrated and anxious. He feels cut off from the outside world and unable to deal with real life. I have met children who tried to solve their dilemma by concentrating on their inner life and were, thus, in danger of losing the most elementary and necessary contact with the outside world. And I have known children who gave all their energies to maintaining their environment and who were therefore not free to feel their own inner needs.

The most common reason why children find it difficult to play, therefore, is that their parents for one reason or another have failed to give them the security they need. Broken, unhappy homes are likely to produce frustration of the second and more serious kind. While a child is with such a parent, it will feel constantly frustrated and will always be on the look-out for someone with whom it can feel secure. Sometimes teachers or older brothers and sisters help to fill the gap. If someone is found, the child may then be able to play out the unsatisfactory home situation, thus lessening the tension and in some way making a compromise with life. We have watched this happening to children in hostels over a period of time.

Another way out of the difficulty is exemplified by the case of a little girl of four who is having to face a very difficult situation at home, where the father's absence in the Army makes life very difficult for her. This child has identified herself with her mother in the effort to keep contact with the outside world. She copies her mother's words and actions and follows her about all day. The only play of which she is capable is sweeping and dusting after her mother. She never plays in any other way. By *becoming* the mother, this child is trying to make up to herself for what she lacks in the actual mother; but so great is her anxiety that she wants her mother always present, so that, for one thing, the real difference between herself and her mother is not lost sight of. This child is so busy keeping her own environment going that she is unable to express her inner needs as a child.

All children, of course, go through stages in which they play at being grown-up. It is a very necessary part of their experience, and many children who find play difficult seem able to come to it in this way. But this child was playing in a compulsive way and was not absorbing her own childish experiences. Her most urgent need is for someone on whom she can absolutely depend before she can give up her identification with her mother and live as a child again.

In the early days of evacuation I met a six-year-old boy who was the most completely cut-off child imaginable. He never spoke of his own accord and only answered questions reluctantly. For a short time at the beginning he refused food. He was completely docile and inactive and walked about in a dazed fashion. He was incapable of learning anything in school, and play was out of the question; he simply sat and watched people. It was not surprising to learn that both his parents had been killed in the air-raid shelter from which he had been rescued. Fortunately he was put into a good foster-home, where the foster-mother understood something of what he was going through. She became fond of him, but did not try to force herself on him. She let him go his own way at his own pace.

After about eighteen months he began to respond and recover. His first efforts at play were pathetic, and he would look sheepish and give up if anyone noticed him. He played only when alone with the foster-mother, when her own little boy was out with the other children in the village. She would plan these occasions when time allowed and would sit knitting or reading. He would play with bricks, stopping always when anyone came in. Gradually the play became more complicated, and one day he actually built an air-raid shelter and played out his parents' death, suddenly asking, "Does it hurt to get killed?" All this time he had been grappling with the experience of his parents' death, and only when he felt secure enough with his foster-mother, when he had grown new roots in his environment, so to speak, could he face the fact of their death and let them go. This he was able to experience again and again through play, till he had accepted it. Of course, this was not the free, happy play of a normal child, there was much anxiety and compulsion in it. The patience and tact of the foster-mother cannot be too highly praised. She helped not only by her fondness for the child but by a passive acceptance of him and his difficulties.

It is more than probable that the child had had a satisfactory relationship with his parents and that this stood him in good stead during the difficult time and made recovery possible. Many other children in this situation would probably have produced some other symptom of anxiety, such as bedwetting or stealing, in a direct effort to maintain live contact with the environment. Many of the evacuated children reacted in this way and were able to keep up some limited form of play activity. Many children in Europe will be in a similar predicament, and their first need will be an environment which is secure, and which they can accept as their own after the necessary time has elapsed, and they can test it out and find its value for themselves. The first need is for people who can love children and stand a great deal from them.

There are other children who are unable to play in the normal way, who try to destroy their environment by aggressive acts and so become further cut off. Children such as these probably really feel over-whelmed by their own inner needs and feel that they may hurt people outside, from whom they want so much. Rather than take this risk, they cut themselves off as completely as they can from vital contact with others and build up an inner phantasy world around themselves, inside which they try to work out their own salvation in thoughts without play. This world may be full of frightening monsters who are going to destroy the child: but it may also contain loving companions who share everything, even meal-times, with him. In this way a kind of equilibrium is achieved, but without play and therefore without contact with reality.

Of course, most normal children go through these phases of cutting themselves off from outside contacts and building up a phantasy world to meet special needs. But the ill child is the one who cuts himself off too completely and lives for too long in a frightening world and keeps no real anchor outside. Such a child cannot play successfully in a normal way, and any contacts he makes will be destructive and tend to spoil the play of others.

We have found in evacuation hostels that these children can be helped enormously if an adult can find a way into their world and take it seriously. In time the child may be able to express in drawings and in play some of his inner world to this person. Such a step is obviously a great achievement for the child and the adult.

Secure contact with the outside world, therefore, is the first thing to be achieved if anxious children are to be helped to play satisfactorily.

Various types of play

In my experience I have found that some children can be helped to come to play through expression work such as painting, drawing, handwork, etc. I suggest that the reason may be that such activities are undertaken only in response to encouragement (and often a great deal of help) from an adult. Thus a bond is made which gives security and a measure of freedom. Herbert Read (1943) in *Education Through Art* explains how he feels every piece of work done by a child to be the direct response to the relationship the child has with his teacher. If the teacher can accept and appreciate the work, then it improves and becomes freer and more creative. Certainly one knows teachers who are inferior artists themselves, who can call forth work of high value and inspiration from their pupils. Such a bond is very deep and satisfying on both sides, and it not at all surprising that, through such an experience, a child becomes freer and develops in other ways. To have one's best efforts accepted and appreciated not only forms a very real link with the outside world, but it convinces the child, as nothing else could, that he is not the guilty, unworthy, or destructive person he felt himself to be.

In a girls' club a very inhibited young adolescent was once helped to play by the discovery that she was exceptionally good at weaving, and she was induced to teach the club leader to weave. This took quite a time, and they became friendly, but she was still very afraid of the other girls in the club. Gradually she gained confidence, and with the help of the club leader she taught two or three of the other girls of her own age. To cut a long story short, there was one momentous day when she was found playing around the building with this little gang. Here, again, undoubtedly the relationship with the adult was the important thing. She was able to give the one real achievement of her life (her skill in weaving) to someone who valued it and made it into a medium of exchange with others.

Some children who are inhibited in play by fear of their own aggressiveness can be helped to play by games which control and use their destructive impulses, for instance, games with rules (with an adult there to enforce them) and team games with ample supervision. Incidentally, group activities often seem to help a child who is afraid and insecure with adults. Such a child feels safe in a group and eventually may regard the adult as a friend and not an enemy. Play with hammer and nails, whip toys, and spades all gives legitimate outlets for aggressive feelings. Also, if the child can make something with tools, his destructiveness is rendered positively valuable as well as socially acceptable. Creation is always the most effective way of dealing with guilt. Just recently, it has been the fashion in one evacuation hostel to have large penknives for carving boats, daggers, etc., from wood. The children go about chipping away at their sticks and are proud of their workmanship, which often shows real skill, but even where there is no skill, the hostel staff appreciate the work when it is shown to them.

So it seems that there *are* ways of helping a child to play, though none of them is easy, and they demand from the adult not only endless patience, but a complete giving of all that he has and is. But it is an exciting experience to see a child launched into play, which may enable him to become a free and independent human being.

CHAPTER FOUR

Introduction
to *Deprivation and Delinquency*

(1984)

I t does not seem an exaggeration to say that the manifestations
of deprivation and delinquency in society are as big a threat as that
of the nuclear bomb. In fact, there is surely a connection between
the two kinds of threat, because as the antisocial element in society
rises, so does the destructive potential within society rise to a new
danger level. At the present time we are fighting to prevent the danger
level rising, and we need to muster all the resources we can for this
task. One resource will undoubtedly be the knowledge gained by
anyone who has had to come to grips with the problems of deprivation
and delinquency by taking responsibility for individual cases. Donald
Winnicott was such a person and was precipitated into this position by
the Second World War when he became Consultant Psychiatrist to the
Government Evacuation Scheme in a reception area in England.

Although the circumstances in which Winnicott found himself
were abnormal because of the war-time, the knowledge gained from
the experience has general application because deprived children who
become delinquent have basic problems which are manifested in pre-
dictable ways, whatever the circumstances. Moreover, the children
who became Winnicott's responsibility were those who needed special

---

First published in D. W. Winnicott, *Deprivation and Delinquency* (London: Tavistock, 1984).

provision because they could not settle in ordinary homes. In other words, they were already in trouble in their own homes before the war started. The war was almost incidental to them, except in those cases (not a few) when it was positively beneficial in that it removed them from an intolerable situation and placed them in one where they might, and often did, find help and relief.

The evacuation experience had a profound effect on Winnicott because he had to meet in a concentrated way the confusion brought about by the wholesale break-up of family life, and he had to experience the effect of separation and loss, and of destruction and death. The personal responses in bizarre and delinquent behaviour that followed had to be managed and encompassed and gradually understood by Winnicott, working with a staff team at local level. The children he worked with had reached the end of the line; there was nowhere else for them to go, and how to hold them became the main preoccupation of all those trying to help them.

Up to this point in his career Winnicott had been concerned with clinical practice in hospital settings and in private practice, where adults responsible for children brought them to see him. In building up his early clinical experience, he had deliberately avoided as far as he could taking on cases of delinquency, because the hospital did not have the resources needed to deal with them, and he himself did not feel ready to be side-tracked into this area of work, which is infinitely time-consuming and would require skills and facilities that he did not have. He felt he must first gain experience of working with ordinary parents and children in their family and local settings. The majority of these children could be helped and prevented from further psychiatric deterioration, whereas he knew that the children who had gone over into delinquency needed more than clinical help. They presented a problem of care and management.

When the war came, Winnicott could not avoid the delinquency issue any longer, and he deliberately took on the Evacuation Consultancy knowing something of what he was in for and that a whole new range of experience was awaiting him. His clinical experience would have to be extended to include the care and management aspects of treatment.

Soon after the start of the area scheme to which Winnicott was appointed, I joined his team as Psychiatric Social Worker and administrator of the five hostels for dealing with children who were too disturbed to be placed in ordinary homes. I saw my first task as that of trying to evolve a method of working so that all of us, including

Winnicott, could make the best possible use of his weekly visits. The staff living in the hostels were taking the full impact of the children's confusion and despair and the resulting behaviour problems. The staff were demanding to be told *what to do* and were often desperate for help in the form of instructions, and it took time for them to accept that Winnicott would not, and in fact could not, take on that role, because he was not available and involved in the day-to-day living situation, as they were.

Gradually it was recognized that all of us must take responsibility for doing the best we could with the individual children in the situations that arose from day to day. Then we would think about what we did and discuss it with Winnicott as honestly as we could when he visited. This turned out to be a good way of working and the only one possible in the circumstances. These sessions with him were the highlight of the week and were invaluable learning experiences for us all, including Winnicott, who kept careful records of each child's situation and the stresses put on staff members. His comments were nearly always in the form of questions which widened the discussion and never violated the vulnerability of individual members.

After these sessions, Winnicott and I would try to work out what was going on from the mass of detail that had been given to us, and we would form some tentative theories about it. This was a totally absorbing task because no sooner had a theory been formulated, than it had to be scrapped or modified. Moreover, the exercise was an essential one for me, because during the week I was used as a sounding board by those in charge of the hostels and as a support at any time in difficult moments. I was then in a position to alert the administrator responsible for the scheme when risks that could have led to disaster had to be taken, and to inform Winnicott about what was happening.

There is no doubt that working with deprived children gave a whole new dimension to Winnicott's thinking and to his practice and affected his basic concepts on emotional growth and development. Quite early on, his theories about the drives behind the antisocial tendency began to take shape and to be expressed. His thinking affected what actually went on in the hostels and how children were treated by individual staff members, and the results were always carefully noted by him. The hostel notebooks still exist and show his careful observation and attention to detail. Gradually new approaches and attitudes were built up and attempts made to get to the innocence behind the defences and the delinquent acts. There were no miracles, but if crises could be met and *lived through* rather than *reacted to*, there could be easing of tension and renewed trust and hope.

As it turned out, I became the one who held the job together, because I was able to be in daily contact with the staff and children in the hostels. I also saw it as essential to keep communications open and as clear as possible between all concerned in the scheme: committee members, local authority administrators, the parents of the children, and the public bodies who were involved. In this way a wide section of the public was kept informed about the effect of separation and loss on the children and about the complex nature of the task of trying to help them. It was the dissemination of this kind of first-hand knowledge from evacuation areas all over the country that eventually provided the momentum for the setting-up of a statutory committee of enquiry into the care of children separated from their parents (The Curtis Committee) and eventually led to that landmark in the social history of this country—the Children Act 1948. Winnicott and I both gave written and oral evidence to the Curtis Committee.

With regard to the actual job itself, Winnicott was the person who made it work. He was the central figure who gathered together and held the experiences of us all and made sense of them, thus helping staff living with the children to keep sane in the children's subjective and bizarre world in which they lived for long periods at a time. For us, one of the important lessons of the total experience was that attitudes cannot be taught in words—they can only be "caught" by assimilation in living relationships.

I have often been asked, "What was it like to work with Winnicott?" I have always avoided answering, but I think I would say something like this: it was to be in a situation of complete reciprocity, where giving and taking were indistinguishable and where roles and responsibilities were taken for granted and never disputed. In this fact lay the security and freedom needed for creative work to emerge out of the chaos and devastation of war. And it did emerge on many levels and brought satisfaction to all of us taking part in it. We discovered new dimensions in ourselves and in others. Our potentiality was realized and stretched to the limit, so that new capacities emerged. This is what it was like to work with Winnicott.

The papers included in this collection fall into a natural sequence, which starts with those written under pressure of Winnicott's clinical involvement in the war and which describe the effects of deprivation as he experienced them. Then follow papers giving his ideas about the nature and origins of the anti-social tendency. The third section is devoted to the kind of social provision needed for the treatment of delinquent children; and finally come three papers about individual therapy and its use in work with the deprived.

Although these writings are of historical interest, they do not belong to history but to the ever-present encounter between the antisocial elements in society and the forces of health and sanity which reach out to reclaim and recover what has been lost. The complexity of this encounter cannot be overestimated. The point of interaction between the care-givers and the cared for is always the focus for therapy in this field or work, and it requires constant attention and support from the professional experts involved and enlightened backing from the responsible administrators. Today, as always, the practical question is how to maintain an environment that is humane enough, and strong enough, to contain both the care-givers and the deprived and delinquent who desperately need care and containment, but who will do their best to destroy it when they find it.

CHAPTER FIVE

Child care in Oxfordshire:
an interview with Alan Cohen

(1980)

Alan Cohen: How did you come into social work then, Mrs Winnicott?

Clare Winnicott: How did I come into it? I suppose through a friend of the family. And in a way my family had always been interested in social work. My father had run a club for unemployed people, my grandfather had been—had taken quite a big part in the social situation where I lived. I think it was in the family.

AC: When was it you first came into social work? Was it during the war or before the war?

Alan Cohen is a retired social worker who completed the Mental Health Certificate at the London School of Economics in 1963, where the lecturers to the course included D. W. Winnicott. An evacuee himself, he worked as a social worker in the areas of family casework, mental health, and intellectual disability, and he taught on social work courses in Nottingham and Lancaster. His interest in the history of British social work led him to conduct a series of extensive interviews with several dozen influential figures in British social work. He is the author of *The Revolution in Post-War Family Casework: The Story of Pacifist Service Units and Family Service Units 1940–1959*. (Lancaster University, CNWRS 1998). This interview with Clare Winnicott was conducted on 27 June 1980.

CW: Before the war. Before the war I went and worked in YWCA
clubs simply because a friend of my mother was in charge of a
YWCA centre, and she invited me to go and work in the centre. And
I did. Then I went to LSE [London School of Economics] afterwards
to take social science. Then I went back into working in the club in
South Oates for unemployed miners, unemployed young people in
Merthyr Tydfil, and I was working there when the war broke out.
But I left in order to go and do the Mental Health Course at the LSE,
so I was there about a year. Then I went and did the Mental Health
Course.

Then I went to the regional office of the National Association for
Mental Health, Reading Region . . . as part of the war-time evacuation scheme, and I was appointed as a junior person working under
somebody else in the Midlands Region. We were connected to the
regional health authority—really working under them, and they
paid my salary.

AC: That was your first job as a PSW [psychiatric social worker]?

CW: Yes, the first job after finishing the training. I think I always
intended to go back and do the Mental Health Course after I'd done
social science, but I had a year in between.

AC: Was it unusual at that time for a PSW student to go into what we
could call, nowadays, community care, as opposed to child guidance
or . . .

CW: Oh, yes, I think it was. Yes, although quite a few did. Yes, I think
most people went into child guidance clinics or mental hospitals, but
the work didn't interest me in the least. I wanted to be in the thick of
social work, not stuck away in a clinic.

I was sent to work in the Oxfordshire evacuation scheme, one
day a week, by the person who was running my office. It was only a
one-day-a-week assignment, to work with Dr Winnicott, who was
coming down once a week to be a consultant to the hostels who were
full of difficult children. The children who couldn't be kept in an
ordinary billet were put into hostels, so on the whole there were five
hostels with difficult kids in. And I was told to go and work there
once a week and put things right.

I think the person who was my boss then actually briefed me by
saying, "There's a difficult doctor working in that area. He comes
down once a week. He doesn't believe in social work, because he

likes to do it all himself. But it's really in quite a mess, and you must go and straighten the whole thing up." That's what I was told.

So I did: I turned up one Friday to the hostel where he was visiting and listened. And gradually wondering where I could come in and what I could do in this situation. And I think one of the things that I did achieve, fairly soon, was to help the staff in the hostels to make use of his expertise, his knowledge, in a way that they were not able to do.

They used to say, "He comes down and talks to the children. He plays his pipe to them, and we like him very much, but he doesn't ever tell us what to do." So I said, "Well, let's never ask him what to do. Let's do the best we can in the present situation, and then, when he comes again, tell him what we did and see if he's got any comment to make on it and if we can therefore learn something from what we did." And that's how it really evolved. And he always said, "You gave me a role and turned the job into a professional job."

One thing I did was to stop him eating all the children's rations in one meal! The staff were inclined to save all the best food for him, and I just slipped in one day, "I suppose you know you're eating the children's butter ration for a week?" He was absolutely horrified! So that's how I started in the hostel scheme. I did stick on to that until the end of the war.

AC: So you had accumulated quite a lot of experience of working with children who'd been separated from their families.

CW: I think one thing I had learned was that the children who were in touch with their parents, whose parents wrote and visited, were in a much better state than the children who never heard anything from anybody. So one of the things I did there was to ask permission to go up to London and to try and find the parents whose addresses we'd got, of the children who'd never heard from them.

And I was taken on, gradually, full-time into this Oxfordshire scheme, so I had more time to do that kind of thing. And I did do that: I spent several days, whenever I could get the day, up in London, and I was allocated a WVS driver, and we went round to the addresses we'd got, and we did find a lot of the parents. Often we found a completely bombed-down finished road, and sometimes we could locate the parent in the rest centre, but not always. And some were killed. Some were killed.

AC: And their children didn't know that?

CW: No. So what I did there was try and make a link between the parents, and actually I got such a name for it that every time I appeared into a hostel, they would rush up and say, "Miss, have you seen my mum?" When did you see my mum last?" And it was quite hard for them when I had to say, "I can't see your mum every week. Only every now and again."

But it did awaken some parents to their own responsibilities in regard to the children. Because I could say, "Look he's missing you terribly. What about a note? Give me something to take to him." Or something like this. So I did work very hard to make links between home.

And I think that was very much encouraged by Dr Winnicott, and the benefit of it was also seen by the staff. The staff realized it. I think this influenced me and my way of working from then on, and I brought this kind of thinking with me into the child care service when I became a tutor [at the LSE].

I think gradually in my office in Oxfordshire other jobs were given to me by the local authority. I was fortunate in working direct to the deputy clerk of the council, so that I didn't have a lot of people to consult about everything I did. It was he who said to me when I first went to the job, "Now I shan't mind what you do, so long as I know about it." So that really taught me a lesson forever, a very valuable one—to keep people informed—and I simply showered him with memos about everything I did. And in this way I felt covered, and he was informed.

One day I had to go to him to get sanction for a lot of the things we wanted in the hostel group, and we wanted something for one of the children in one of the hostels. And I was going over to his office; on the way over to his office from mine, I found myself getting extremely worked up, to wring his withers and try to get out of him the concessions that I wanted. And I suddenly stopped dead in the passageway and said, "This won't do. I must carry the emotional strain of this job. It's not his job, and I must simply put the facts before him as well as I can and take the decision, whatever it happens to be. Even if I don't like it. Because otherwise he's not going to see me. He's going to start not seeing me." So I think for me and my personal growth as a social worker, that was an important moment.

AC: Did that relate back to the teaching you had from the Mental

Health Course? Or things that you've done subsequently? Where do you place the course in all that?

CW: Yes, it's interesting. I don't really know where it relates back to. I can't think we were taught that on the Mental Health Course. I can't think we were just taught that sort of thing.

AC: About tuning in, perhaps?

CW: Perhaps, yes. I don't really know, because if you're working in a hospital or a child guidance setting, you've always got the doctor, the psychiatrist, to turn to. In a local authority you haven't. You've got an administrative officer. I think I don't know where that came from, and why I should make that decision suddenly. I think it was partly because I found myself so worked up, and I just thought, "This mustn't spill onto him like this, otherwise he's going to. . . ." Yes, I think we had talked a great deal in the PSW course about a professional role—what it means to be a professional. And that you have to carry a great deal, that you can't necessarily share with other people.

This suddenly extended it into this decision that an administrative officer with authority can't just be twisted round my little finger, or he's going to get sick of me. And I'm not going to get anything done. I must take the backwash of this. And it did make me very much more careful in what I did pass on to him, or to the committee, really.

AC: You were making creative use of ideas which had been discussed in the context of relationship with the hospital doctor or clinic doctor. You then related it to yourself working in a local authority.

CW: I think I was much more concerned with. . . . I don't really think it came just from teaching. Certainly we thought about what it means to be a professional person, but I don't think it came from that. I think it simply came from practicalities, that if I do this kind of thing, I'm not going to be acceptable in this situation. I'm going to be either not seen, or chucked out—One or the other! People aren't going to stand this. They've got their own responsibilities. They've got to be responsible for raising the money, for persuading the treasurer to spend the money, etc., etc., and that's their job.

Mine is to put facts before them on which they can make a judgement. It also helped me to sort out facts quite a lot. And to be selective. Facts about children, or the situation, or what I wanted. How to present facts to committees, or to people in authority, or people I needed to be in touch with about the work itself. Not to pass on the emotional burden of it but to pass on the result, or the facts about the case, *and* accept the judgement, even if it's one I didn't agree with. But I'd got to face up to it, that I would have to do that.

AC: Was it about this time, too, that you told me a story about a pile of files landing on your desk?

CW: Yes, it was about this time too. I had to make my way in Oxford-shire. I was one of the first of the few qualified social workers ever to be in a local authority. And it took them a long time to get the idea about the work, and they would send over—the clerk would send over to my office—and I wasn't there, and where was I? I had to answer. "Why were you not in your office? I sent over for you."

I said, "Well, there are things to be done. My job isn't to be in the office all the time. My job is to be out visiting people and seeing what's going on in the world. And I can't be expected to be in the office." And I would often go straight out from home in the morning and not go into the office. If I'm going out in one direction, where I live, I'd go straight out, and then come into the office later. It took them a long time to get used to the idea that they might find the blackout up in my office, in the morning, when they sent over. So that there was a lot to do—I had to fit myself into a local authority situation—make myself as acceptable to them and as useful to them as I could. And it was tough at first. And I remember saying to myself, "If the situation isn't any different in three years, I'm off. But if it is different, if they are more accepting or understand the work better, then I'll stay and get on with it."

But, you see, to begin with I was never allowed to sign a letter, not even to a client, a mother of a child in the hostel. It had to be signed by a representative of a clerk's department. Well, I found this very difficult indeed to do. I had to dictate the letters, and they were phrased in my kind of phraseology but never signed by me. I found this terribly irksome and very confusing for the client, or the hostel member, whoever it was. But that altered fairly soon: I got that altered. They saw that . . . It was perhaps a way of keeping a check on me and what I did, but when they saw that I could write a fairly sensible letter, or that what I was saying to the client was appropriate, they let me sign my own letters in time. So there were things like that, that were very difficult to put up with.

They gradually did two things, I think. Some of them saw that I could be useful to them, so I got landed with a lot of difficult cases—mostly from the mental welfare officer who was dealing with what were called sub-normal children. I got some very difficult cases from her to go and investigate and report on.

Then I was asked to help . . . the public assistance people who were responsible for boarding out children. I was amazed to find that Oxfordshire boarded out children from all over the country. They were used as a boarding-out reception area, partly because there were a great many big houses and wealthy people who would eventually take these children as maids or servants of some kind.

And I remember going down to the public assistance office to discuss this particular case they wanted me to see, where a woman was complaining about her maid, who was a girl brought up in the Oxfordshire children's home, a large children's home. And this girl was so noisy and rowdy she couldn't stand her. And then, of course, I inquired into what happens with these children. You know . . . "do you go and visit them automatically" or "how often?" And they said, "no, we don't visit, but we should soon hear if there was trouble."

"And then how do you do your boarding out?"

Well, it was all done on cards. You took out the name of the child wanting a foster home, and you took out the name of somebody wanting a child, and you put the two things together and hoped for the best. And there was almost no follow-up.

But I did take on and I did visit this child for them and found a child from a very large children's home suddenly placed in a kitchen of a very large house, in the basement part of the kitchen, and very lonely indeed. And very much missing all the other children. She used to sing loudly to fill up the space round herself. And she was even accused by her mistress of being so silly as to take her shoes off and go and dance in the garden when the snow was on the ground.

Well, I found that very enlightening, just dealing with that open case. And, of course, I did make arrangements with this girl to come up to my office and see me on her day off, and we helped her. The whole office helped her, actually. So that was one. I got a foot into the way the public assistance people worked.

I also got an invitation from the Deputy Medical Officer of Health to go and visit this particular children's home, and I can't quite think what that was for, but I know it was the first time I'd been in one of these large children's homes. And I found an extremely noisy situation going on in one room, where all the kids had been locked into one room for the afternoon, a bare room, because they'd been naughty and there was nobody to play with them anyway. And just to keep them under control, they were simply locked in a room. There was no grown-up in there with them. I was asked to meet the staff there, I think. I can't remember the details of it, but I know it gave me the first opening I'd ever had into this kind of situation.

I also visited children in the Poor Law Institutions where they'd been placed from a children's home if no job could be found for them, and this usually meant the dull ones, the ones who were handicapped in some way or another, were put into the grown-up institutions under the. . . . You know, I don't know what Act it would be, but they were in the Poor Law Institutions for the old people mostly.

AC: In an ordinary work-house?

CW: Yes, they were in the old work-houses. I visited two of them and actually saw this was happening.

Then I was asked to do something else for the local authority: go and investigate a case, that's right. The Chief Education Officer asked me if I would go and visit a school where there'd been some sex play reported by the headmaster. He got very cold feet about asking me to go in and do it, and as the time got nearer for my visit, he got more and more agitated about it. He actually rang me up and said, now, you're to go to that school and find out if this sex play went on inside the school playground, or if it was outside. If it was outside, come away without saying anything. If it was inside, well, please do what you can. So that was how he felt about it. [*Laughter.*] Sounds incredible, but it did happen.

I came into my office one morning and found a pile of files on my desk, 18 files, and I looked at them, and they were all the children boarded out under the 1933 Education Act. Fit person cases. They were in the care of the local authority, and they had to be boarded out. The 1933 Children and Young Persons' Act stipulated that these kids were not to be put into children's homes, they were to be boarded out.

These were children who'd been before courts. Well, nobody had said anything to me about them, so I rang the clerk to the Council and said I'd found these files on my desk, what about it? And he said, "Oh, yes, the Education Committee last night decided that you could take these on." Well, I was very interested to do so, and I did take them on.

But when I got in touch with the Chief School Attendance Officer whose job they'd been before mine and said to him, "Look, there are no addresses, names or addresses of the children, on the files. Where do I get those from, the children's parents?"

And he said, "Oh you don't want them. You won't be working with the parents. They're finished. They'll never go back to their parents again. These children have been brought away. They're wicked parents, and that's it."

So I felt this isn't the way I work, I'm not used to working this way. So I spent the morning in the public library, got out the '33 Act and combed it right through, and there's nothing in it that said that a child must be kept away from parent, or that they may not meet. Nothing in it to this effect.

So I went back to the office and explained this, first of all to the Deputy Clerk, and then to the Chief Attendance Officer, saying, "There's no reason whatever under the Act why these children and parents should not meet, and if I take this job, I must work this way, with the parents of the children." And they just said, "Well, if you want to give yourself a lot of trouble, carry on."

So I did take on that load. So in a way I had collected not only the evacuation job, I'd collected the fit person cases, and I'd done quite a bit with the public assistance and was likely to be asked to do more.

Yes, I was asked to go and visit a nursery. I had a lucky turn in the nursery. A stroke of luck happened to me that really established my credibility in the sight of the Authority more than anything else. I was asked to go and visit a nursery, and the Deputy Medical Officer, a woman, said she would take me to the nursery. Everybody in the nursery was bedwetting, and they were very concerned about it. So I remember being driven there, and I was absolutely panic-stricken! When it stopped at the traffic lights, I wanted to get out and run, but we got there. And I just had to think to myself, "Look, you don't have to know the answer to this lot. All you have to do is to sit and find out what's going on and relax."

So, in fact, this is what I did. I took out my notebook and really wrote down. . . . I said to the matron, "Tell me what happens in the nursery from the time you wake the kids up in the morning. Who does it, and what happens all through the day?" And I wrote it down, hour by hour by hour. And even she, at the end of this performance, said, "Well, they don't get much time to themselves, do they?" And I said, "It does look it."

I didn't make any specific suggestions, except to say, "When do they play? When can they get messy? Do they have a time when they can get messy?" In fact, they didn't: they were always permanently cleaned up. And if they got messy, they were cleaned up and sat down and not allowed to move again. But she really saw that herself by the end of the afternoon. I didn't press it home.

I came away from the nursery and, of course, never heard another word about it for a long time. So I rang up the Deputy Medical Officer and said, "Look, what did happen? Is that nursery still in trouble? Do you want any more help?"

"Oh no, no. It's all cleared up. The bedwetting cleared up, and none of us can think how you did it. And I can't believe you've only had a year's training," she said.

AC: This is all within the space of a year we're talking about?

CW: A year's training? No, this isn't in the space of a year; this [transpired over] two or three years. But, actually, what had happened, I'm quite sure, is that the staff had lost their anxiety about it. I don't believe the bedwetting had stopped. It might have, in one or two cases, but I think it may have gone because the atmosphere relaxed. It may have had an effect on it that way. But I don't believe there was no more bedwetting.

However, I mean I didn't just have carte blanche to go into their side of the work, unless I was invited. But it was developing that way, and I remember saying to the Deputy Clerk and also to Dr Winnicott, as he still was then to me, "Look, it's very interesting: I'm collecting not only the evacuee children, but I'm collecting. . . Everything to do with children I've had a finger in this authority, there really could be an office devoted to children, and workers devoted to the work for children."

And, of course, I got into schools automatically, because the evacuee children were attending schools. So I had a right to go in and inquire in the school how the children were getting on. And in fact I used to place children in foster homes in villages where I knew the school would be cooperative and really avoid some areas because the schools hadn't a clue about how to deal with difficult children.

And I knew there would be trouble. In fact, there was big trouble at one point, with 11 kids who couldn't be held in school—a boys' hostel where 11 kids ran away one night and raided all the orchards round the whole area, and I had the job of collecting them all up from all over the county, far and wide, and then we had to . . .

The school authority said, we are not having them in school, that's it. So we had the good fortune to find a retired teacher from London, actually evacuated, himself, to Oxfordshire. We had the luck to find him and say, "Look, will you come and take school for our kids in this one hostel?" Well, that had a very interesting result, because he did do this work for a year or two with this group. We got a hut somewhere. They weren't in the place where they slept. There wasn't enough room, anyway. So we had a special little school hut, but they got to know him very well, and he always had tea with the staff before he went home. And he was the right sort of person. After a couple of years or so, they so made up in their school work that they really were ready to go back into the school.

A lot of luck came, in that the school itself lost one of their chief teachers, and they were short of staff. And we were able to say, "Look, supposing we bring our teacher with us, could you admit us back into school?"

So, as a matter of fact, that did happen. He went back into the school with our 11, who proceeded to show up very well with the rest. They wouldn't let him down! And not only that, they became prefects, and unbelievable things happened to them. But we obviously had to exclude them for those years; we had to!

So that was an interesting bit of light on the school problem, I thought. If you can really give them a lot of attention, they can make up on school: if you get the right atmosphere, you can. They were thrilled—very proud of the school, very proud of him, and it was really a very happy incident. Didn't look that way when it started.

Well, I suppose, because I'd collected all these bits of jobs together, and I'd had contact with every department in the local authority, and I could see that other jobs would come my way if I had any time, I did say, "We've got really the nucleus of the department here for children. Wouldn't it be exciting if we could have one? Not just as an evacuation thing, but as a permanent feature?"

And I think I was at some point . . . I think the Curtis Committee was being set up towards the end of the war, and I was invited to give evidence at it myself; and then my husband. (He wasn't my husband then.) But I was also asked to write something about it for evidence— to give written evidence. I think he and I together, in about 1945, had written an article on the way the hostels worked. How we used the various people; what the pattern was; how we selected staff; how we selected children for the various homes. And that was published in *Human Relations*. The first volume, I think, of that thing that the Tavi published, Tommy Wilson published, and he asked us to do it: invited us to do it on the work of the hostels.

Then I was asked to speak at the first National Association for Mental Health [NAMH], the first clinical conference that was held after the war. I was asked to speak about the work in Oxfordshire.

And from that I was then invited by the NAMH—because the war was coming to an end, and obviously my job would come to an end—to go on their staff to do this kind of work: to go around discussing with people working with children the kind of things we'd been doing, the things we'd learned. So I was really on their staff for a year, organizing short courses for people working with children in children's homes, boarding-out officers.

AC: Can I ask you my last question? Hold on to your seat. You don't have to confine yourself to this period for this question: any time span you like. What do you look back on as being the best social work thing you have done in your career? It's intentionally vague: you can say as many things as you like—something you think back on with pleasure and pride that you did, and you're pleased about it.

CW: I think taking a stand on the fit person cases, that morning I went and got out the 1933 Act. I knew I must be sure of the Act and really making a stand on that one because I think that was absolutely vital to do that. Somebody had to do that at some point. I think that's the thing I'm most glad I did. Not particularly the thing I enjoyed doing most—that is another subject. I think I'm pleased with myself for not falling into their trap and taking on something in this limited way. And I got away with it. I was allowed to do it, put it into practice. And it was very important to me. I think it was noticed by other people, it did.

AC: Can you think back on any individuals or families that you've helped?

CW: I've got individual cases that followed me around wherever I went. One very, very delinquent boy with a very high IQ: well, I rescued him over and over again. He was stealing all over the place. He'd got a ghastly mother, a very intelligent mother, and he was probably the illegitimate son of somebody quite high up. Nobody could hold him anywhere. He'd been in every hostel. I'd got five hostels, and nobody could hold him. I was absolutely desperate about him, and I suddenly thought of the school, of the council caretaker, the man who really looked after the council buildings—a man I knew and met every day going in and out, and I knew he had been a policeman, and I knew that he was a football referee in his spare time. So I thought he'd be marvellous for my so-and-so.

So I went and asked him. I said, "Look, I've got the most difficult case in the world, but he's terribly worth while if we can hang on to him." So he said, "We'll have a go at him." And, of course, he could report to me everyday and tell me every day what was happening. And the boy knew this. And I also did another very drastic thing, which I'd no legal right to do in that case. I said to the mother, "I am not giving you his new address." And he came himself, the boy, by then 15 or 16, into the office and said "What's all this about my mother not getting my address?" I said, "Listen, I'm giving you a chance. I'm giving you the only chance you'll ever get to make your own way without your mother ruining everything"—because she was the one who came and ruined every foster home, every hostel he'd been in, and he'd been everywhere. So I stuck onto him, and this worked with this man, and I did not let her visit. I'd no right to.

And he made good. He got a school certificate. He had several more stealing episodes into his mother's flat, which you'd expect. He then came to see me when I was teaching at the LSE. He arrived one day and said, "What are you doing in this dump?" in a very snooty way. He said, "I want you to know that I've changed my name by deed poll." And he'd taken quite a famous name, and actually she was his aunt. She was quite a famous writer of children's books.

I was asked to go and speak at a conference. It was after my husband's death, so it must have been within the last ten years. I arrived there, and the person who opened the door said to me, "Do you remember Carrie Taylor [a pseudonym]?"

So I said, "Yes, I'll never forget Carrie Taylor."

Well, she said, "I'm the other social worker in Middlesex, and you were in the reception area. She came from my area into yours." And we had some words together about it. She said, "I'm still in touch with her, and she's an air hostess, and she speaks several languages. And she's gone up the scale. She's really quite a senior person now in British Airways."

And I was absolutely thrilled with this, because she was so difficult, this girl. I'd picked her up in an American army camp, aged 14, with a great scar across her dead-white face, caused by her mother throwing her on the fire at a younger age. And she was in care as a physical harm [case]: mother had done her physical harm. And straight flaxen hair and a deadpan white face and this scar and glasses.

Anyway, I took her to one of the hostels, and we had a terrific job to get her to settle. But fortunately the couple in charge really worked hard with her. They wanted a lot of support. She stole the woman's ring immediately. The ring was found, and we discussed. I said, "Could you lend her your ring on Sundays, and say to her, 'It's very precious to me, but you could have it one day a week'?"

Anyway, we all went through hell, one way and another, and she emerged. Her mother used to come down to take her out. She'd get completely drunk in Henley, and the police would bring Carrie home, back to the hostel. This went on repeatedly. It always happened like that. The police knew her very well. And I remember Carrie showing me a parcel she'd had from her mum. She was thrilled, and it was half a pound of grapes bought from a barrow and simply wrapped in a piece of paper, all soaking wet. It's a wonder they ever got there, but they'd come from her mum. There was something there. We all struggled with this mum, and it was very hard work. We got very disappointed, and, you know. . . . But fortunately the mother one Christmas Eve was in a pub brawl and died—fell, and actually died.

Then we all wondered, what was going to happen to Carrie now? She said to the cook, who was a great friend of hers, "Can I come and sleep in your room?" And they let her. She moved her bed into that room. She slept there for about a week and then went back to the others. And she did a lot of other things. She really had a regression, and the staff let her do it. She bought a baby's bottle, filled it with milk, and went to sleep sucking it. And they let her do it. They were frightened stiff doing it, but they did let her do it.

That didn't last long, and anyway we got her through and at last it was time for her to leave school. We got her a job with some friends of the hostel staff on a farm. She was one of these kids who, like every other girl, is mad on horses and animals, and we got her a job on a farm where she could go for her half-days back to this group, all beautifully settled.

And Middlesex [the local authority] said, "That's not enough money for her to earn. We've paid out all this money all these years. We're not going to supplement her any longer." So I got on the blower to Middlesex and said, "I want to speak to the Director of Education," because she was under his authority. So they said, "He's in a meeting."

So I said, "Will you get him out, its urgent", and he came out and spoke. And I said, "Look, we've got a girl in our care", and I told him the story. "We've all been through hell. She's making it, and we're not going to have it disturbed now for anything. And if you make any more objections to this, I shall see that you get into print. I'll get it reported in the papers."

So they gave in on this. We were allowed to do what we wanted. And I'd heard no more of Carrie Taylor until recently, so that was a case I'm very pleased with. Because if I hadn't intervened in a heavy-handed way. . . . I nearly said to this social worker [at the conference]: "You aren't the one on the other end who had a finger in that pie?" I don't know. But that's the sort of thing you look back on and are very pleased about.

PART II

WORKING WITH CHILDREN

Casework techniques in the child care services

(1955)

W hile it is true to say that there are basic techniques by means of which we practise casework in any field in which it is applied, it is, nevertheless, important to realize that techniques are always being altered and improved upon. They are not fixed and final but must remain flexible and capable of adaptation, not only to the needs of individuals, but to the setting in which they are being performed. The most important thing about techniques is their flexibility, for if they lose it and are allowed to harden, they will soon cease to be effective instruments and become weapons for defence or attack in the hands of those who use them. This is always a potential danger in our work.

One of the difficulties about improving casework skills is that the knowledge derived from one experience cannot just be applied as it stands to the next case. This specific knowledge will never be required in just the same form again. It will only be of value in so far as it adds

Presented at the United Nations European Seminar for the Advanced Study of Social Casework, Leicester, August 1954. First published in 1955 in *Case Conference*, 1 (9): 3–15, and in *Social Casework*, 36 (1): 3–13; reprinted in 1964 in C. Winnicott, *Child Care and Social Work*. Hitchin, Hertfordshire: Codicote Press.

up to something in us, enriches our general understanding of human beings (including ourselves), and increases our confidence in our techniques. In this way a particular experience becomes part of ourselves and part of the professional equipment we take with us as we move on to the next case. The point is that we shall be better people in the new situation—we shall not have just learned a new trick.

Perhaps it is true to say that basic techniques, although they are derived from the specific, can be seen to exist only in theory and in relation to the general, for in practice, in the live-casework situation, they become part of the professional relationship, absorbed in the experience and implicit in all that is done, rather than applied to what is done.

This does not mean that I am suggesting that casework is not a highly self-conscious business. It must always be more and more so. I am suggesting, however, that only as the worker becomes unaware of her techniques as such in her contact with the client will she be free to be self-aware and self-conscious and will her work be truly dynamic and productive. I know that this is all very obvious, but I find that I have to keep reminding myself of it as I talk about techniques, otherwise I can easily find myself believing in them as if they were a kind of formula which gives the required answer and solves the problem. And I have to remind myself that this is not so. Techniques are only ways of doing things within the framework of a professional relationship and in a given setting.

The presenting problem of work in the child care service can be fairly clearly and broadly defined in terms of "environmental breakdown involving the child". It is this environmental factor which differentiates the service from that of other casework agencies and sets a pattern for the role of the caseworker.

Of course, casework in the Child Care Service merges at many points with that of other agencies, particularly with family case-work agencies, child guidance clinics, and the probation services; and as workers in the child care field concern themselves more and more with the prevention of family breakdown, their work becomes more similar to that done by family caseworkers. I shall not discuss this preventive aspect of the service here, although I am very much aware of its significance for the future development of casework in the child care setting. I shall concern myself with the work done for children who are in fact deprived of a normal home life, because this work is the especial concern and responsibility of the child care worker.

I should like to discuss briefly:

(1) the impingement of the environmental factor on the casework process;
(2) the nature of the professional relationship which is the child care worker's basic technique for doing her job;
(3) casework with children, foster parents, and parents, for it is in these three sets of relationships that the fullest use of casework skill is demanded.

1. Environmental factor

I remember clearly how, when I moved from working in a child guidance clinic setting to working in a child care department of a local authority, the whole emphasis of my work changed. No longer was it concerned with working towards adjustments within a given environment (of course, the environment could always fail or break down—but at least it was there to work with). In the Child Care setting environmental breakdown is a fact. It is the reason for the referral and becomes the focal point of the work. In this situation the question which naturally arises is—could this parent, or parents, continue to care for the child if helped to do so? Sometimes this may be possible, and the child care worker then takes responsibility for maintaining the environment, and for the standard and quality of the care given to the child. In other cases it will not be possible to maintain the home environment, and the immediate question will often be, "where is this child to sleep tonight?" And to provide a roof and someone who can care for and manage the child is the first responsibility.

No matter how carefully the work is planned so that breakdowns can be anticipated and plans worked out and worked through, the fact remains that the child care worker will always be exposed to the sudden crisis or emergency and will have to take immediate responsibility for the environment. She will find herself in action, rather than in her more familiar role of enabling people to act and think for themselves, and in her subsequent casework with the child she will have to spend time working backwards, explaining her action and helping the child to come to terms with it and with her. This is very different from the usual method of working forward—so that action is understood and accepted and the momentum to put it through is gathered together for the event.

This "working backwards" is a modification of casework technique which is often imposed by the environmental factor in child care work (by that I mean the direct responsibility to provide an environment which devolves on the child care worker). Of course, other caseworkers are called upon to help clients to work backwards over previous experiences in order to come to terms with the present, but, unlike the child care worker, they have not been the centre of the drama as the actual people who have acted. Thus, it is easier in other situations for the client to talk about difficult experiences because the caseworker has not been involved in them.

Not only does the child care worker need to work backwards over situations in which she has had to take precipitate action, but she has to deal with the fact that she is a person who holds the power to change an environment. This always complicates her casework relationships and must be talked about and worked through with children, parents and foster parents, and the staff of children's homes. For the child care worker is not just the accepting, understanding person that they need her to be and which she wants to be—she is also a powerful person who can be a threat or a saviour, according to individual attitudes, needs, and circumstances. Unless she fully recognizes the implications of this fact and carefully explains her function, and at times brings into the open the possibility that she may be felt as a threat or a saviour, she will find her relationship confused and difficult to handle.

I remember a girl of thirteen whom I had placed successfully in a home two years previously, who suddenly began to avoid me and would slip out at the back door as I came in the gate. The foster mother told me that she was terrified that I would take her away. Although I had always had a good relationship with this child, it was obvious that the happier she became in the home and the more she valued it, the more of a threat did I appear to be. This had to be talked over with her repeatedly, until she could gradually tolerate my visits again.

It is important that the child care worker should come to terms with her own power and responsibility in relation to the environment. Of course, she can always avoid the issue by placing the power to act firmly on to a committee or senior official, but this does not solve her casework problem, for even if decisions are made at a higher level, she must take responsibility for them in relation to her own cases, for it is she who must carry out the plan. If she is not to avoid the issue but is willing to take responsibility for her actions, the worker must be able to know about her own guilt feelings in relation to the power and responsibility she carries. She must be able to tolerate her guilt at depriving parents of their children as well as children of their parents, and she must be able to avoid dealing with her guilt by feeling that she is rescuing or saving children from a bad environment in order to provide them with a better one of her own choosing. The rescue motive is to be avoided in social work.

The environmental factor complicates the casework relationship and requires the modification of casework techniques in yet another way. The child's primary need is not for a casework relationship but for an environment which can provide for him and within which he can be cared for successfully. The main therapeutic experience for the child will not be in the relationship with the caseworker but in his relationships with his foster parents. Of course, the caseworker will be needed to help the child to deal with his feelings about his own parents and to adjust and make use of his foster home, and to select and support the foster parents. Casework of a high order will be required to do this part of the work.

With older children who are unable or do not need to make use of a foster home as a home (as young children do), the situation is different. With them, the relationship with the caseworker will very often be of greater value and importance than the placement relationships. They will establish the caseworker–client relationship with which we are familiar, except that the worker's power and responsibility to act in relation to the environment will also be present and must be made explicit if necessary.

I should like to add one word about the source from which the child care worker derives her power to act in relation to the environment. It is surely derived from the constructive integrating forces in society. The desire is that all children shall have as good a home life as possible. The direct motive, therefore, is not punitive or educational or to make the children healthier: it is the simple, straightforward motive of attempting to meet their need for love and happiness. The power, therefore, expresses the love and sense of parental responsibility that exists in society towards children.

2. Nature of the professional relationship

Our professional relationship is in itself the basic technique, the one by means of which we relate ourselves to the individual and to the problem. But what of the professional self that relates? If we look at it objectively, we find that it is the most highly organized and integrated part of ourselves. It is the best of ourselves and includes all our positive and constructive impulses and all our capacity for personal relationships and experiences organized together for a purpose—the professional function which we have chosen. In other words, it is a function of the super-ego, with which the ego has easily identified because it has evolved from loving identifications with early parental figures. Of course, if there is a pathological super-ego development based on fear of demanding parents rather than on identification with loving parents, we shall make impossible demands on ourselves and on others and shall fail as caseworkers.

In our professional relationships, then, we give the best part of ourselves, and when we ask the question what do we get out of them, we find that it is a very great deal and fundamental to our well-being and our continuing ability to do our work.

Briefly, we get reassurance about our value and goodness—because people can take and use what we give. We get the chance to contribute to the world through our professional function and thereby relate ourselves to society and feel more secure in it. By giving, we get the ability to tolerate our guilt feelings (because we all feel that we owe a debt for life itself and for our own greed and what we have demanded and taken from others). Thus our work helps us to achieve a balance between the constructive and destructive, positive and negative, good and bad sides of our nature (as with all chosen constructive work). Our professional relationships are more balanced and more reliable than our personal ones, and it is important that they should be. We look to our *personal* relationships for the satisfaction of our personal *need* for relationships—for instinct satisfaction. (By instinct satisfaction I mean the need to love and be loved in a personal, intimate way.) Personal relationships are, therefore, less reliable because they are subject to our needs and demands, to our moods and our jealousies and rivalries.

If our personal needs do intrude into our professional relationships, difficulties of all kinds can arise. For one thing, we shall be frustrated in both sets of relationships, and in the long run we shall fail in practice because we are out of touch with the needs of other people. Moreover, we are liable to exploit the needs of others for our own personal satisfaction: for example, we may continue to supervise an older boy or girl long after there is a need to do so and when we should be helping them to gain independence from us; or we may stop supervision when there is a need for it because we cannot tolerate failure or lack of response. It feels too much like a personal rejection, and we become hurt and frightened and hostile ourselves. The need to be loved and liked personally always makes us afraid of hostility, and so we may placate people instead of taking and working through their hostility. If we are looking for personal love ourselves, we can be jealous of a child's love of a foster mother or intolerant of a mother who rejects the love of her child.

In so far as we offer our clients a personal relationship and not a professional one, we fail them, because it is our professional relationship which is of more use to them and which they need in order to establish their own relationships on a more satisfactory basis.

I have said that the professional relationship is in itself the caseworker's basic technique, and I have said something about the nature of the relationship and how it affects the work. I should now like to try and put into words what I think the technique actually is. I think it lies in the provision of a reliable medium within which people can find themselves or that bit of themselves which they are uncertain about. We *become*, so to speak, a reliable environment, which is what they so much need: reliable in time and place—and we take great trouble to be where we said we would be, at the right time. The time factor is important in another way too, in that it limits the duration of the relationship. From the beginning we are working for the end, and that helps us to tolerate the demands made on us. The client also knows that he is not making a relationship for life and that we shall not enter his personal world—and is, therefore, more free to make demands on us and express his feelings because we give him a limited, but reliable, amount of time for a period only.

We are not only reliable in time and place but in the consistent attitudes which we maintain towards people. They know how they will find us. Here again we take deliberate trouble to remember all the details about a client's life and not to confuse him with other cases. We can "hold" the idea of him in our relationship so that when he sees us, he can find that bit of himself which he has given us. This is conveyed by the way in which we remember details and know exactly where we left him in the last interview. And not only do we hold a consistent idea of people, but we hold the difficult situation which brought the client to us by tolerating it until he either finds a way through it or tolerates it himself. If we can hold the painful experience, recognizing its importance and not turning aside from it as the client re-lives it with us in talking about it, we help him to have the courage to feel its full impact; only as he can do that will his own natural healing processes be liberated.

I have deliberately used the word "hold" in what I have been saying, because while it obviously includes "acceptance" of the client and what he gives us, it also includes *what we do with what we accept*.

To sum up, the professional relationship is the technique whereby we provide a limited and enclosed environmental setting which is personal because it contains all that the client has put into it himself, and which is reliable because it is accepting and holding. Through it the natural integrating processes are given a chance. This integrating function of the relationship is particularly important in working with children who have been moved from one home to another and have never known a continuing environmental setting.

Recently a child care worker was discussing the possibility of a new placement with a 16-year-old girl who had been in her care for a long time. The child expressed a wish to go and live near the matron of a hostel where she had once lived, adding: "You know, I think that Auntie Mary (the Matron) is the only person I've ever really loved." After a pause, she went on to say: "Oh, except you, of course, but you're different, if you know what I mean." The child was really showing that she recognized the difference between a personal and a professional relationship and that she could make use of both.

3. Special aspects of the relationship

(a) Work with the children

I said earlier that the main therapeutic experience for children deprived of a normal home life will be in the foster home or children's home in which they are placed. In other words, it is in the environment that their need for personal relationships must be met. But the caseworker will be needed by the child to help him to make use of his foster home by talking over his new experiences and relating them to his own home and what has gone before, thus preserving a thread of continuity for him.

In her first contact with the child, whether it is in his own home or in a Reception Home, the worker must explain who she is and why she came and what she hopes to do for him. In doing this, she must talk in detail about the event which led to her coming, why the child's own parents cannot keep him any longer, where they are, and when he can expect to see them again. These simple explanations must be given straight away even to very young children and even if they appear not to be listening or understanding. In subsequent interviews these explanations may have to be repeated over and over again, together with any new facts about himself and his feelings which the child may contribute to the conversation.

The main area of our casework with children will always be around their parental relationships, and our acceptance of their love of parents who have perhaps seriously failed them is all-important if we are to save their capacity to love for future relationships. We must also know about their anger towards, and their disappointment in their parents and how those feelings increase the pain of separation. These feelings must also be talked about with the children when they give us the opportunity—as they will if they trust us and if we have established the sort of relationship in which they know they can be themselves and say what they feel without shocking us or risk losing us.

Child care workers sometimes feel that they have done their job in regard to parental relationships by arranging for the parents to maintain contact by visiting. As we know, these visits can cause much confusion and difficulty for the child, for what really matters is not the visits themselves, but what the parents are like when they visit. And I do not simply mean, how did they behave—but what sort of people *are* they fundamentally. Because this is the child's real problem, and one with which he will need all the help that we can give him. There may very well be times when the child should be protected from his parents' actual visits, but he will always need to know that the worker is available and that he can talk to her about them at any time and thus gradually come to terms with his feelings.

A case recently came to my notice of a 13-year-old boy whose mother had died when he was 3 and who had lived ever since in a foster home where the father was also a lodger. One day when he was 12½, the father went away with no explanation to the boy and then after some weeks reappeared with a wife, having settled down to live in another town. In the meantime the boy had been taken into the care of the local authority but remained in the same foster home. The father then wanted the boy to go and live with him in the new house, and everyone concerned felt this to be the best plan—except the boy, who said to the child care worker, "If you make me go and see my father, I'll be ill." When the day came for him to go and visit his father who hoped to be able to persuade him to stay, the boy was, in fact, ill.

What was urgently needed in this case was for everyone to stop trying to manage the external situation and for the worker to apply the casework technique of helping the boy to put into words his feelings about his father. By recognizing the boy's underlying anger with his father (which found expression in terms of illness) and by giving him the opportunity of expressing it more fully, the worker could give him the chance of eventually getting to his positive feelings, for he was in fact deeply attached to the father. The jealousy of the new wife would have to be talked about too, and the love of his foster mother and the conflict of loyalties which that aroused.

Of course these interpretations or verbalizations or whatever we call them do not immediately solve problems, but they are the first step towards the possibility of a solution. They give to the child the feeling that somebody sees his point of view and understands and can tolerate his feelings, whatever they are.

In order to illustrate further the use of casework techniques in relation to children in care, I should like to quote parts of two case records.

The first concerns Jean, a girl of 16 who was committed to the care of the Local Authority by the Juvenile Court. This interview is the first contact of a new child care-worker with Jean who had been in care for a few weeks and had proved difficult. The worker was suddenly called in to deal with a crisis over a new job.

"This first interview lasted over an hour. Jean appeared in the sitting-room untidy, sullen, and apparently determined not to enter into any conversation. I introduced myself and began to talk about the Court hearing, telling her of the work of the Court officials, explaining the meaning of a *fit person* order, and telling her how the County Council entered into the picture. I talked about the Children's Department—our work—our place as her legal guardians, what we might be able to do to help her—how she could help build up her own life free from home ties—how some people were always happiest living away from their own families, especially as they grew older and wanted to be independent—how I expected she wondered why the hostel had asked me to call—all this was said in a friendly casual conversational manner, not expecting her to say anything in reply.

Gradually she showed signs of taking some interest, and eventually I said I expected she had wondered what I would be like—Jean smiled and said: 'Yes, I thought you'd come and tell me off, because I won't work on the farm.'

I replied that there didn't seem to be much point in her taking a job she didn't like, and that if she didn't want to stay at the pie shop, we would have to look around and see what other kinds of work were available. Jean's reaction was immediate—she said she wanted to work on the farm, but her Granny said she oughtn't to change her job again so soon and that she didn't approve of her working on Sundays.

I asked if it would help if I saw her grandmother to explain matters.

Jean brightened and said it would, and then her face clouded—she became sullen and said she didn't want to change her job.

I then said that working on a farm was very different from kitchen work, and I wondered if she felt it was too big a change to make and perhaps she was looking ahead wondering what would happen if she didn't like the farm.

Jean looked up quickly and said: 'They'd make me stay there, wouldn't they?'

I said 'No,' I thought that the farmer would probably like her to go for a week or two's trial and then, if she didn't like it, she'd be able to leave.

Jean thought about this and then remarked anxiously: 'But he might not like me, then would I have to go?'

I answered her in a non-committal tone: 'Well, he'd hardly keep you if you played him up, would he?' Jean caught my eye and grinned. She said: 'You'd have to tell me off then, wouldn't you?' I said: 'Certainly', and we both laughed.

Jean's manner changed: she became bright and friendly, eager to discuss the new job."

Obviously the attitude of the worker had been all-important in establishing this contact. The worker's manner was friendly and conversational, with no hint of criticism; her approach to the job problem was objective, with no pressure brought to bear on Jean one way or the other; the relationship was not forced, and the explanations were given with no effort to evoke a response. Then, as Jean relaxed, the worker took the opportunity of making a direct link between herself and the child by putting into words what had obviously been in Jean's mind about the worker, that is to say, what she was like and what had she come for?

As the conversation continued on a realistic basis about the job, Jean was able to come to grips with it and, with the worker's help, to express her fears and explore the possibilities and uncertainties of the future. In the first interview she did not make any final decision. The worker's ability to identify with the child and to understand her feelings and put them into words had not only laid a basis for her own future relationship but had taken the immediate problem one step towards a solution.

Jean's last remark is an interesting one: "You'd have to tell me off, wouldn't you?" This was obviously a half-serious attempt to test out the worker in relation to any possible bad behaviour on her part. The worker's laughing reply: "Certainly", was, I think, the only one she could make, for it was impossible for her actually to sanction bad behaviour.

The next case record illustrates the way in which the child care worker can "keep the home together" and keep relationships alive for children, even though they are separated only temporarily, and shows the obvious need they have for this kind of help.

The three P. children—Doreen, 6, Arthur, 5, and Tommy, 4 years of age—were placed in a Children's Home run by a voluntary society when their mother was admitted to hospital. They were expected to be in care for about a month, but their mother's stay in hospital was followed by convalescence, and at the time of the interview they had been away from home for five weeks. The worker who saw them had had no previous contact with them, as they had been placed in her area by a neighbouring authority.

"When I called at the Home, I was ushered into a large waiting-room with dark upright furniture. The nurse in charge told me that the children were very happy and had settled in with no trouble. They were brought to me one at a time from different parts of the building, and as they came in, I asked their names and exchanged a few odd remarks. After a few minutes the nurse left, leaving the children standing before me in a row, staring at the floor and looking uncomfortable. Nurse had been talking about an outing to the zoo which had happened the previous day, and for a few minutes we had a desultory conversation about the animals they had seen. Tommy said nothing at this point, and the other two spoke in a whisper and largely in monosyllables. While we were talking, I got the children to fetch a couple of stools from the other side of the room, and they settled down in a circle round me. This eased the tension to some extent.

The children had not met me before, and I knew nothing about them except that their mother was in hospital. I introduced myself and said I knew the lady who had arranged for them to come to the Home, and she had asked me to call and see how they were getting on. I asked who had actually brought them to the Home, and Doreen said they had come in a lorry with Mummy and Daddy. I did not know what contact they had had with home since then so asked if anyone had been to see them—they said no-one, so I added that at least I had come now. I asked if they had heard from home at all and was told they had had a parcel at Easter.

I asked Doreen if she and Arthur had seen much of Tommy, and she said 'No'. I said to Tommy: 'You feel rather lonely then, I expect' and then asked if they had been together at all, and Arthur told me that when they first arrived, they had been in the Nursery with Tommy for a few days. At this point Tommy, without any show of emotion, said: 'I want to go home' (this was the first remark he had made). I said I expected he did, that everyone felt like that when they were away from home, and it must seem a long time to him. He said nothing. I asked them where their home was, and Doreen said they lived in Badenham. I said I knew Badenham, and it probably seemed to them to be a long way away. Tommy then said: 'I 'spect Badenham's in the pond.' I explained to him that because he had come away, it did not mean that anything had happened to Badenham and that his home was still there waiting for him to go back to.

It was evidently a great relief to him to talk about this, and from being a silent spectator, he began to monopolize the conversation. I suggested to him that he thought he might never be going back, and he told me of his fears in this respect and again said that he thought Badenham had gone away. The other two followed the conversation closely, and I reminded Doreen that she had been away for a while before, but had gone home again, saying that therefore she knew that she would be going back, but that Tommy, never having been away before, could not feel sure about this.

We then talked about Mummy going into hospital, and I reassured them that she was getting better and that soon they would all go home.

I asked Tommy what he had had in the parcel from home and explained that Daddy had sent the parcel, and that it meant that Daddy was thinking of him the way he thought about home. The others joined in and told me what they had received. I asked them what things they had at home, and they all started to talk about their toys and what they did at home. As they talked, the picture of home became more real to them, and they laughed and chatted to each other and to me. I think that to Tommy, in particular, the idea of home was becoming rather remote, and it was noticeable how much more animated he became as, with the help of the others, he began to remember more and more about home and to talk about it.

Altogether, I spent about an hour with the children, and when I left they asked when I would be coming again. I said I would do so in a few weeks, but they would probably be at home by then. They went off quite happily, Tommy leaving the other two without trouble and looking much more confident."

Here we see the child care worker in action in rather difficult circumstances. Her friendly understanding but professional and unemotional approach to the children gradually wins their confidence and creates an atmosphere in which they can talk. Her interpretation of their remarks in terms of their own fears helps them to express their anxieties openly. This reassures them and enables them gradually to reconstruct home again, and the ability to do this gives still further reassurance. At no point does the worker force the issue. The main work of the interview is done by the children themselves, and at the end of it they have had a complete experience.

Another casework technique which applies to work with children as well as adults is that of working from the positive factor in any situation to the negative rather than the reverse. For example, a child of 9 years who was well settled in a good foster home started stealing money to buy sweets to give to his foster mother. The worker's first remark to the child was, "You are very fond of Auntie, aren't you?—and you want to show her that you love her and you want her to love you." After this, the worker went on to say that Auntie liked to know the child loved her, but she didn't like the stealing, and nobody liked stealing. The same approach to the problem was made with the foster mother in this case, and, to cut a long story short, this home was saved by the fact that the positive feelings behind the episode were recognized and worked on and brought into the open, so that they formed the basis for a new adjustment.

I would like to stress the absolute need there is for the children to be able to talk to the child care worker about their relationships and their fears and conflicts about the past, the present, and the future. This involves a full discussion of all plans with the children themselves. And it does not mean *telling* them about plans but, rather, giving the children the time and opportunity to help in *evolving* the plan.

(b) Work with the foster parents

The child care worker's relationship to foster parents is a special one and unlike any other that we meet in casework. It is essentially a relationship of shared responsibility for the child, the foster mother being responsible for the day-to-day management and well-being of the child and the worker taking the overall responsibility for enabling her to do this effectively. In the choosing of foster homes, therefore, it is important that the worker chooses people with whom she feels she can establish a good working relationship, because if they are insecure in their relation to her, they are unlikely to stand the strain that the child will at times impose on them.

In interviews with prospective foster parents, the worker's aim is, first of all, to help them to understand the nature of the work they are contemplating, so that they can come to a decision about it based on a realistic consideration of all the factors involved and not merely on an emotional impulse. Secondly, while helping the foster parents to assess themselves in relation to the job, the worker's aim throughout the interview is to assess them herself.

A great deal has been said about the assessment of foster parents and their motives for doing the work. It seems to me that what we are trying to find is ordinary, normal people with the average number of faults and failings. We are not looking for perfect parents, because they only exist in theory and in fantasy.

By "normal" we really mean people who are not driven by guilt and anxiety but who are able to get something out of life and enjoy it, as well as contribute to it. Thus, the question: "What is it that these people get out of life, how do they get it, and in getting it, how do they at the same time contribute?" is a central one for us. We want to get at the balance they have achieved between their negative and positive impulses. This can come out clearly in the interview as they talk about their own family life in general and in relation to the foster child. They should also be asked about their own childhood and encouraged to talk about it as fully as possible, because it will reveal their attitudes to their own parents and to life more clearly than anything else. The important thing to find out is what sort of people are these and how have they dealt with the experiences of life. How tolerant are they of themselves and others? Their attitude to what has happened to them is far more important than what actually did happen.

I remember interviewing a prospective foster father who had been brought up in a large Public Assistance Home. When I asked him about life in the Home, he said: "Well, of course, we missed our parents and nothing made up for that, but it wasn't too bad. The staff did their best for us, but they were dreadfully overworked, and so we children had to help each other to get on as best we could." All this was said without bitterness or resentment because somehow he had come to terms with what had happened. He was aware of what he had missed, but it had not prevented him from getting something positive out of the experience. He proved to be an excellent foster father, although in theory one would have had serious doubts about him.

Our attempt to build up a picture of the prospective foster parents as people is a better method of assessment than a deliberate search for their unconscious motives in wanting a foster child, because the motive is part of a total pattern and cannot be understood or seen as a thing in itself. We must ask: "How rigid is the pattern? Is it flexible enough to include a foster child?"

In the assessment interviews the worker will need to discuss the child's relationship with his own parents and the conflicts and problems that these will present both to him and to the foster parents themselves. The foster parents will need help to understand that difficulties which may arise (such as bedwetting, stealing, lying, etc.) are symptoms of the deprived child's natural urge to regress to dependence in any new environment which gives him hope. In other words, the symptoms are inherent in the fostering situation—and will not be the foster mother's fault when they occur. While these discussions will do something to prepare the foster parents for events to come, they will not, of course, prevent an emotional reaction when the events actually occur; these we have to meet later on when the time comes. The discussion of these problems gives the child care worker the opportunity to put herself in the picture in relation to the work the foster mother is undertaking. She anticipates what may happen and is aware of both the difficulties and the satisfactions of the work and will be available regularly to talk them over with the foster mother within the framework of shared responsibility.

The actual role of the child care worker in relation to the foster parents is not easy to define, and I think we must say it is a composite one—supportive, educational, and supervisory—with emphasis on each of the functions as need arises, but mostly with all three being carried out simultaneously. If the relationship becomes the worker–client relationship which we know in casework, something has gone wrong in our selection of the foster parents. We have then taken on a case, not a working partner, and the work with the child will suffer in consequence.

The supportive role which is a passive one goes on all the time as part of the relationship. The supervisory role also is implicit in the relationship and is continuous, for we are always assessing the work and re-evaluating it in the light of new developments. The educational role is more active and positive. I should like to say a few things about this aspect of the work.

We are not attempting to give a professional education to foster parents. Such education would include a theoretical understanding of deprived children. We are really doing something more difficult and delicate—trying to help them in their personal adjustment to the child. The educational method we use is the casework technique of helping them to see what they are doing by putting their experiences into words. In this way they inform both themselves and us about the child. It is important for us to share with them the satisfactory experience as well as the difficulties; for in times of stress we shall all need to remember them in order to see the total picture and the pattern of development as it emerges. It is impossible for the foster mother to see the total pattern when she is immersed in an emotional situation—but we are always concerned with the pattern and can help her to see something of it too. Foster parents (like parents) need continual reassurance about their positive feelings for a child as well as about their negative feelings. The guilt about having and loving someone else's child is ever present and may reveal itself in over-protectiveness and anxiety about health and in an inability to discipline the child.

When the foster mother asks for direct advice about the handling of a child, we shall need to apply our casework technique of talking out the problem rather than just giving an answer. Recently a child care worker was asked, "What time do you think Mary (aged 9) should go to bed?" This seemed a simple seeking for information on a subject about which the foster mother was ignorant, as she had not previously had a child of this age in her care. But the worker had to consider how this information (if it were to be given) would be used. Would it be held as a threat over the child's head? Was the foster mother trying to put onto the worker the responsibility for disciplining the child? So she did not give the answer but discussed bedtime problems in general and how one could tell when a child was getting enough sleep.

In her educational work with foster parents, the child care worker helps the foster parents to objectify their experiences by talking about them and by seeing them in relation to a developing pattern. But there are times when she can do more. She can give the foster mother a new insight into a particular piece of behaviour. For example, a foster mother complained that her foster child (aged 7) would not leave her alone for a second. He was continually under her feet and in the way while she was in the kitchen trying to get her work done. The worker said: "I think he's afraid of losing you, and unless he can see you, he can't be sure that you are still there. He's lost people before, and he's determined not to lose you." This foster mother was quite capable of understanding the situation, especially as it was really a compliment to her. This same foster mother later told the worker about the child's enormous appetite. The worker said that many foster mothers found that this happened with children who had been deprived. When the foster father came in, the foster mother said "Miss . . . says that children who have not had a happy home life always eat a lot"; then she added: "I suppose they're making up for all the other things they haven't had."

Sometimes the casework will centre round the foster mother's own feelings in relation to the child and not around the child's feelings or behaviour. For instance, foster parents continually seek to explain adolescent behaviour in terms of bad heredity. The caseworker's only possible reply to that sort of statement is: "Yes, I can understand that you are much less sure of yourself with this child than you would be with one of your own." If the worker falls into the trap of embarking on a discussion of heredity and environment, she will not only entirely fail to convince the foster parents but will miss an opportunity of helping them.

Thus the work of interpreting and "making sense" of what happens goes on. Naturally some people will understand more easily than others, but we often under-estimate the foster parents' capacity in this direction, or we fail because we offer our own explanations and do not talk in terms of their own experience or in their language.

(c) Work with the parents

There is no doubt that some of the most difficult interviews that the child care worker has to conduct are with the parents of the children who are in care. The most strategic moment for the first contact to be made with the parents is when they apply for their children to be cared for. At this point every possible avenue can be explored to prevent the break-up of the family, and workers are realizing more and more the necessity for intensive and supportive casework to be done at this stage. Even if preventive work is not successful and the children have to be received into care, this can be done as part of a plan for the whole future of the family with the co-operation of both children and parents.

In working with parents either before or after the children come into care, one of the things we shall be trying to assess is their capacity to make and maintain satisfactory relationships with their children. The main focus of our work will, therefore, be the parents' own problems; and if we are to help them at all, our acceptance of them as they are is the first essential, as in all casework. This does not mean that we like or accept what they have done, but that we see and understand their point of view. So often a rejecting parent feels rejected and, in many cases, is actually rejected by the marriage partner (or the rejection may go back to earlier relationships). Our acceptance of the parents can be in itself a therapeutic experience for them, doing something to counteract feelings of rejection.

About two years ago a child care worker was called in to interview a young mother in a maternity hospital who was threatening that if she was made to leave the hospital with her baby, she would kill him or herself. She had refused to feed the baby, handling him roughly and throwing him to the end of the bed. (She had repeatedly said: "Why should I be expected to want my baby, when my mother never wanted me?") The worker had first interviewed the girl's husband, who revealed the fact that she had entirely neglected their two-year-old child and that he, the father, had done everything for this child from birth. This had been possible because he was doing a residential job and they lived on the premises, but he was unable to manage the second child.

He also explained that his wife felt very bitter because her own mother had not wanted her, and she had been brought up in a children's home.

In her interview with the mother at the hospital, the worker did not argue or persuade her to keep her baby. Everybody else had taken that line with her, and it had made her all the more determined to get rid of the child. She had become hardened and embittered by this approach. The worker simply said: "I understand how you feel and that you are unable to want your baby because you feel your mother did not want you. I will therefore arrange to take your baby to a foster home for the time being. Perhaps later on you may want to see him, and that will be possible." The effect of this on the mother was to produce a flood of tears and the words: "You are the only person who has understood how I feel." Of course, the mother did not immediately want her baby after this, and the child was, in fact, placed in a foster home and later adopted. But this acceptance and understanding of the mother was the beginning of the possibility of a change of attitude. One day she might have a child and want it.

In all cases where parents have failed to keep their children, there is a tremendous sense of guilt which can be completely paralysing. They feel that however much they do, they can never put right what they have done to their children. The result of this feeling is the apathy and depression we know so well or the projection of their feelings onto some external factor or person whom they feel to be to blame for what has happened. The sense of guilt and resulting hopelessness can be so great that they repudiate the relationship altogether and feel no sense of responsibility. This is one of the reasons why parents find it so difficult even to write a letter or send a parcel for the child's birthday. The mere act of putting pen to paper means that they have to think about the child to whom they write, and so they do not want to write. Thus the feeling of guilt is increased, and a vicious circle is set up.

In our handling of interviews with parents we have to be careful not to increase their sense of guilt, because this either puts them on the defensive or makes them reject the child still further by becoming more irresponsible about the relationship. In some cases it is not a good idea even to say, "the child misses you and wants to see you". It is more of a relief for them to hear that he is settling down and getting on all right, because this means that they have not done him irreparable harm. Our visit in itself does a great deal to keep the child alive for them. As we talk about how he is and what he is doing, they can gradually relate to him through us, provided that we have established a relationship with them by talking about their own problems and seeing them as people with a point of view and not as the bad parents.

Often this means that we have to take on a parental role in relation to the parents for a time, so that in building up a dependence on us and working through it they can come to tolerate their children's dependence on them. We can gradually enable them to see ways in which they can help us to help their child. They can begin to help us by telling us all they can about the child, and the taking of a case history can be a valuable experience to the mother as well as of use to us.

The visiting of children should be talked about and planned with the parents. We must try to help them to see the point of view of the foster parents or house-parents who are caring for the child; their own jealousy about the child's love of foster parents will need to be brought into the open.

As I have already said, the parents of children in care are the most difficult group of people with whom we have to work in the child care services, and we have to face the fact that some of them are too emotionally immature and unstable to respond to the casework methods we have been discussing here. Many urgently need psychiatric treatment which we may be able to help them to obtain. Others may respond to the kind of help that the Family Service Units can given in England. But when all available methods of help have been considered, we have to recognize that some parents will never be able to establish satisfactory relationships or a happy home life for their children. In these cases the only thing we can do is to help the children to establish stable and permanent relationships with foster parents and to enable them as they grow up to come to terms with and tolerate their parents' illnesses and difficulties. This is a long and difficult task for the caseworker and for the child and will demand the fullest use of casework skills and techniques.

CHAPTER SEVEN

Face to face with children

(1963)

First of all I want to make a comment on the title of this paper: "Face to Face with Children". The words seem to conjure up a very definite picture of social worker and child confronting each other in an alarmingly direct way. The alarm would, I am sure, be shared at least equally by both parties. In fact, in practice this face to face situation is one which we never let happen. We know that the directness of it constitutes a threat from which any child will either withdraw or defend himself in other ways which put him beyond our reach. In working with children, we devise, or more often improvise on the spur of the moment, all kinds of ways for reducing the tensions inherent in the one-to-one situation.

In case of misunderstanding here, I want to say immediately that I am not suggesting that children cannot make use of direct help, and especially I am not suggesting that they need us to provide for them endless diversions and sidetracks from their personal problems. Other people will provide distractions enough, and children will anyhow find them for themselves. Our task is quite a specific one, and that is to

---

Study Conference, Association of Social Workers, Oxford, April 1963. First published in 1963 in: J. King (Ed.), *New Thinking for Changing Needs* (London: Association of Social Workers, 1963); reprinted in 1964 in C. Winnicott, *Child Care and Social Work* (Hertfordshire: Codicote Press).

create a situation in which children can be themselves. The social worker is perhaps the only person in the child's life who represents his real self, and who tries to be in touch with the whole of him, and not just with the part that shows. But the child will only allow this to happen on his own terms and in his own time, and in order to let it happen at all he must have the chance to see the social worker as a real person and to assess his or her attitudes and intentions towards himself.

I realize that I have already raised questions concerning the technique of casework with children—questions to which I will return later on. At the moment the point I want to make is that "face to face with children" gives a misleading impression of what in fact happens when we are working with children. As a title, however, it is dynamic and very much to the point, and I think I can see why it was chosen. It gives us no possible loophole for escape from facing the nature of our direct professional responsibilities for the children who are our clients. And this, if I am not mistaken, brings us face to face with out own uncertainties, not only about our techniques but about our role in relation to children.

What *sort* of people are we, and what attitude is it helpful for us to adopt towards children? We find a confusion of roles available: for example, is the social worker an upholder of the establishment, or a kind of helpful supportive super auntie or uncle, or a reliable big brother or sister? Or is the social worker a sort of psychotherapist? Or is there something else still undefined that the social worker should be? These are real questions which we need to answer in the course of time. At the moment I shall attempt to clarify some of the problems because this is the obvious first step in a search for answers.

To begin with I should like to consider why it is that we social workers often hold back from giving to children the kind of direct casework help which we are prepared to try to give to our adult clients. With children, more often than not, we seek to establish a positive ongoing relationship, to assume an over-all protective attitude towards them, and to keep a supervisory eye on their interest and welfare, stepping in and taking appropriate action when necessary. This kind of work is, of course, basic and will always be part of our function in working with children, and sometimes it may be all that is necessary, but we know that we are often in a position to do more than this, and that the majority of children need more than this from us.

I think there are real reasons for our hesitation to go further. I have already mentioned the question of our own confusion about our role in relation to children, but it seems to me that there are perhaps more fundamental questions which it would be useful to look at because they really affect our whole approach to this subject. I will mention some of them.

Historically the major influence in our thinking about social casework in this country (and in U.S.A.) has come from social workers in the psychiatric settings. Naturally this would be so because for one thing psychiatry itself has been the source from which a greater understanding of human nature has been derived. I suggest that this influence from Psychiatric Social Work has been both an inspiration to workers in other fields, shedding new light on the problems which confront them, and yet at the same time it has acted as a limiting factor to the development of social work skills appropriate, and fully geared, to the functions of the various agencies. This includes making use of the opportunities presented by the function of each agency.

It seems to me that we can discern the influence of Child Guidance methods on certain of our attitudes towards casework with children. For instance, in the tendency of social workers to think either that the problems of children lie in the problems of those caring for them, and/ or to regard the children as so disturbed that they need psychotherapy. As both these assumption can often by fully justified by the facts in any given case, the result has often led to a concentration of effort on helping the adults concerned, because anyhow the children seem beyond the scope of social work help.

Of course in any agency dealing with children, work with parents and others will always be an important part of the social worker's job, and this work can bring real relief to the children. But in regard to the children themselves, we have to face two facts. The first is that, as we know only too well, the amount of psychotherapy available is minute in comparison to the need for it. The majority of the children therefore, although they may be urgently in need of this kind of help, will not be able to obtain it. The second fact is that if psychotherapy were available, not all children who need it could make use of it, because their conflicts are not only intra-psychic conflicts projected on to the outside world, but also real conflicts which exist between themselves and the people in their environment, conflicts which are beyond the capacity of the child to deal with. Workers in Child Guidance Clinics recognize the reality of this problem, and Psychiatric Social Workers have always aimed to work with the parents of children in treatment. However, in spite of help to parents, we know that some children will fail to make use of treatment because their parents cannot, because of their own problems, let his happen. Other social work agencies may pick up these cases at a later date along with other cases in which the child's environmental circumstances are threatened in some obvious or subtle way, or are impoverished or chaotic, and the presenting problem is first and foremost a social problem. But the problem is the child's problem, and although the adults in his world will also need help, work with them is a long slow job, and their ability to take help is often limited. We knew there will be many cases in which we cannot afford to concentrate on work with the adults and wait for this to affect the child, however logical an approach this seems to be.

I suggest that another reason why we often hold back from direct work with children about their problems is that the needs of many of the children who come our way seem overwhelming. We are horrified at some of the experiences they have been through. We see only too clearly the gaps in their lives and recognize that their basic needs are not being met. We know that as Social Workers we ourselves cannot fill these gaps or meet these needs and we feel impotent. At this point we can lose confidence in the relevance of our social casework techniques and abandon the attempt to reach the child's feelings because they are altogether too painful. Before we know where we are, we find ourselves concentrating on filling the gaps for the child at the expense of the other part of our job, which is to look at the gaps with him.

To work effectively with children, the first and most fundamental thing we have to know about is the strength of our own feelings about the suffering of children. All adults find this a difficult proposition, and we are familiar enough with the ways in which other people deny or minimize the reality of the child's feelings. But we too are only human, and we shall find that our own tolerance level will fluctuate.

In casework practice with children or adults, there is a general recognition of the value of acknowledging and surviving the hostile feelings which are present in the majority of our clients at one time or another. This is important, but possibly we could be more consciously aware of the suffering behind the hostility and of the need our clients have for us to acknowledge and share this too with them. The capacity to suffer is a sign of health in the individual, an inevitable part of the process of integration of bringing together good experiences and bad ones, love and hate.

I now want to look at another question that I have already mentioned, and that is the difficult one of the role of the social caseworker in relation to children. And by role I mean in this context our own self image of the way in which we operate in carrying out the functions of the various agencies concerned with children. Of course, agency function will determine the pattern of our relationship and provide the meeting point between child and worker, but it will not determine the usefulness or quality of the relationship.

When children are referred to social work agencies, I think we really know that they need from us more than that we maintain a friendly consistent relationship with them. They need professional help with the problem for which they were referred to the agency, although they may be totally unaware of their need. Our role therefore is a therapeutic one, with the long-term aim of enabling the children to find and maintain in their own world their own relationships, which can be theirs for always in a way that our relationship cannot be. For a time, we may have to stand in as the good person, but there is a real danger here in that if we prolong this state of affairs, when we let them down, as eventually we must because of the nature of our job, they can be left in a worse state than if they had never met us.

Perhaps an analogy can be drawn here between the giving of money to adult clients and the giving of friendliness to children. These gifts may be truly needed, but they deal with the moment only. Our giving in this way can only be justified if we are also prepared to try and relieve the underlying problems which give rise to these needs.

Social workers are always rather alarmed if they think that the work they do with clients might be termed therapeutic, especially (and for obvious reasons) if the clients are children. But need we really be so alarmed when we find that the *Oxford Dictionary* defines therapeutic as "tending to the cure" of morbid conditions? Surely this concept is wide enough to include what we do? However, I know that the real point is our difficulty in distinguishing between psychotherapy and the kind of therapeutic help that we can give. We are afraid of becoming psychotherapists, especially when we work with children many of whom need psychotherapy. If we assumed a psychotherapeutic role in social work, not only should we be frowned on by the psychotherapists, but we should be regarded with the deepest suspicion by our fellow social workers: quite rightly, because we should be failing to carry our social work responsibilities and to use the opportunities that go with them.

In *The Boundaries of Casework* [Goldberg et al., 1959] published a few years ago, much sorting out was done for us by a group of social workers about the question of the differences between the technique of psychotherapy and that of social work. As this is a social work classic,

I shall assume that the content of it is familiar and shall not attempt to re-capitulate it now.

In considering work with children, it seems to me that a very simple and clear distinction can be made between psychotherapy and social work on the basis of the place that each starts from with the child because of the nature of their work and the functions of their respective agencies. The psychotherapist starts from the inside and is concerned with inner conflicts which hamper social development. He or she remains, usually until the very end of treatment, a subjective figure in the child's world. The effectiveness of treatment depends on the degree of subjectivity that can be maintained. The social worker, on the other hand, starts off as a real person concerned with the external events and people in the child's life. In the course of her work with him she will attempt to bridge the gap between the external world and his feelings about it, and in so doing she will enter his inner world too. As a person who can move from one world to another, the social worker can have a special value all her own for the child, and a special kind of relationship to him which is quite different in kind from the value and relationship that a psychotherapist has. In my view there is no risk of the social worker becoming a psychotherapist, because she is not in a position to do so. She can never become entirely the subjective object which the psychotherapist becomes, she is bound to external reality because she is part and parcel of the child's real world and often is responsible for maintaining that world. The social worker with children is therefore in a strategic position in their lives because she is in touch with a total situation representing a totality of experience. The question is, how to use this position and to operate effectively from it. We still have much to think out here.

Undoubtedly a very valuable part of our relationship with children lies in their knowledge that we are also in direct touch with their parents and others who are important to them. For a time, perhaps, our relationship is the only integrating factor in their world, and we take on a significance which is beyond what we do or say. We make links between places and events and bridge gaps between people which they are unable to bridge for themselves. As we talk about real people and real happenings, feelings about them soon become evident, and before we know where we are, we have entered the inner world of the individual, and so we bridge another gap, that between fact and fantasy.

I remember very clearly in my own experience as a social worker this awareness I so often had that I was bridging gaps between people.

It struck me first one day when a mother said to me with incredulity on her face: "You *saw* Brian *yesterday*—it doesn't seem possible." To her, Brian was more than a matter of miles away—he almost didn't exist any more—but as I told her about him, ordinary things, that he was learning to swim and had lost some more teeth since she'd seen him, gradually her feelings came to life, and he existed once more in her inner world. But his could not have happened if I had not really known her child. First of all, there had to be the real live link. With the children, too, this kind of thing was happening all the time. It seems to me that this kind of work is not only relevant when there is a real separation experience. With children in their own homes or in foster homes it can be just as necessary when relationships are strained to breaking point. If we can enable children to express their feelings about their parents and refrain from defending the parents, there often comes a point at which the child can momentarily relate to them again, and this experience can have an effect on the real relationship.

It has been suggested that in this work of enabling people to relate to each other through us, the social worker becomes a catalyst (not an analyst). This term is used in chemistry to describe certain substances which by their presence produce changes in the reaction of other substances to each other while remaining unchanged themselves. Perhaps there is food for thought here.

The social worker with children has to be rather an agile person moving as quickly as the children move backwards and forwards from the world of fact to the world of fantasy. Obviously it is no good to answer questions or statements which belong to the feeling world in language which belongs to the world of facts. But in acknowledging the reality of feelings, we remain in contact and link together the real and the subjective.

At this point all kinds of questions arise. How far should we go into the child's inner world? How deep should we go? How much should we verbalize his feelings? Should we even make interpretations about feelings of which he is not aware? And lastly the question behind it all concerns the dangers which seem to be involved in this kind of work. It seems to me that if we are to make the most of the opportunities we have for working with children, we have to be able to reach them and respond to them at any given moment and be willing to follow them as best we can. Of course, we shall not always understand what is going on or what they are trying to convey to us, and often this does not matter. What matters most is that we respond in a way which conveys our *willingness to try to understand*. And it must be obvious that we really are trying all the time. This in itself can provide a therapeutic experience.

It is difficult to be specific about this question of how far should we go. Some of the simplest things that we do go the deepest, like the sharing of painful or frightening experiences by acknowledging the feelings involved. A child who was being moved from a Children's Home to a foster home said to the Child Care Officer: "Did Peter cry when he went away?" The Child Care Officer was able to say: "It's all right to cry, because it is sad to leave places." She might have denied the sadness in the situation by buying the child an ice cream or talking about the new foster home. Of course she could do both these things later on, although the timing of them would be important.

It seems to me that in work with children we are really trying to reach the suffering in them arising out of their deprivations and handicaps. Obviously we cannot force children to suffer, and some will not be able to reach this point; all we can do is to give them an opportunity to reach it by being able to stand it ourselves and by believing in it. If we do not do this, nobody else will, and the child will either be left with the burden of it or will develop defences against all real feelings.

In case of misunderstanding, I must say here that I am not suggesting that we should all wallow in suffering with the children. The child may only touch down into it for a moment, but in that moment he has reached the vital tip of himself which is his growing point. He will need us to nourish this growing point by providing opportunities for its development.

In her book *Casework in Child Care*, Jean Kastell (1961) says, "Direction is often a feature of casework with the child in care, for in a way we are not only caseworkers, but also teachers to help the child to learn to make something better of his life" (p. 300). While I agree with the idea behind this statement, I personally would not have used the word "teacher" in this context, because children cannot be taught to live, they can only be provided with the opportunities for achieving a more satisfactory way of living. Undoubtedly the social worker with children has a responsibility for seeing that opportunities for positive development are provided, and for helping children to make use of them.

However, the dangers that we talk so much about have to be faced. What are they? I can see two real dangers, and two that are subjective—that is, dangers to us.

The first real danger relates to the transference situation. In social work we know that transference operates between ourselves and our clients, but we take and live through it and survive it. Occasionally when it seems relevant to do so, we relate its manifestations back to previous relationships in the client's life. This way of working holds good for children, and I think it would be dangerous to make direct transference interpretations to them, because we should induce a degree of dependence in the children which we could not meet, and this would lead to difficulties for other people as well as for the child.

The second real danger might arise if we went ahead of the children and verbalized or interpreted their feelings out of our theoretical knowledge and not on any evidence they have given us of a readiness to accept or deal with these feelings. The danger here is not that we shall do untold harm to the children, because children can defend themselves as well as anyone else against what is unacceptable. The danger is that we shall damage our relationship with the children because they may well reject us along with what we have said.

Recently a ten-year-old child said to her psychoanalyst: "It doesn't really matter if you say a lot of things that aren't right, because I know what's right and what's wrong." In this case the fact that the child wanted to keep coming to her sessions was the only way in which the analyst knew that he must have said enough things that were right so that she still believed him.

Now what about the other dangers, the ones which I have called subjective because I think that they arise out of our feelings about the work. They are both connected with this question of "how far should we go with children into their inner feelings?"

The first concerns our feeling that at any moment we shall be out of our depth because we shall fail to understand what the child means. This feeling can be very threatening to us, because not to understand can feel like not being in control of the situation, and to be in control makes us feel safe. At this point we can easily rationalize about the dangers to the child and re-establish control by adopting a reassuring or a patronizing or even a moralistic attitude. Or, alternatively, we can sit back and be prepared not to know but to hold on and believe in the processes going on in the child, and that he is using us to work out his problems in some way of which we are not fully aware. It is a great relief to be able to believe in processes and to realize that people can use us in their own way in spite of the inadequacy of our casework skills.

Then I suggest that the other subjective fear arises for us out of our fear of the unconscious. We tend to regard the unconscious as simply the reservoir of primitive destructive forces which the ego is struggling to control, and we tend to forget that the constructive creative forces in human nature also arises from this source. This tendency leads us to wonder what will happen if we let children express their feelings too freely in the interview situation. Is there not a danger that the destructive forces will take over? It feels to us as if this might be so, but in fact we know that the expression of feelings to someone who can be trusted is a means of gaining control of them. To be trusted by the child, the social worker not only relates to him in a positive personal way, but creates and maintains a professional relationship to him which, among other things, eliminates fear of retaliation. Feelings which have to be repressed because there is no one strong enough to take them and acknowledge them are not within the control of the ego and are likely to be acted out in difficult behaviour.

If we are honest, I suppose we have to face the fact that the true source of our sense of danger in doing the work as I have described it is that at any moment the destructive forces in our clients can seem to threaten their own integration of the destructive forces in ourselves.

I have been trying to debunk the dangers which loom up when we consider working with children on a feeling level, but I know that the dangers cannot just be debunked by words, and that if they seem real to us, we shall, in fact, limit what we do to our own danger line.

Now I come to the second part of my paper, which brings me to the children themselves. Before I could get to them, however, it seemed important to consider some of the dilemmas and problems which face us as we face them. I want to use some case material about individual children because this raises and illustrates the problems in a direct way.

In adapting our casework techniques to work with children, one of the first things we discover is the value of an indirect approach in making contact with them, and that in the majority of cases it helps to have something between us and the child, a third thing going on which at any moment can become a focal point to relieve tension. In this connection car rides can be important, or it may be drawing, or playing, or walking round the garden, or even the presence of the cat or dog or whatever.

I am reminded of a case in which productive work was done by a Probation Officer with John, a 13-year-old boy. This boy was able to reach to his deepest feelings about his own deprivation and lack of mothering by talking week after week about his cat and kittens: John's care of the cat, and her care of the kittens, and then the loss of the kittens because his mother would not keep them any more. This was the theme, and the Probation Officer was able to use it and sensitively linked this drama with the boy's own inner feelings and with his real life story. There was nothing superficial about this work, and it went very deep indeed.

Here is a case in which a record-player played its part in more senses than one. This is what the Child Care Officer says:

"Mary, who is nearly 15, was committed to care in June 1952 when her mother was charged with neglect. She has been in her present foster home since December 1952. She had the same Child Care Officer from that date until 1959, then another change in 1960, when I took over. I had great difficulty in making contact with her as she was very resentful of the changes. She had blocked completely on the question of her mother and the reasons for her being in care. At the time of this visit, she was wanting to see her mother but was unwilling to know what had happened.

I saw Mary after having received a letter from her mother saying that she would like to see Mary. At first Mary said, rather truculently, that of course she wanted to see her mother. I took the opportunity to try to get her to discuss her feelings about her being in care, and what had happened to her, and why it had happened. As usual, Mary was at first very reluctant to talk about the matter, but after a while she asked me one or two questions. The whole interview was interspersed with listening to records, and at one point Mary asked me what I would like to hear, so I chose Helen Shapiro singing: 'Don't treat me like a child', and half-way through this Mary said: 'Well, what *did* happen?' For the first time ever, I felt I had really got through to her. This led to my being able to tell her why she had been taken into care and why it was that her mother had never been able to look after her. There now seems to be a prospect of making a positive relationship with Mary."

I think we would agree that this interview conveys to us a sense of purpose in the Child Care Officer. Nevertheless it was vital that she allowed herself to be caught up in the record playing. In so doing, she followed Mary's lead into her world and accepted Mary's conditions for communication. In other words, Mary made her own terms with the social worker, and they were accepted.

Another case, that of Joan, age 14, who is in the care of the Children's Department, gives a vivid picture of how Joan used her relationship to the Child Care Officer in the process of coming to terms with past events. The Child Care Office describes it in this way:

"As a result of recent discussion with me, it seems obvious that Joan is now verbalizing and coping with her previous unconscious feelings surrounding her mother's death. At the moment she is absorbed with death and suicide and the gruesome things of life, which may be an indication that the terrible scene she witnessed when very small connected with her mother's previous attempt at suicide did have an effect on her.

During the journey back to school in the car, she suddenly said: 'I wonder how I will die.' I laughingly said, 'Like anyone else, I suppose', and she, in a joking way, said: 'How do you know, I might commit suicide.' I took this up with her, and gradually the conversation dropped to a serious level, and I knew then that she had really meant more than she said. I tried to tell her that there are certain times in the life of everyone when they feel desperately unhappy and that no one escaped this, but hat one hopeful thing is that one could always say: 'This will pass', but if one committed suicide, there was no chance of saying, 'It will pass.' Joan then said that sometimes her unhappiness lasted for days and days, to which I replied, 'But even so, it passes' and that she had got many more years ahead of her. She suddenly adopted a humorous attitude again and said: 'You haven't, have you?' There was also a lot of talk about what would happen if we had a crash and my head went through the windscreen and I was lying all bleeding and cold. I immediately thought of the picture Joan had seen of her mother when she had cut her wrists and had been lying in a bed full of blood."

So it seems that when you set out for a car–ride, you never know where you will get to, or what will turn up on the way. It must be quite difficult when you are driving a car to be suddenly faced with suicide. However, the Child Care Officer was aware of what was going on and by taking it seriously, she really met and accepted the child's suicidal feelings and knew the connection between them and the mother's suicide.

The child was struggling to recapture a memory, one which will haunt her until she can do so. Of course she will not recapture it all at once, the memory will come and go until she is ready for it to become a fact in her life.

It would be interesting to speculate in this case what would have happened if the Child Care Officer had linked Joan's fantasy of the

Child Care Office lying bleeding and cold with the fact of the mother's suicidal attempt which the child had seen. For instance, she might have said: "Perhaps this reminds you of something you have seen." We cannot tell what the result of some such remark would have been, but we do know that the really important thing was the Child Care Officer's ability to face suicide with the child, because this would take some of the fear out of it and would make it safer for her to take one more step towards the assimilation of the experience.

The last case is a longer one, and it brings together many of the questions raised in the first part of my paper.

Philip, aged eight, is having difficulty in settling down at home after a long hospitalization following poliomyelitis. Because of his difficult behaviour and some ill-health of her own, the mother is also having difficulty in accepting him back into the family circle. This is an interview with Philip by a young social worker in a voluntary agency (The Invalid Children's Aid Association). It takes place at his school, where the social worker has been attending a committee. The headmistress lent her room for the occasion.

"Philip had seen me in the school and seemed pleased at the idea of having a chat together. At first he was rather embarrassed as he realized I was going to talk about home, so I explained that I was very worried about him, as I knew he was not happy at home. I said that I expected that he thought I was Mum's friend and that I sat down with her every week to have a good grumble about him. Philip nodded his head. I said this was understandable, but in fact this was not the case, though his Mummy spent a great deal of time talking about him. She told me many times about when he was a baby, and she had nursed him—before he went to hospital.

Philip asked me if his Mummy had fed him and cuddled him in her arms—and as he asked me, he demonstrated what he meant. I said she had, but to Philip it must seem such a very long time ago, and of course he would not remember. His Mummy had been very upset when Philip had been taken away from her to hospital and cross with the doctors and everybody for keeping him so long. I knew Philip had been well cared for, but it meant that for a long time he did not see his Mummy and he must have wondered what was happening.

Philip asked me if he had had the irons when he was a tiny baby, and what Polio really was. I explained this in a simple way, and then said he must get very cross at times that he has not got strong legs like the others. I also said he must feel very angry about suddenly coming home to a family he does not really know, and it must make him feel cross with everyone—his parents, his teachers, and me as well, because so many people had been talking to him. Philip nodded his head and then listened intently whilst I told him about other children who soiled their pants and the bed when they were feeling very angry with their parents. I said I expected that Philip felt the same.

Perhaps Philip felt that he ought to be a baby again, and go back to when his mother last looked after him. I said he must be upset to see all his brothers and sisters, especially the young ones, as they haven't had to be away from home. He must think they are an awful nuisance at times. Philip agreed, and I told him of a conversation another boy had with his mother, when he was cross with her and had soiled himself. Philip asked me what the little boy had said to his mother, and I passed the question back to him. He then started to tell me a very long and involved story about the little boy, which gradually changed into first person.

He said that the little boy had been playing outside with the others, and his mother called him in. She then asked if he had messed his pants, and he said no, but then he smiled. (Philip explained to me that whenever the boy smiled it really meant 'yes'.) His mother was very cross with him and brought him indoors. The boy then saw his mother, and is brothers and sisters, all eating the biscuits, and so the boy went outside and stole some sweets out of the cupboard. His mother asked him if he had taken them, and he said 'no'. but she told him off, and the boy was very upset.

All of a sudden an enormous bear came up and broke the cupboard door and then turned on them all; the boy was very cross with his parents and started to throw them against the wall, and they fell down as if they were dead. Philip said he was there, and he saw me coming down in my car towards their flat. He said he was going to tell me all about it. He took me into the sitting-room and gave me a cup of tea and a biscuit. Then the bear came into the room and started to break the chair I was sitting on. I then said to Philip: 'I expect the bear then started to break all my bones—legs, arms, nose, and gave me a couple of black eyes as well.' Philip laughed and said: 'That's right, he did.' Then he started to take all my skin away, and I became a skeleton, and then Philip became a skeleton as well. Then he put his parents in the coal chute, and they were covered in black. The 'coppers' and ambulance then came and took them all away, and that was the end.

I said to Philip that he must feel like hitting his Mummy and Daddy—and all of us, in fact. He must feel like having a real fight, and I said I thought it was understandable when he was feeling so cross. I said I thought it would be nice if he could go around with a great big hammer hitting everyone on the head who made him cross. Philip laughed at this and pretended to have one in his hand and hit people.

I said it must be difficult for Philip to show his feelings in this way because his legs were not strong enough, and this must upset him at times. Philip asked me if he had had polio when he was a baby, and if he had had to wear the irons. Then I told him about other children who had had the illness and how upset they were at times as well. I said that I expected he wished his legs were strong, and Philip said something about wanting to be a strong man when he grows up. I said I thought it would worry him at times, but that he was going to be a wise old bird when he grew up, because he was an intelligent boy, and he would also understand how other people felt when they said how they had been in hospital, or been away from home. Philip then said if they said they had sat at home all the time on a chair and not spoken, he would understand.

(He then went back to his story.) The little boy would sit on the chair, and when his mother asked him if he wanted a biscuit, he wouldn't answer. The third time she asked him, she said 'dear', and then he answered her as nicely as he could. Philip explained to me that the boy had been waiting for his mother to say 'dear'. I said I expected he wished his Mummy would be kind to him and show him that she really loved him, and he agreed. I said I could understand this, and I thought that she really did want to love him, but that she found it difficult to show at the moment.

I reminded Philip how both he and his mother would be in the same room, staring at one another, and both waiting for the other to be kind first. In the end they both made one another thoroughly cross, and then it was very difficult for them both. Philip smiled at this and I said that I thought he was trying to be so naughty to see if they would get rid of him and send him away. He nodded his head, and I said that I knew his Mummy did not really want him to go away, although at times she gets so tired, she may say it. Philip asked me this again, and I pointed out to him that they were both really strangers to one another, it must be hard for them both. I said that she was not well at the moment and that this was a pity, as it made it more difficult for Philip. If she were feeling better, she would have been able to help him more.

I said one of the most important things about him was that he had a very good brain and that everybody had thought so. Philip then asked me if I knew the boarding-school he had been to, and I said I did, and I said I expected at times he wished he could go back there. I then said that I could remember his telling Miss L that he didn't really like going back, and that it was very serious being away from home. He was interested when I said Miss L still asks after him when she writes to me, and I told her that he was coming home. He asked me if we could both come and see him together and smiled at the idea. I said I knew he wanted a home and a Mummy and Daddy of his own and that once they got over this very difficult time things, would be different. In fact his Mummy would probably love him specially because of the difficulties they had had together.

Miss W (the headmistress) then came into the room to leave the car key, and Philip asked me if it was my car. I said it wasn't and that it belonged to the people I worked for. He asked me whether I had it at the week-end, and I said it depended where I had been, as I travelled about quite a lot. He asked me if I was going to get my own car when I was very rich, and I said I didn't suppose I would ever be very rich. He asked me if I lived near and if I had cream biscuits at home. I said I expected he wondered if I had nicer biscuits than he did. In fact, I didn't have nearly as many as they did at his home, and if I had any, they were the same as his Mummy's. Philip asked me if I had biscuits like the ones that were on the plate in Miss W's room (the biscuits which we had had for Committee), and I asked him if he would like one. He was delighted at the idea and chose a chocolate one, which he munched busily while he was talking.

I said how he must be feeling cross with his brothers and sisters at times as there are rather a lot of them, and I expected he thinks they are bullies sometimes. He didn't comment.

I said how much easier it would be if Philip could tell his mother how annoyed he was feeling at the moment and how upset, as she naturally got even more cross with him when she had to clear up all the mess he was making. I wondered if he wanted to go back to being a little baby again, as that was when his mother last looked after him and he wore nappies. I told him how everybody had quarrels and felt annoyed with people even though they were very fond of them. He asked me if I did. I said that I did and that I bottled it up for a couple of days, but in the end I knew it was best to talk about it and how much better I felt afterwards. I expected he would feel the same, but I knew it was difficult for him at the moment to sort out what he did feel.

I had spent about an hour with Philip, and it was obvious that the headmistress wanted to come back into her room. When she did come back, she was naturally very interested that we had been so long and said to Philip that she hoped he was kind to his brothers and sisters and wasn't a bully and that she hoped he was going to be good to his Mummy. I said that I expected everybody felt cross with their parents at times, and Miss W fortunately told Philip of a time when she had been very upset with her own mother. Philip was very interested to know what they said to one another, and I emphasized again that this feeling was natural in a family and that he was by no means the only one.

Miss W said how well he was getting on at school, and Philip asked me if I would like to see his composition. I then asked Miss W if this was all right. I then walked to Philip's class-room and said that what he had told me would stay a secret and that I would not tell his Mummy, and he looked up at me and said it was 'just between you and me'. I said I would like to have another little chat, and perhaps his Mummy would let us. He thought this a very good idea and asked me when I would be coming. I said I would fix that up with his mother on Friday when I saw her."

I think that in this case we see a social worker at grips with a total situation, and she is able to maintain this position and at the same time to relate to the individual child in such a way that his feelings can be expressed and the reality of his situation can be faced. She is at home in his real world and can enter his fantasy world, and at no point does she confuse the one with the other but uses both levels of experience for the main purpose of helping the child to adjust to his personal handicap and to his social environment. She also does more—she gives recognition to Philip's potentialities for making something of his life.

To sum up, I would say that our "face to face" responsibility for children involves us in three overlapping areas of work with them.

First we try to reach the children, to establish communication, and to construct a working relationship with them which is personal and yet structured.

Having reached the child, we try to look at his world with him and to help him to sort out his feelings about it: to face the painful things and to discover the good things.

Then we try to consolidate the positive things in the child himself and in his world and to help him to make the most of his life.

These three areas of work add up, it seems to me, to the process of social casework with children.

As a last word, I want to say that even if we are unable to help the children as much as we should like to do, we can at least attempt to prevent muddle from arising in their lives; or, if it has arisen, continually make the effort to sort it out for them so that things add up and make some sort of sense, and in this way we can prevent and relieve a great deal of distress.

CHAPTER EIGHT

Communicating with children—I

(1964)

S uppose that we could agree that a rough definition of communication would be that it is quite simply a matter of giving and
taking between people. A moment of communication is a moment of reciprocal exchange. The essential ingredient of communication is, of course, the will and the ability to communicate, and these
depend on the individual's balance of trust and suspicion, which in
turn depends on what is stored up in his or her inner world of the
unconscious memories of previous communications, including the
very earliest, and on his or her ability to use symbols. A symbol is
simply something that is allowed to stand for something else. Words
and gifts are symbols which have their own accepted meaning, but we
who use them give them meaning over and above their literal content
by the way in which we select them and use them. Words and other
symbols can also be used defensively to hide ourselves and our feelings and to come between us and other people. But this is in itself a
form of communication showing that we are unwilling or unable to
communicate.

Presented at the Association of Child Care Officers, Southeast Region, March
1964. First published in 1964 in *Child Care Quarterly Review*, 18 (3).

The capacity for symbol formation in the individual is an important part of normal development and is a crucial matter in the capacity to communicate and to become socialized.

Put briefly, a symbol is a secondary phenomenon which can be accepted and allowed to stand for a primary one, so that the primary one can be relinquished temporarily, and later permanently, as it becomes part of the phenomena and processes of everyday life. To put this in its simplest terms, the infant, whose primary needs for food and care are continuously met in a way reliable enough to bring him satisfaction and a sense of well-being, stores up memories of these experiences and becomes able to fill the gaps in care, when mother is not actively caring for him, by finding pleasure and satisfaction in other things—the blanket or the woolly toy or whatever is available, his own thumb perhaps, or a dummy. This other thing gives satisfaction because it stands for the primary satisfactions and keeps alive memories of them.

But there is more to it than this, because the other thing stands, at one and the same time, for the satisfaction-seeking infant and the mother who satisfies. The blanket or the woolly toy is therefore a symbol of unity between the self and the not-self and is evidence that the first vital link is being made between the infant and the outside world. Later the word "mum–mum–mum" will be used to stand for the satisfying experience and the caring person, who is gradually recognized as a person. And so a whole new area for communication is opened up, based on the medium of words, which have to be learned.

But this use of language will only go on developing if primary needs go on being met by the person who is the embodiment of the words. No wonder then that small children, and even older ones, separated from their mothers, so often lose the capacity for speech, or lose the sense of the meaning behind the words. It is only by sensitive patient care that the words will be given meaning again, but this will take time. If there is not good-enough care, then the words, although fluent, will remain meaningless and serve only to come between the child and other people. The words will no longer be a vehicle for communication, and moreover previous good experiences, and the stored memories of them, which represent the inner world and true self, will remain cut off from present feelings and everyday life, and growth will be impoverished or distorted.

Our task, therefore, with children in this position is first to see that the day-by-day care of them is not merely adequate, but is as fully geared to their individual needs as it can be, because this is the basis for preserving, restoring, or establishing the capacity for real communication, real giving and taking.

It seems to me important that we social workers should remind ourselves that in the kind of communication that we hope to establish with children we are always cashing in on the work of others, on the work of those who have cared in the past, and those who are caring in the present, for the children's basic, day-to-day needs. The quality of this care will determine to quite a large extent the relative success or failure of anything that we can do.

I think we would agree that communication between people takes place on different levels of existence or experience. There is the ordinary everyday exchange between people which may take place on a somewhat superficial level, but nevertheless it serves to keep communication channels open and has an important binding and socializing effect. It keeps civilization going, and the world ticking for us all, because it reduces suspicion and the latent paranoia in us all.

Then there is the communication, the prototype of which I have already described, which takes place between certain people and in which the feelings and needs of each are recognized and reciprocated. The true self of each meets and responds to the true self of the other.

The third kind of communication is that which concerns the exchange of ideas either in words or in art forms of all kinds. This is, at its best, a sophisticated elaboration and extension of the true self communication; at its worst it can be an attempt to hide the true self and even to become a substitute for it. Strictly speaking, when this happens, communication is not taking place, although it may seem to be. What is said or painted onto canvas is then the private concern of one person—and the world guesses.

We know that when we are in communication with other people, not only does it take place on different levels, but different ways will be used to convey meaning. What the voice *says* will only be part of the story, and sometimes the least important part. The rest will be in terms of attitude, posture, tone, gesture, look, or touch—or the non-verbal signs and sounds we all make when what we feel will not go into words.

Then, too, often the things not said speak more loudly than the words said. For example, a woman patient in a hospital said to the Almoner: "This has been a good year for roses, I wonder what they will be like next year" (Lambrick, 1962). The real communication here was not about roses but concerned the patient's knowledge that she would not live to see them next year. It was this knowledge that she wanted to communicate. Or another example would be that of a child being moved from one home to another, who said to the Child Care Officer: "Did David cry when he went away?" The real communication here was not about David, it was quite simply: "I want to cry *now*."

For those who would be in communication with others, simply everything counts, and all our faculties are needed if we are to receive and interpret with approximate accuracy what others are expressing in what they are, or what they do and say. Fortunately experience increases our awareness of what people communicate and how they do it, but nevertheless we find that each case presents a new task in understanding simply because each individual is unique.

In order to reduce this fascinating but vast subject of communication with children to manageable proportions, I shall confine what I have to say to three aspects of it. The first is to try to put briefly into words what we are *aiming* at in communicating with children. Then, secondly, to raise questions concerning how we communicate, and thirdly to spend some time in discussing five kinds of cases which present special problems in communication.

With regard to the question of what we are aiming to achieve in communicating with children, I would say first of all that we are not *aiming* to collect information or to take a case history, although of course we do all the time incidentally collect information about the children and gradually piece together their life story as seen by themselves. This is important to us, and to the children, because it helps us in our assessment of their problems, and it helps them to become aware of continuity.

But behind this, our real aim is to keep children alive, and to help them to establish a sense of their own identity and worth in relation to other people. By keeping children alive, I am of course referring to maintaining their capacity to feel. If there are no feelings there is no life, there is merely existence. All children who come our way have been through painful experiences of one kind or another, and this has led many of them to clamp down on feelings and others of them to feel angry and hostile, because this is more tolerable than to feel loss and isolation. Our work, therefore, is not easy, because it will lead us to seek contact with the suffering part of each child, because locked up in the suffering is each one's potential for living and for feeling love as well as feeling hate and anger. To feel a sense of loss implies that something of value, something loved, is lost, otherwise there would be no loss. Awareness of loss, therefore, restores the value of that which is lost and can lead in time to a reinstatement of the lost person and loving feelings in the inner life of the child. When this happens, real memories, as opposed to fantasies, of good past experiences can come flooding back and can be used to counteract the disappointments and frustrations which are also part of the past. In this way the past can become meaningful again.

So many of the children we meet have no sense of the past, and therefore they have no sense of the present and of the future. The child who has reached his or her own loving potential is then in a position to discover new loving relationships in the present and the future. If we attempt to reassure children and to jog them out of their despair, we can deprive them of the chance to reach their own potential, i.e. to reach the love they were capable of before they suffered loss.

I now want to turn to the question of *how we set about* trying to get into touch with a child's real feelings. We find that usually it is no good if we set about this task in a deliberate way by trying to delve into the child's inner world because we shall be resisted if we do. The question-and-answer method simply does not work, and, moreover, we recognize that children have a right to their privacy, and only as we gain experience in implicitly recognizing this can we hope to gain their confidence. We know that we must relax and see first that we adequately fulfil our rôle in relation to the children. Our rôle will be broadly determined by the nature of the responsibilities we carry on behalf of our agency. This will need to be made clear so that the child gradually comes to know what he or she may expect of us, and who we are, and why we are there anyway.

Then within our rôle there is the question of what we ourselves are like as people. Do we talk to the grown-ups and ignore the child, or do we ignore the grown-ups and make an immediate fuss of the child in an attempt to evoke a response at all costs? Do we give time to the child, and do we also give our undivided attention? Are we reliable? Do we keep promises, or do we forget? Are we the cheerful type, or the quiet type, and are we the same every time? There is a great deal about us as people that children need to establish, and they, even more than grown-ups, are quick to find us out, but this they must do if they are to know how to use us.

As I suggested earlier, real communication which involves direct giving and taking between people does not go on all the time. It happens at certain moments and with certain people, and on the whole we select very carefully the people with whom we communicate in the deepest sense which involves our real feelings. Communication involves giving away a bit of ourselves, and we are careful to whom we give it. Usually the people with whom we communicate are those whom we have come to trust and with whom we have something in common. In our work with children we therefore find that we spend a good deal of time creating the conditions which make communication possible. We try to establish between ourselves and the children a neutral area in which communication is indirect. In other words, we participate in shared experiences, about which both we and the children feel something *about something else*, a third thing, which unites us but which at the same time keeps us safely apart because it does not involve direct exchange between us. Shared experiences are perhaps the only non-threatening form of communication which exists. They can concern almost anything in which we both participate—walks, car rides, playing, drawing, listening to something, looking at something or talking about something.

A Child Care Officer found that the only way that she could feel in touch with an unhappy 4-year-old was to sit quietly beside him watching his favourite TV programme. This was not a waste of time, because the programme brought them together and united them in a way which was tolerable for the child. When this had happened a few times, the child was able to sit nearer to the Child Care Officer, so that she could quite naturally put her arm round him. Thus was achieved non-verbal communication. If the Child Care Officer had tried to put her arm round the child to begin with, he would have felt threatened and would have resisted.

Shared experiences form invisible links between people which become strengthened as they begin to have a history. Gradually experiences will be referred to and talked over and relived in retrospect, and we shall find that there evolves between us and the child a language for talking in, which is quite special to each child because it contains his or her own words and way of remembering and imagery, which we take the trouble to learn and to use. If we first take care to learn a child's words and his or her special meaning for things, then in time the child will incorporate and use our words and meanings as his or her own.

Once indirect communication has been established by means of shared experiences, then there exists an area of life within which direct communication, direct giving and taking, is possible. In fact, anything is now possible; the floodgates could be opened or the sparks could fly. Both these events would be signs of life and evidence that real relationships between people, which involve giving and taking, loving and hating, were being established.

For instance, the end of the story of the Child Care Officer and the 4-year-old boy watching television together was that once having established communication by means of her arm round him, he then on a later occasion was able to throw himself into her arms and cry for his mother, who was in hospital. The intensity of his love and longing for his mother was felt in these moments, and this in a sense restored her again for him and made the mother more real. He could not have reached this point alone. After this event he was noticeably less depressed and unhappy and began to eat more. On later visits this little boy did not want to cry again, nor did he want the Child Care Officer to put her arm round him again. He wanted to go back to the indirect communication of shared experiences. He brought her his books and his toys, and she read and played with him. He certainly looked forward to the Child Care Officer's visits and needed them because he knew that at any time communication of his real feelings to her was possible.

And so it is that indirect communication involving a third thing— the shared experience—takes the strain out of life, because it enables people to meet and at the same time to maintain their separateness, because they feel about something else, not about each other. Within this neutral area no demands are made either way, although at any minute they always *could* be made.

When we have created the conditions for communication between ourselves and the children, it is important that we recognize it when it happens, and when they speak to us in the language of feeling, we must answer in the same language and not in the language of facts. Feelings are illogical, and it is no good our being logical about them: this simply shows the child that we are not on his wavelength after all.

To illustrate what I mean, there was the case of a 12-year-old boy in a Remand Home being visited by a Child Care Officer who had known him before. Towards the end of the interview the boy's father was mentioned, and suddenly his eyes filled with tears. The Child Care Officer said: "Are you worried about your father?" The boy said: "Yes, I worry about him a lot because his health isn't good and he often seems ill." The boy looked very distressed, and there were more tears. The Child Care Officer said: "Perhaps you sometimes even feel that your father might die?" The boy said: "Yes, I do think that, often, and I hate it when he goes out on his bicycle because I always think that he will be brought home dead." At this point the Child Care Officer lost her nerve and said: "Well, when I saw your father last week, he didn't look at all ill, in fact he was looking very well." This statement is in the language of facts, and it simply does not reach feeling, and moreover it creates a gulf between the adult and the child. In this case the Child Care Officer might have said something like this: "I know you are very fond of your father, but perhaps sometimes you feel very angry with him too." Actually this boy had a great deal about which to be angry with his father, because the father had left the boy's mother, taking the boy away too, and was now living with another woman. At this point the boy started stealing.

So the question of language is an important one and means that we have to be constantly aware of which language the children are speaking in and to answer them in the same terms, otherwise we shall block communication and leave them frustrated and even more hopeless than ever of being understood.

I now come to the third aspect of my subject, and this is to consider why it is that some children present special problems in communication. This matter is, of course, related to the subject of the social diagnosis in each case. This involves an assessment of the developmental problem with which each child is struggling and the ways in which he is dealing with it. This kind of assessment, which is part of our professional responsibility, is in fact an extension of something which we do automatically in ordinary life. When we meet a child, we quite naturally wonder what sort of a child he or she is and what sort of an approach on our part is most likely to meet with a response. In our work, however, we do all this more deliberately and with conscious effort and care because more depends on the success or failure of our efforts and, moreover, if we cannot get on to the wavelength of the individual child, we ourselves, as I have suggested, can become the block to communication.

In each case the reason for the difficulty in communication will be a complex one and a highly individual one. The reason will not be an actively deliberate one but will be related to unconscious processes and the drive for self-preservation which is behind all symptoms. The word "reason" therefore, is a misnomer, because it implies conscious thought and choice.

I should like to discuss five kinds of case in which the ability to communicate is seriously impaired or virtually non-existent because the will or drive to communicate is no longer present. These cases will be familiar to all social workers. They are: *the suspicious; the hostile; the withdrawn; the restless extrovert; the depressed.*

1. First, then, there are the children who keep themselves to themselves because they are *suspicious* of anyone or anything outside them-

selves. The world outside is a bad place, and the only way to ensure self-preservation is to have no dealings with the world. A certain amount of suspicion is of course normal and is part of the natural tendency for self-preservation which is present in us all. Usually, however, we do not remain suspicious—we take the next step, which is to test out the situation or the person to prove if our suspicion is realistic or unfounded, and then we act accordingly. This is happening all the time without our thinking about it. Children are less experienced than adults and therefore have the right to be that much more suspicious.

But some people, for a variety of reasons, have lost the courage to test out the situation because they have a deep conviction that their worst fears will come true and they will find that people in the world are as punishing and vindictive as they are feared to be. So they never try to find out, and this at least keeps disaster at bay, although the cost of doing so is high in terms of all that they miss. In many cases suspicion of the world is not a total thing. It becomes fixed on to one thing, e.g. food, or certain places or people or certain activities. This can be difficult to handle, but so long as the suspicions are respected, it does at least give elbow room for development in other directions.

The establishing of communication with a child who is unduly suspicious will obviously take time and patience, because any attempt on our part to break in will only increase suspicion. These children need the opportunity to see us in action so that they can weigh us up and assess our attitudes towards other people and towards themselves, and then one day they may have the courage to test us out in some way or other, when they are ready to do so.

I remember seeing a boy of 9, who was a deeply suspicious person, come up to his house-father saying that there was something in his eye. Fortunately the house-father took this very seriously, because it was the first time this boy had asked for any personal attention, and although there was actually nothing in his eye, it was bathed and treated with great respect. This was the beginning of a gradual lessening of suspicion. The child communicated, and the communication was received as such.

Another example is that of a Child Care Officer who, over a period of many months, had spent much time in the playroom of a Children's Home with a suspicious little girl of 4 years. As soon as the Child Care Officer came into the room, this child never took her eyes off her and surreptitiously watched every movement and every contact the Child Care Officer had with any other child, but strongly resisted any move made towards herself. After months of this seemingly futile attempt, the Child Care Officer was one day sitting on the floor talking to another child, when the child in question rolled a ball very slowly across the floor until it touched the Child Care Officer. The Child Care Officer then rolled the ball equally slowly back to the child. The rolling game continued at each visit for a long time, and by means of it tension was lessened and communication was gradually expanded.

In the kind of case in which suspicion dominates the scene, we know that what is happening can be stated in theoretical terms as the projection by the child of all his or her hostile feelings on to the outside world in an attempt to preserve the goodness within him- or herself.

2. The next kind of case I want to discuss presents the opposite picture. The child himself feels so *angry and hostile* that he fears that he will destroy everyone and everything in sight. Therefore, in order to preserve the outside world, which somehow he at the same time values, he hangs on to his anger and attempts to keep it inside and under control. Such a child will be unable to communicate his real feelings because he fears their destructive potential. When we attempt to get near to him, he seems indifferent, passive, and uncooperative. These children are often easier to help than the suspicious ones, because deep down they do believe in goodness and are capable of love.

First of all, however, we have to meet and survive the hostility and aggression such children truly feel but dare not communicate. We have ample evidence of its existence. Usually it shows on their faces and in their attitude of calculated indifference. Before we can get anywhere, this needs facing and putting into words. I am reminded of a probation case in which a 12-year-old boy remained actively passive for many weeks and obviously found great difficulty in making the slightest response to the Probation Officer. One day the Probation Officer went to collect the boy from the waiting-room, and on the way out of the room the boy suddenly punched another boy in an angry way. The Probation Officer took him away quickly before a fight started up and said to him: "You must be pretty mad with someone to hit out like that, and I don't think it's with that boy in the waiting-room. I guess you're pretty mad about having to come here at all, and with me for insisting that you do." The boy admitted that he was angry at having to come and thought it was all a waste of time, etc. As this boy's hostility was met, and recognized, it became possible at last for the two people to meet on a realistic basis. Obviously the boy intended the Probation Officer to see his anger, and it was then possible for the Probation Officer to deal with it. But he could not have done so earlier.

3. A third kind of case in which communication in the real sense of the word is very difficult to establish is that of the child whose effective personality is *withdrawn* into him- or herself as a protective measure against dependence and the frustrations and disappointments that go with it. Inadequate personal care and loving attention or the sudden withdrawal of it, or the actual loss of the person depended on, can result in this state of affairs. The child withdraws and so to speak "looks after" him- or herself. These children do not seem to suffer actively, nor are they overtly hostile or suspicious, because they have put themselves beyond the reach of the ordinary feelings that are part and parcel of all relationships.

Outwardly they comply just enough to maintain their existence with the least effort. We must expect to fail to communicate with many of these children, but that does not mean that we should give up trying and write them off. Perhaps they need our presence in their lives as *the person with whom they do not communicate* and from whom they have withdrawn. This may involve us in silent sessions or in some activity such as reading a story, which makes no demands on them. If we can accept this rôle of the person with whom they do not communicate, without seeking to force our way in, then one day the situation could alter, but if we do not put ourselves in this position and contract out, there is little hope that it will alter.

I remember trying to help a young woman in her twenties. She had been a very withdrawn child, actually spending most of her time in a large cupboard under the stairs. In here she kept her toys and her possessions, including her radio for listening to "Children's Hour", which she never missed. She only really felt secure when she was in this place. She actually slept in it as well, and as far as possible she kept everyone else, especially her mother, out of it. Many times when I saw her I had to say, because I felt it was true: "Today you are in your cupboard with all your possessions, and I know that I must not come into it."

Some months later she had a dream that she was in an under-ground cave—it was warm and cosy—"rather like her cupboard", she said, and there was plenty of food, and I was there, and we were going to cook a meal. So there had been an alteration in the situation, and for once I was allowed into the cupboard. But I am sure that this would not have happened if I had not accepted the rôle of the person who was *there*, but who was kept outside. In this rather negative way eventually something positive could happen, but what a pity it could not have happened years before.

For some of these withdrawn children, maybe only a regression to dependence on the person who is actually living with them and caring for them will bring them through to the place where a real relationship based on the meeting of dependence needs is possible: in other words the place which enables them to give up "looking after themselves" and be dependent on someone who can then take them forward in the natural way until they can be truly independent within the setting. If this is to happen, the person caring for the child will need much support from the Child Care Officer. I have known people who can take children through this kind of experience, but they do not do it easily and need constant reassurance.

4. By contrast with the children who withdraw from the problems of everyday life, there are others who may deal with their problems by the opposite kind of reaction, which we call a "flight to reality". We may regard them as *extrovert* and find them full of activity, talkative and co-operative. We can easily be misled by these children, partly because they are such a relief from the more unresponsible children on our caseload. But in time we notice that their activities change too frequently, and they lack sustaining power. They talk too much, and too easily, about anything that comes to mind for comment. What they are doing is clutching at anything that is available outside themselves to present themselves from feeling, because feeling would lead to despair and hopelessness.

In working with these children, we have to beware that we ourselves do not get caught up in their endless merry-go-round that leads nowhere. Here again we have to play a waiting game, establishing ourselves in their lives as someone who can be trusted and with whom they might eventually share their hopelessness. But they have to make quite sure first that we are not taken in by their excitability. If they could reach with us a moment of true feeling, this might enable them to reconstruct their lives on a sounder basis. In other words if they can *feel*, even if it is only to feel the pain of loss and despair, then the way is open for other feelings to come to life again. Many children will not be able to reach this point because it is altogether too painful, and they will construct their lives on an artificial basis. Some may achieve much and be the life and soul of many a party, but they will be inwardly dissatisfied because they are incapable of any real relationship.

5. The last group of children I want to mention as presenting to us problems in communication are those who are obviously in *a depressed state*. They are difficult to reach because they are preoccupied with their own anxieties, which may concern their health and bodily func-

tions or their lack of achievements or relationships. Life feels futile because they feel dead inside. We know from experience that any effort we make to encourage these children out of their depression or to distract them or cheer them up, although it may seem to work temporarily, is, in the long run, of no avail, because it simply does not reach them. Children in this state cannot believe that anything is good because they doubt their own goodness. They may say, "Mother is not good", or "My parents are bad", but even if this is true, it is only another way of saying that they themselves are no good.

It seems to me that the only way to reach these children is that we ourselves should believe in and acknowledge their feelings of badness and deadness, because they are *real*. We may know that this is not the total truth about them, but at the moment it is. To attempt to cheer them up or get them to snap out of their depression is like a rejection of them, and as such it confirms their feelings about themselves and removes them still further from us.

If we can "hold" them as they are in their despair—and understanding is a kind of holding—then there is some chance that they might come to life again. Of course we may find that we do actually hold them physically at times when it seems appropriate. The point is that we cannot bring them to life again in any artificial way by trying to inject them with our belief in their goodness and that life is worth living. Only their own belief will enable them to find it so.

When we fully acknowledge the hopelessness and despair that many children we meet carry around with them, not only is this evidence to them that we are in touch with them, but it means that their feelings are now a stated fact and, as such, are objectified and put outside themselves. This can bring relief and the possibility of an alternative way of living. But if nobody acknowledges the existence of the despairing self, the children themselves have to keep it going. It is here that people tend to say that the child is wallowing in despair, but what else can he do with it except to lose touch with feelings?

I have spent some time describing various kinds of case in which we find communication difficult to establish. I am aware that I could add to this list and that I have, for instance, not mentioned the children who are overtly hostile, but it seems to me that in practice they are not so difficult to communicate with as the cases I have mentioned.

When we feel we are failing to make contact with a particular child, it is only fair to ourselves, let alone to the child concerned, that we should give careful attention to this question of diagnosis, because this affects not only what we do but how much we can reasonably expect to do. We all too easily blame ourselves when we fail to establish communication and feel that our techniques are inadequate (and then we blame those who taught us, or did not teach us), but I suggest that, more often than not, it is our assessment that is not adequate.

To sum up, I would say that if we believe in the reality of children's feelings, we shall not find it difficult to communicate. If, on the other hand, we do not have this belief, we cannot get round the difficulty by learning techniques. It is better then to leave alone the subject of communicating with children.

CHAPTER NINE

Communicating with children—II

(1977)

The social work task in relation to children is, as we are well aware, a formidable one—formidable in terms of the wide statutory responsibilities laid on the social services: to promote the welfare of children so as to prevent their reception into care or appearance before a juvenile court, to take action to protect children from physical or mental suffering, and to provide suitable personal care for each child whose family cannot do so. Daunting as these fundamental practical tasks are, even more formidable is the emotional task laid on social workers who have to face the children themselves, in the difficult circumstances that bring them to the notice of the department. The uncertainty conflict and anguish has to be met and understood by the social workers if the child is to have the chance to salvage anything of value for the future. If the pain in the situation is not recognized and shared, it cannot be experienced and worked through, and there is then no alternative to the building up of resentment which can last a lifetime, and waste a life, and lead many to prisons or mental hospitals.

Presented at the Child and Family Care Conference, British Association of Social Workers, Manchester, April 1977. First published in 1977 in *Social Work Today*, 8 (26), 7–11.

As I see it, if we could only learn to respond effectively to children at the crisis point in their lives which brings them to us, and at subsequent crisis points which are part of growth, we might save many of them from becoming clients in one capacity or another for the rest of their lives. I am aware that this has implications for the priority system within the total social services, and I suggest that work with children does need to be reconsidered realistically within that context.

In my present work as a psychotherapist seeing young adults who for one reason or another need help to get on with living more harmoniously with themselves and others and/or to avoid mental illness or suicide, I have been struck with the fact of how early it was in their lives that things began to go wrong, and once wrong, how the difficulty perpetuates itself so that there is almost no escape from it without help, and sometimes not then. Out of twelve people I am involved with, only three have had what could be called a fairly normal home-life: that is, that in spite of difficulties the children have felt loved and cared for and had both parents available, and no traumatic separations in early life. The other nine people suffered early losses or traumas of one sort or another due to break-up of marriages (one sent away at 2½ and another at 3), mental and physical illness of the mother causing early and indeterminate periods of separation, and quarrelling parents resulting in a chaotic home situation from the individual's birth onward.

All of us working in the psychotherapeutic field are recognizing that in the majority of cases the problems and illnesses of our patients had begun much earlier than had been recognized by previous workers in this field. In fact we now know that we can find that the illness pattern of the adult patient had been laid down in infancy and in early problems of relating to other people, in the first place to the mother. Theoretically I have known that this is likely to be so, but every time I meet it I am still surprised to discover how terribly true it is and how devastating can be the results.

All the time my patients are teaching me over and over again, not so much in direct words, but by implication and by the way they live and feel and think, that if only there had been someone at the point of crisis to encompass the child, to recognize that the child has feelings about what is going on, and to help him through the shattering effect of losing all that is familiar, then perhaps some of the shock and trauma could have been absorbed and need not have disturbed the individual's development as it did from then on. But in each case this did not happen, and individual development has been stunted or impaired, resulting in much unhappiness and depression.

Recently, a 14-year-old who had exhausted all the local authority's children's homes, assessment centres, and several community schools said to her social worker "None of you lot can hold me, I can do what I like. There isn't a place in the whole country that I can't get away from if I like." And we know that she is right, the holding was needed long ago in infancy or very early in childhood. Then it would have made sense, and might have been accepted and made use of.

Of course, the pain of separation from those we love is for all of us a devastating experience, but for a dependent child the whole of his world collapses and everything loses meaning. The worst thing that can happen is that the trauma can be so great and the child feel so helpless in the face of it, that all feelings are clamped down on, leading to deadness and depression.

My own work of the last six years has therefore brought me back to a re-evaluation of social work with children and the hope that in the social services we will not be content simply with social work for children. The opportunity I have had to look back on the life stories of those who have come to me for help and support has provided ample evidence of the need for direct communication with children and special measures at times of special need and crisis, and I feel convinced of the prophylactic nature of the work that could be done in this area and of the need to concentrate on it and extend it.

Whenever a social worker intervenes in the life of a family which includes a child or children, there is a story behind the intervention, and the social worker needs to know that story and its effect on each child and to live through the experience with the child as fully as possible, without denying the pain, and accepting the sadness, anger, and depression that the situation gives rise to. In this way, moments of great pain can become moments of truth on which a future might be built in time. In crisis situations, communication will not be confined to words only. The actual presence of the social worker reduces isolation and loneliness and communicates concern and support. In times of acute distress, the actual physical holding of a child is likely to be the only means of bringing any relief. Adults, too, often need the reassurance of a protective arm or an outstretched hand. The whole demeanour and tone of voice of the social worker conveys just as much, if not more, than the words he/she uses.

The freedom that social workers have to use themselves in these situations will depend on each one's capacity to identify with others and to imaginatively encompass the experience of their clients in any given situation. This is hard work and takes its toll in terms of emo-

tional strain which has to be recovered from. Social service departments need to allow for this strain on their social work staff, to understand it, and to devise ways of meeting it within the structure and
organization of the department. I suggest that this needs a lot of thinking over, especially in regard to periodic recuperative holidays.

So far I have talked about communication with children in crisis
situations because my recent experience with young adults has
brought home to me very vividly how much suffering might have
been avoided if there had been someone outside the family to whom
the boy or girl could have turned for help and understanding when
things began to get difficult. Such a little help at that stage could have
gone so far; but nobody in the child's environment recognized the
distress signals, and often the children were considered naughty or
rebellious. Perhaps social workers have a responsibility here in helping other professional groups who work with children to be more
aware of distress, the situations likely to cause it, and how it could be
relieved or prevented.

I should now like to discuss ways in which social workers communicate with children in the course of their day-to-day social work
responsibility for them. First, I want to think about the purpose of
communication, and secondly how we might try to do it, and finish by
considering the important question of the role of the social worker in
relation to the child.

The immediate purpose of communication, as I have already suggested, is to get into touch with the real self of the child, which is what
he is feeling about himself and his life at the moment of meeting. We
want to help children to remain in contact with themselves and maintain a sense of their own unique identity and worth in relation to other
people—at this moment—in relation to the social worker. As all children who come our way have been through painful experiences of one
kind or another, we shall need to seek contact with the suffering part of
each child, because locked up in the suffering is each child's potential
for living and for feeling love as well as for feeling fear, anxiety, and
hostility. In these situations there is a strong temptation to seduce
children away from the reality of their feelings and to offer distractions
of one kind or another. If we do this, we lead them up a blind alley
from which they may never return. The greatest reassurance we can
give to children is the feeling that they are understood and accepted,
right down to the painful sad bit in the middle. If we do not deny this
painful bit of themselves, they need not do so, and their natural resilience can then take them on into life again. But if there is denial, this

natural resilience can be used to distract them from true living (and how many people there are who go around saying they do not feel real).

In order to develop into a whole human being, each child needs to be recognized and known as a person in his own right, with his own particular ways of thinking and feeling and expressing himself and with his own special thing to say, which distinguishes him from everyone else. It is when this is listened to and appreciated that life be comes worth living, because the thing most real to him is real to others, and this links him to the world, to life, and to shared experiences and meaningful relationships.

Recently a past student sent me a poem written by a 14-year-old boy. It speaks for itself and for all children.

Poem[1] from *Books for Your Children*, 1975:

He always
He always wanted to explain things, but no one cared,
So he drew.

Sometimes he would just draw and it wasn't anything.
He wanted to carve it in stone or write it in the sky.
He would lie out on the grass and look up in the sky, it would be
only the sky and the things inside him that needed saying.

And it was after that that he drew the picture,
It was a beautiful picture. He kept it under his pillow and
Would let no one see it.
And he would look at it every night and think about it.
And, when it was dark and his eyes were closed he could see it still.
And it was all of him and he loved it.

When he started school he brought it with him,
Not to show anyone, but just to have it with him like a friend.

It was funny about school
He sat in a square brown desk like all the other square desks and he
thought it would be red.
And his room was a square brown room, like all these other rooms.
And it was tight and close. And stiff.

He hated to hold the pencil of chalk, with his arms stiff and his feet
flat on the floor, stiff, with the teacher
Watching and watching.

The teacher came and spoke to him.
She told him to wear a tie like all the other boys.
He said he didn't like them and she said it didn't matter.

After that they drew. And he drew all yellow and it was the way he
felt about morning. And it was beautiful.
The teacher came and smiled at him. "What's this?" she said
"Why don't you draw something like Ken's drawing?
Isn't it beautiful?"

After that his mother bought him a tie and he always drew airplanes
and rocket ships like everyone else.

And he threw the old picture away.

And when he lay out alone looking at the sky, it was big and blue,
and all of everything that he wasn't any more.

He was square and brown inside and his hands were stiff.
And he was like everyone else.
All the things inside him that needed saying didn't need it any more.
It had stopped pushing. It was crushed.
Stiff.

Like everything else.

Perhaps it will not surprise anyone to know that this boy committed suicide soon after writing the poem. Of course, the problem existed before the boy went to school. He was cut off from communication in his home. The teacher had a second chance, so to speak, and if she could have taken it, things might have turned out differently, but that is not certain. It is not an exaggeration to say that a moment's communication of genuine appreciative recognition can be life-saving.

Now I want to move on to the question of how we communicate with children. It is obviously impossible to generalize, but I will put forward some thoughts for consideration. I have already suggested that our presence, our attitude, behaviour, tone of voice, are all communicating something to the child, and we need to be fully aware of this situation, and sometimes put into words how the child might be feeling about us. In fact, the method used by Virginia Axline and others of "reflecting back" to the child, in simple direct words, what he is doing and how he is behaving is a very useful simple way of helping him see himself objectively, and come to know himself, through being recognized and known by us.

We recognize it as important that the purpose of our presence in the lives of children and their families is made clear as soon as possible, in a way that a child can understand, so that he is not left anxiously guessing or suspicious or afraid. We are powerful agents in the lives of children, and we need to convey our concern for them as individuals, so that they have the opportunity to feel us as supportive, benign agents. Often this can be done quite simply by our remembering something about the last time we saw the child, something that we did together perhaps, or something that they said to us. I have purposely mentioned the value of our remembering something that the child said, because this will have more significance for him than anything we may have said, and the fact that we remember will carry more reassurance than any of our words could do. He will feel known, special. I feel very strongly about this question of listening to children.

How desperately some children need us to listen to them and to try to understand what they say, and how easy it is to be too busy to listen. Inside each child there is a story that needs to be told—a story that no one has yet had time to listen to. It is through expressing himself that the child gets to know himself and sorts out his confusions and develops his own self-image and sense of himself in relation to someone else who will stop to listen. Of course, other people who are nearer to the children have more opportunity to listen to them, but social workers do need to listen if they are to gain the child's confidence and help him to gain confidence in himself. Moreover, there are things that cannot be said to those who are too near. Here are some actual things that have recently been said by children to their social workers. All the children express their fears, their doubts and uncertainties, their hopes, and their love and hate, sometimes in words, or by implication.

Children talking

Heather is 9½ and lives with her grandmother of 73 and her elder brother, following the death of her parents and younger brother in a car crash in which she herself was injured. She said to her social worker, "When I wave before turning the corner on my way to school, I wonder if it will be the last time I see her. Nan's all I've got left, that's why I cling to her. I don't want to go to boarding school. I'd be unhappy there. I just want to be with my Nan." There had never been any question of sending this child to boarding school, so the idea was entirely her invention and really expressed her not surprisingly severe separation anxiety.

Anna, aged 3½, was placed with foster parents at her mother's request, and the mother is undecided about wanting the child home. She has been in care for three months, and on a recent visit said to the social worker, "I don't want to go home. When my Susan mummy came I cried. I'll go home, but only for a tiny while. I'll come back here, won't I?" How clearly this 3½-year-old knows what she can do, and what she wants and where she is wanted.

Desmond, aged 9 years, is in boarding school following the break up of his home after his father left. The social worker took him out for a ride in her car during his half-term holiday, and during the course of the journey he said, "I really hate my dad, now that I know the truth— he used to hit my mum, and it was his fault the baby died. There are lots of things I hate about him, but some that I like. Can you give me his address so that I can write to him?" Here is a boy struggling to come to terms with his difficult home situation and his hate of his father, which does not exclude some positive feeling too. In this process of coming to terms with his life, the listening ear and the accepting attitude of the social worker is absolutely vital.

Susan, aged 17 years, was previously in care and known to her social worker over a period of three years. She is now married, with a girl baby of one year. She has shown a repeated pattern of taking herself off when things go wrong, staying away for days, even weeks at a time. She said to her social worker recently, "That's the trouble with me. I go off whenever things go wrong. I want to talk about it, but something inside tells me not to, so I run away, it doesn't matter where, but it doesn't help." I suggest that the reason why this girl doesn't talk is her great fear of her own violent feelings. If she expresses them, she fears that she might lose control, they would sweep her along, and who knows what the end might be, for the baby and for herself. I may be wrong in this conjecture, but I would certainly have these thoughts in mind with someone who runs away when things get difficult.

I want to mention the other aspects of communicating with children that are relevant to the practical technique of trying to do it as effectively as we can. They are:

1. the approach to children;
2. the establishment of a neutral zone of shared experiences;
3. the language of communication.

These three questions are inter-related, and in attempting to describe them, I am aware that I am not really describing techniques, but a whole approach and attitude to the work, which implies in the social worker a philosophy that can embrace this attitude and approach. This is not simply something that can be learned in a training course, although it can be discussed by students; but its roots lie in the individual social worker's value system. It raises the question of what kind of people we are, as opposed to what we do.

In approaching children for the first time, or in later times of special difficulty, we find that we avoid a direct approach, because it could be felt as threatening. If we ask questions, we either do not get answers or get fictitious ones that spring from the child's imagination and/or his attempt to hide from us. So we have long since given up this approach. Nor can we expect to talk downwards to children from our grown-up height, so we sit on the floor or on a low seat. Then we remember to start up the conversation by talking about something else—not about the child himself directly. I remember a terrified child being greeted by the words: "Hello Linda, how nice of you to come and see me in your red shoes." The response was immediate: "And my red gloves, and my red scarf", which she proceeded to display. But the ice was broken, and the child was willing to go on co-operating. The idea is to pick on something to talk about at the beginning that the child might be, or already is, showing interest in. The social worker might say, for example, "Has Teddy got a name?" or "That looks a nice game, shall we see if it is?" Or the social worker can simply sit down and do something herself, like drawing, that would be likely to gain the child's attention.

This indirect approach is useful for older children too, and even for adolescents who would resent being expected to sit down opposite the social worker and talk. In fact the procedure of getting alongside rather than face to face with children is an important way of facilitating communication. Then we have to remember that children will want to find out what we are like, and it is important that we show our hand and let them find out for themselves. On the whole they are more astute at this game than are our adult clients.

I now come to my second point about the technicalities of facilitating communication, and this concerns the whole area of shared experiences, which is such an important part of life and of relating and of being related to. The ride in the car, or the game played together, or the TV programme watched, or even the visit to a clinic or hospital, all give opportunities for shared experience, and this is perhaps the most non-threatening form of communication there is. It can build up confidence and mutual trust and provide a neutral safe area within which direct communication is possible when needed.

Moreover, shared experiences can be talked about, and relived over again, thus enriching the inner life of the individual and at the same time building up his/her personal history, which can be validated by the person who has shared it. An experience shared can be a complete experience and a permanent possession. If social workers are to know the children for whom they are responsible, they will seek to create an area of shared experience between themselves and the child, however limited it may have to be. Once established, this area can be widened out to include other people and new experiences, which will, hopefully, outlast the social worker's responsibility, which has a time limit to it.

Language and emotion

Now I come to the question of the language we use in communicating with children. This is an immensely complex subject because it is multi-dimensional and takes place on many levels at the same time. What is said is not necessarily what is heard, because what is heard reflects the capacity of the hearer not only to comprehend, but to deal with the emotional implications of the communication. If social workers are to be anywhere near the mark in communicating with children, they will need to hear what is said in terms of their total knowledge and understanding of the child's situation and how he/she is likely to feel about it.

For example, a 4-year-old boy was keeping his new foster parents awake in the night. When the social worker arrived, he said at once, "Auntie's keeping me awake at night." Was he telling a lie? I suggest that this has to be understood and responded to in terms of the child's anxiety in the new home and his uncertainty of the new foster parents and how alarming it is to be sleeping for the first time alone in a room of his own in unfamiliar surroundings, instead of the safety of the nursery from which he had come. Aunty was keeping him awake.

Another example is that of an 8-year-old boy who asked his social worker when they were alone together, "Do you like Aunty Margaret?" (his foster mother). Clearly, what this child wanted was not to hear the social worker's opinion of his foster mother. He had his own views on the subject and badly needed permission to express them.

The point I want to make is that it is no good to answer questions which involve and expose feelings, in practical terms, because this means that although questions may have been answered, no communication has taken place whatsoever. Social workers have to train themselves to listen with a third ear; only thus will they catch and understand the real purpose of the communication and be in a position to respond appropriately and help the child to a new understanding of himself and his anxieties.

I do not wish to give the impression that communication with children is not concerned with sharing factual information with them. They certainly need explanations in words that they can understand, about what is happening to them and their families and about past and future happenings and plans. A great deal needs to be discussed and sorted out about real things that have happened, so that children can build up a realistic picture of themselves and what goes on around them.

Recently a social worker student introduced her husband to a 10-year-old boy in care, and he asked, "What's a husband, Miss?" and later he asked if this man was her only husband. A 9-year-old fatherless boy living in a children's home with his younger boy cousin, John, asked, "If my Uncle Peter dies, will I be John's father?" This was a genuine question. What a puzzling world it is when you have so little experience to call on in order to sort out its complexities and how much factual help is needed to get things into some sort of realistic perspective.

Often social workers are in the position of having factual knowledge of a devastating nature about the lives, or the death of the parent (or parents) of a child in care. In the end the child will need to know these facts, but how are they to be imparted? Everyone will have their own views on this question, but I suggest that the imparting of painful and damaging information could be a long job and that first much hard work has to be done to build up the child's confidence, and trust, in the social worker through what I have called shared experiences. As these shared experiences are talked over and become part of the child's remembered history, it is likely that sooner or later questions about the past will be raised, tentatively at first, and then bit by bit the details will be filled in as the child becomes strong enough for the next part of the story. If the first question can be answered briefly and factually without anything added or commented on that is not implied in the question, then the process of finding out the truth is likely to progress at the child's pace. Let us only hope that the social worker stays long enough to see this process through to the point when the child can come to his own terms with the knowledge. But perhaps this is too much to hope in these days of rapid promotion and a high staff turnover rate?

Time limits

To finish, I want to say something about the social workers' role in relation to children who are the responsibility of the social services. As I see it, the best work can be done when the professional nature of the role is fully accepted—because it has built into it a discipline based on knowledge and objectivity, and it includes an awareness of a time limit. This discipline therefore adds a realistic dimension to the work and provides a focus for it. If we side-step the professional nature of our work and mislead children into thinking that we are available indefinitely as their best friend, we are badly letting them down. What we are in a position to offer is warm, friendly, personal help aimed at enabling them to come to terms with themselves and their situation and to provide opportunities for them to establish relationships and build up loyalties for themselves which can last a lifetime, and on the basis of which they can take their place in society.

True professionalism

I know that in social work today there is a swing away from professionalism because it is seen as tending to create a barrier between "us", the social workers, and "them", the clients. I feel sympathy with those who want to break through these barriers where they exist, but I do not think they have anything to do with what we call professionalism. In my view it is only if we can, as social workers, accept within ourselves the common humanity that binds us and our clients together that we shall be able to empathize with them and understand their vulnerability because we too, are vulnerable. Perhaps the most valuable gift that we bring to work with children is our own capacity to remain vulnerable while accepting our professional discipline and role.

In conclusion, I hope I have suggested that there is a very real need for much more concentrated and specialized work with children in the social services than has yet been attempted, and that its expansion would in the long term be likely to relieve the total burden on the service. The kind of work I have envisaged in this paper is not so much highly skilled (although skill will grow), but it is highly sensitive and demanding, and a high degree of self awareness and powers of observation are needed by those who do it. In my view, special training is absolutely essential for this work, and I suggest that it could best be provided by specialized ongoing in-service training (in the form of group supervision by a suitable expert) for all social workers engaged in work with children at a given time. Such training would also secure the necessary support for the staff involved in this highly charged and challenging work.

Note

1. There was no author or additional information about this poem.

PART III

SOCIAL WORK

CHAPTER TEN

The "rescue motive" in social work

(1955–56)

July 1955:   (Comment by *CCQR* Editor: "Miss Britton wrote in a paper reviewed elsewhere, "The rescue motive is to be avoided in social work" [chapter 6, this volume]). Our reviewer writes, "Perhaps one day she will tell us [what the motive in child-care work should be]." Miss Britton sends us the following brief comment.)

Dear Sir,—It is certain that the rescue motive was of prime importance to the pioneers in child care as in other fields. Our debt to them is great. But the point is that motives grow up just as people do, and the motive of the past is not appropriate to the present.

First published in July 1955 in *Child Care Quarterly Review*, 9 (3): 120, and in January 1956 in *Child Care Quarterly Review*, 10 (1): 12–13.

Editor's Note: These letters appeared in the July 1955 and January 1956 issues of the *Child Care Quarterly Review* (CCQR). Clare was initially responding to an unsigned review of her article "Casework Techniques in the Child Care Services" (chapter 6 in this edition), which had been published in the first part of the July 1955 issue. In the second letter, Clare responded to several letters in the October 1955 issue of the *CCQR* and referred specifically to communications from E. Phylliss Corner, Chairman of the National Association of Probation Officers, and Mark Fineman.

Child care has now reached a stage at which the rescue motive hampers. There is no longer a need to collect funds or mobilize public opinion. The rescuer is not suited to the more delicate work of modern child care which demands of the worker a more direct, straight-forward drive, one that is close to that of parents who care for their own children.

Rescuers can always be found a place, but the time is past in child care for their kind of enthusiasm. The present issue is confused by their need to save rather than to find and foster what is good in a situation.

Yours sincerely,
  Clare Britton
London School of Economics

January 1956:

Dear Sir,—I have been very interested to read the comments made by your correspondents on the rescue motive in social work which I discussed in my paper "Casework Techniques in the Child Care Services" [chapter 6, this volume], and on which I added a further note in your July issue of the *CCQR*.

As so often happens in correspondence when one particular theme is taken out of its context, the original of which it was only a part is lost sight of. If my paper is referred to, I think it will be seen that I actually said or implied many of the very fundamental things that are raised in the letters, especially in the one from Miss Corner.

It is a little difficult to see why the idea of growing out of one motive into another causes such alarm. I am not denying that love is the motive in social work today (see my original paper), and I entirely agree with Mr Fineman that "love—the desire to help one's fellow men" is essential in the social worker of today as it was in those of yesterday, and I would add that without it we do not even *begin* to help anyone however skilled our case-work techniques. What I am suggesting is that the *quality* of love should be akin to that of parents for their children, and we know that parents help their children and go on loving them through good times and bad, through distress and difficulties of many kinds as the children come to grips with the essential problems of life and find their way through them. This is often difficult for parents and many long to rescue their children from the difficult things, but by doing so they would deny to their children the right to live their own lives and to discover their own potentialities to overcome difficulties.

As I see it, the social worker of today has to be able to tolerate and help her clients to work through the difficulties and conflicts which disturb their lives. The social worker has to be able to *contain* in herself and her relationship to the client both the good and the bad in a situation and in the individual. If she cannot bear the conflict herself and seeks to end it by rescuing the client from what she considers to be the bad influences in his life, she is only doing half her job, and, moreover, she is denying to the client the possibility of discovering the strength which comes through finding his own personal solution to his problem. The rescuer will feel better for the act of rescue, but the social worker who encompasses the *total* situation will feel worse, because she has to stand the *conflict* of good and evil which the rescuer avoids.

That there are situations from which the social worker of today may have to rescue a client because all other methods have failed in spite of the help given, I would agree. But that is quite different from being *motivated* to rescue. Furthermore, the social worker is aware that the problem is not solved by the act of rescue. It is transferred from one place to another, and it has to go on being solved in the new setting.

In her letter Miss Corner suggests that perhaps the essential difference between us and our predecessors lies in our aims and methods and not in our motives. It seems to me that as social work has gradually evolved as a profession and new aims and methods have become established over the years, we would expect that people entering it as a later stage should have a different motivation for doing so—one more in line with the new aims and methods and the new conception of the kind of responsibility that society has towards those who need help.

Perhaps we must not hope to reach agreement on these very fundamental questions, but that makes it all the more necessary for us to exchange ideas freely and honestly so that we can learn to understand each other's language and ways of thinking and to respect all points of view.

Yours faithfully,
Clare Britton
London School of Economics

CHAPTER ELEVEN

The development of insight

(1959)

I found the reading of last year's report on the Conference on Personality Development a stimulating experience, because the wealth and range of the ideas put forward, quite apart from their own intrinsic value, revealed the new orientation to professional education which is gradually taking place in the fields of education and social work by the increasing application of dynamic psychology not only to what we teach, but also to how we teach.

The report on last year's Conference had another effect on me, however. As a speaker at this year's Conference I wondered what on earth there was still left to say. Insight was mentioned many times last year, and Paul Halmos (1958) stated that in the teaching of personality development the first aim is that students shall acquire insight. Others supported this view in words or by implication.

I see my task as an attempt to separate out and examine at close range some of the meanings of this word insight and its development. In doing this I shall assume that members of the Conference are familiar with what was said last year on this subject.

Conference on the teaching of Personality Development, Leicester University, March 1959. First published in 1964 in *Child Care and Social Work*; reprinted in C. Winnicott, *Child Care and Social Work* (Hitchin, Hertfordshire: Codicote Press).

I start off by wondering why it is that we value insight so highly. Why has it become for us the pearl of great price which is worth all the cost of acquiring, and in comparison with which other possessions seem to have less value? I cannot believe that it is simply a utilitarian matter, that insight is important simply as part of our professional equipment. I suggest that we value it not only in terms of its usefulness but because it opens a new world to us, a world in which we are in touch with our own potential and aliveness as well as with that of our pupils or clients. We are constantly testing our own capacity for comprehending the truth about ourselves as well as about others. Another way of saying this would be that we are engaged on the age-old search for inner truth, truth about ourselves and the nature of man; but today we have additional equipment to help us, that which Freud made available when he discovered and chartered the unconscious and applied the scientific method to its study.

We recognize that insight into the feeling of others implies insight into our own similar feelings. In fact, the very word insight starts us off with this supposition. It implies a two-way process, as if the one were not possible without the other. Why should this be so? Paul Halmos (1958) made some convincing comments on this question last year, and I should like to quote the conclusions of his argument:

> When one truly "understands" human motivation one succeeds in fusing the affects of one's own previous experience with the affects called up by the observation of another's present behaviour. Or to express this more accurately, understanding consists in recalling those sentiments in one's own life which in fact appear to characterize the other's observed behaviour. So you see this ability to recall will decide whether we have the full flavour of another's experience. The ability to do this telescoping of past and present experience is what the psycho-analysts call "insight".

I agree with Dr Halmos that the crux of this matter of insight is the ability to recall the affects of one's own experiences when confronted with similar experiences in clients or pupils. We are unable to see in others that which we have for years defended ourselves against seeing in ourselves, defended ourselves because the feelings aroused are too painful and threatening to us.

Of course we all employ defence mechanisms of one sort or another to protect ourselves not only against the vicissitudes of external reality as it impinges on us, but also against internal pressures arising from conflict. What is important so far as insight is concerned is the degree of rigidity of the defences. Where there is rigidity, effective sublimation cannot take place, and where this state of affairs exists, work drains rather than sustains and strengthens the ego. The stronger the ego, the less need there is for a rigidity of defence, and consequently the greater the capacity for insight.

This subject of ego strength could occupy almost all our attention because it is germane to the subject of insight. It will be agreed that the only fruitful way of discussing ego strength is in terms of the individual's growth.

In selecting students, we look for ego strength. In the early history of the individual, a very important factor contributing to ego strength is the environment which has certain qualities such as reliability, and which is free from gross abnormalities, as, for instance, a chaotic state in the mother at the time of infantile dependence. When the early environment is satisfactory, there builds up in the individual a personal pattern for the management of instinct and for dealing with frustration. There is opportunity for the establishment of what Melanie Klein calls good internal objects, which enables the individual to trust and to believe in the self and in others. The same conditions facilitate the capacity to accept substitute experiences and objects (symbols). Signs of ego strength include a capacity to tolerate anxiety, doubt, guilt feelings, and depression. This toleration gives the individual time for the development of those internal solutions which we call sublimation. Sublimation could be said to be the most satisfactory defence against anxiety.

It is interesting to recall that in his early development of the technique of psycho-analysis Freud discovered that to give reassurance to the patient tended to strengthen the defences against further insight. Freud also recognized that it was sometimes profitable to produce a degree of anxiety in some patients to enable them to break through their defences and gain insight, and that this could be therapeutically effective within the framework of the analytic relationship. In the last few decades psycho-analysts have increasingly realized that anxieties are inherent and that from them comes some of the stimulus to sublimation.

Today in teaching we recognize the value of a degree of anxiety in our students and that it can be the prelude to the breaking down of defences and the gaining of new insight. But we must add immediately that if anxiety is too great, new defences against it will be organized. In fact, if we look, we find that we guard against this danger. We do this by the whole organization of the course within the time limit prescribed. We see that the programme and the arrangements are reliable.

We are careful in the timing of the introduction of new ideas. The relationships between students and staff and within the student group develop a stability within a framework of mutual experiences year by year. In other words, we are giving ego support to the students in exactly the same way as a mother lends, and later the two parents lend, ego support over a period of time according to the needs of the immature infant ego.

At this point I must mention a complication which can arise. Undoubtedly there are some people who are near to having insight into themselves but who have not quite achieved it and are impelled to try and to understand people with similar experiences to their own in the unconscious attempt at gaining insight into themselves. In other words, their work with clients or pupils is part of their own psychotherapy, which in the long run may work, but in the meantime objective assessment is obscured by subjective needs, and the amount of help and guidance that can be given cannot rise above the tolerance level of the worker and has relatively little relation to the client's needs.

Insight, then, is a complete phenomenon which occurs in relatively healthy individuals and can be regarded not so much as the hallmark of health, but as part of the integrative forces in the ego making for health. Ernst Kris (1956) writing on "Insight in Psycho-Analysis", says: "It has been said that insight is not a curative factor, but evidence of cure. The statement is I believe fallacious since it overlooks the circularity of the process . . . . However, the complexity of the ego functions which participate in the process of gaining and using insight may well account for the wide variations of the impact of insight on individual cases" (p. 453). From our own experience of trying to help students to acquire insight, we know that there are great differences in the degree to which they can acquire it, differences which have their own history in the development of each individual.

I think it might be useful if I listed five points of interest which I consider to be vitally related to the study of the development of insight.

1. The first I have already referred to in pointing out the relation between the capacity for insight and health in the individual. (By health I mean psychiatric health.) The existence of rigid psycho-neurotic defences shown in phobias, hypochondriacal fears, obsessional behaviour, or in regression to over-dependence on people in the environment leading to hostility to those in authority, can all be seen to hamper the development of insight to a greater or lesser degree. The keyword in neurotic defences is repression, which means that areas of

childhood experiences are not available to consciousness. I would also like to refer to health in terms of the absence of psychosis or the more severe type of mental disorder. A good example would be a severe degree of splitting in the individual ego which may be difficult to detect, since parts of the personality can appear to be exceptionally understanding, although there is a failure on the part of the individual to be in touch at one and the same time with all aspects of the self.

It also has to be remembered that there may be a "false self" defence which is highly successful not only as a defence, but also as a way of life. It is rigid, however, in the sense that the individual cannot gain insight without first experiencing some degree of breakdown.

Individuals who are severely ill do not usually come forward for selection, and if they do, their illness is detected in the selection process.

2. The second aspect of insight which I should like to mention is that which can be stated in terms of the richness or poverty of the individual's inner psychic reality. There is great variation here, and we recognize some people as more alive than others. This means that by the processes of introjection and projection such people have taken into themselves the experiences of external reality and fused them with their own imaginative experiences. In this way they have made the world their own both internally and externally, and they can move about with ease and freedom, absorbing and building in new experiences as they arise. The richer the individual's world is, both in terms of actual experiences and the internal imaginative elaboration of them, the greater the potential for insight.

3. I now turn to the process of identification and its relation to insight. Last year Paul Halmos spoke about identification in drawing attention to the fact that intellectual understanding is not enough. Insight into other people's problems involves being able to live their experiences imaginatively, but with only temporary involvement and without loss of self. In this context I am concerned with something which can be referred to as over-identification, in which there is a loss of self and the identification is not imaginative but affects the life of the individual, and the process of recovery from the identification is delayed. Here insight may be acute and perceptive, and yet we note pathology. Ernst Kris points out that the underlying infantile phantasy in such cases can be one of primitive merging (Kris was referring to analysis, but his remarks are in my opinion applicable to our more general field). I am suggesting therefore that there is such a thing as over-identification in which experience of life is obtained vicariously.

If in the pattern of the individual fear and not love underlies the process of identification, then for that person identification has ceased to be a vehicle of insight, chiefly because the personality of the individual tends to be subservient to that of the person identified with. Miss Freud (1936) refers to this problem in her concept of "identification with the aggressor".

4. My fourth point concerns the relation of the mind to the development of insight. I am not, of course, falling into the trap of thinking that an intellectual grasp of psychological processes is insight. Indeed, we know that one of the most subtle defences against feeling is a flight to intellectualization. It is possible, however, for the mind to be working along with what might be called the psychesoma—that is to say, the experiences of the ego which are closely related to bodily functions and feelings.

Assuming this easy relationship between the mind and the living person, we demand of our students when we ask them to achieve insight that they shall allow themselves to separate off an observing ego whose function I shall describe by quoting from Marjorie Brierley (1951). After referring in her book *Trends in Psycho-Analysis* to the insight of poets, artists, and mystics, who show "the most lively sense of psychiatric reality", she says that "the forms in which they express their insight, though true to feeling, are unsatisfactory as formulations of fact." She goes on: "The would-be tester of psychological reality has to cultivate the emotional sensibility of the artist and yet bring his intelligence to bear upon the data so provided in order to express subjective facts not merely in terms consonant with subjective experience itself, but also in terms consonant with objective knowledge" (p. 162).

In other words, true insight involves our being able at one and the same time to feel and to think about what we feel, and to relate all this to what others have said and written on the basis of their own experiences. In teaching we are helped if we are aware of the mind, which is an ally, and of intellectualization, which is an enemy, of insight. I suggest therefore that this ability to observe and to feel and to interpret, at one and the same time is a highly sophisticated process and is the essence of insight, or its highest refinement.

5. My fifth point refers back to the two aspects of the word insight. Looking into oneself gives the ability to look into others and to understand their experience, but in order to do this there must be the drive or desire to do so. Possibly this drive is included in the meaning of the word empathy, and behind empathy lies the wish to extend

one's own experience or to get reassurance through sharing, or to satisfy the urge to help people. Empathy seems to be a positive extension of insight by giving it an outward direction. It is different from identification which is a mechanism employed by everyone automatically to a greater or lesser degree. I think that empathy involves enriching the self by the shared experience, as well as giving oneself to it.

I should like to take up now some of the practical implications of what I have said, and I suppose the most obvious one is that of the selection of students. I have already mentioned this question, and it is not my task to go into it fully. I merely want to draw together the ideas which arise out of my discussion of the subject of insight and its development.

At last year's Conference Miss Waldron's (1958) very useful discussion of selection interviews showed the constructive use which can be made of them. I appreciate her conclusion quoted from Miss Ashdown and Miss Clement Brown that the interview is "not only a means whereby the selector selects but (is) a co-operative effort to solve a vocational problem". In the context of what I have already said, however, I should like to stress the first part of that sentence and say that the main task of the selector is the elimination of those who have personality problems which would prevent them from making use of training. For however well we plan our courses and however dynamic our teaching methods, some people will never achieve insight.

We are helped in the work of selection by the fact that candidates have already selected themselves for training when they make application to us. This self-selective process means that the majority of people who come forward are ready for training and are suitable for it. There will, however, be a marginal group who have chosen their profession in order to solve personal problems which cannot be solved by the choice of a career, and there will be others who are not yet ready for training. Even among this marginal group there will be a few who, with training, may be enabled to solve their own problems and at the same time to contribute to society in their chosen profession. It is on the marginal people therefore that we have to concentrate in selection, and we all know that they take a disproportionate amount of our time and thought, and are a greater test of our skill, than the more straightforward candidates who are, fortunately, the majority.

As I have already suggested, we seek to eliminate from our training those who have rigid defences and an inflexibility of personality, those who have too marked a mood swing and who appear markedly elated or depressed throughout the interview, those who have a poverty of inner world experiences, and those whose imaginative elaboration of their experiences is out of touch with reality. I suggest that others to be avoided are those who are over-shy and suspicious throughout the interview. The people I have referred to as those having a split in ego structure so that they are never in touch with the whole of themselves at once are difficult to detect in an interview. The false self which they put forward can be quite convincing, but when they come on the course, we find that they do not make full use of it or of us and fail to gain insight.

Another group of candidates who come forward particularly for work with deprived children are those who have suffered deprivation themselves. What matters of course is the amount of emotional deprivation that exists, because we know that associated with it there is likely to be some antisocial tendency. I made my worst mistake in selection here. I fell for the candidate's spontaneity, warmth of personality, and deep understanding of deprived children. But during training she did not make the expected progress and became difficult to help. However, she received adequate practical work reports and passed the examination. At first she was well-liked in her job, but at the end of two years I had a letter from her employer saying that she had absconded with the petty cash, leaving many debts behind her. This behaviour was entirely understandable in terms of the student's own deprivation, but not understandable of course from society's point of view. I had seriously underestimated the extent of her difficulties.

I suggest that we also have to consider with special care those candidates with very high or very low IQs. In some the high intelligence can have been exploited to the cost of the rest of the personality. Those with low IQs, apart from their own personal problems of inferiority with the rest of the group, are just boring to teach, unless we are orientated to the type of teaching that they would need.

After the process of elimination, there will still be the problem of selecting the best people, and here we pay attention to positive ego strength and the way in which the individual has dealt and is dealing with life, and further, we shall consider this in relation to the training and what it could contribute to each individual at this stage in his or her development. And I hope we shall always deliberately take one or two risks each year by admitting people with good potential who have difficulties but who have some awareness of their difficulties and are already on the way to working through them. Such people can make excellent use of training for their own personal development as well as in professional development. Obviously the number of risks we take each year must be well controlled because too many people with difficulties can undermine the stability of the student group. Careful noting of risks taken and subsequent checking up on the performance of those students whom we consider to be risks would teach us much about selection. In my experience some people who turned out to be exceptionally valuable in the end were risks at the time of selection.

The basis of selection seems to turn on this question of insight. We choose, if we are lucky, those who already have the capacity for insight, and we hope to help them to develop their insight as the dynamic process at the core of their self-aware professional personality. How do we seek to do this? I should like to draw attention to one or two aspects of this question.

I have suggested earlier that the development of insight begins in infancy with the relationship to the mother and later to the two parents and then is extended to others. It is said that the child's first mirror is his mother's face, and in it he sees what he himself is like by the reactions he produces in her, and at one and the same time he sees what she is like. This two-way process is one and the same process. The fortunate child builds up a true picture of himself in the natural responses of the mother to what he is like at any given moment. If the mother's responses are inhibited or coloured by her own mood, the child never quite gets a clear picture of himself. Of course he will seek it from others and may get it, but the struggle to do so may be considerable.

Our students, if we have selected them carefully, come to us with the capacity for insight already to a greater or lesser degree established in their early years. In order to establish themselves as professional people during training, they require from us, their teachers and tutors, something very like that which they earlier required from their parents: a true and objective picture of what they present of themselves to us as they change and develop into professional adults. They rely on us for this, and we all know the students' thirst for criticism so long as it is objective and constructive and is based on what they themselves can see of themselves in what we say. Students absolutely need to be able to rely on us not to let our personal problems or moods cloud the picture of themselves which they need for personal and professional growth. It is this sort of reliability that they in turn have to give to their clients and pupils, and if they have not experienced it, they will find it impossible to give. Alas, we are only human and we have our off-days, and the students and clients and pupils suffer in consequence. But our occasional off-days are not disastrous, because it is the total experience of training which matters.

The next comment I should like to make links with something which Professor Tibble (1958) said in his "Afterthoughts" on last year's Conference. He said: "What we are overtly discussing with the student is the problem he is aware of in his pupils or clients or in the work situation, but what we are also implicitly discussing are the students' own personality problems."

I think this is very true, and, speaking for my own field, although our teaching is in terms of clients and their problems, the clients become in fact aspects of the students and their problems, and by this process of identification which is possible in a protected learning situation much personal insight is gained by the students without any direct interpretation of their own unconscious feelings. So that during training clients are more often than not aspects of the students, whereas in a job clients are clients, for when the students get to the job, they have taken over into themselves the role of their teachers and supervisors.

In connection with the presentation of case material for discussion, it seems important that when we begin on this method of teaching, the cases should not be too penetrating in the revelation of the client's problems; faced with too clever a piece of work, the students may feel suddenly exposed and may become resistant to the whole process of learning in this way.

I should like to raise another question about teaching method. If students are to gain insight, the teaching groups must remain alive and dynamic, and this surely means that not only must we time the introduction of new ideas, but that we must allow time for the students to exercise their ability to express their own subjective experience in terms of the theoretical concepts with which they are grappling at the moment. It can very well be found that an example brought forward by a student does in fact illustrate and illuminate the particular bit of theory which is being taught at the time.

Here we get what might be called an unconscious co-operation, something which in an analysis is dealt with by an interpretation, but which in our teaching work is dealt with by a linking up of the experience with the theory. In order to use the student's contribution effectively in such moments, we have to call upon our own insight and actively enter into the process of learning with the students, so that we together reach a moment of truth in which experience is objectified and integrated into the theoretical body of knowledge which the students are acquiring. I would like to add that in my personal opinion when the teacher has ceased to learn anything in the teaching process and to learn from the students, this has a deadening effect on the whole process, an effect which blocks the development of insight for all concerned.

The acquiring of insight during training is a painful process for the students, involving as it does the shifting of defences, the lessening of rigidity, and the rebuilding of more satisfactory defences based on the insight gained. We feel it to be quite normal therefore for students to go through phases of doubt and depression and hostility. The hostility we recognize as a new reality testing which we must meet and live through. Perhaps these aggressive phases during training are the most vital for new growth, and we know that we just have to "take it" without probing for content; if we did probe for content, we should get the wrong answer. It is interesting to compare this phase of training with what the psycho-analysts call the negative transference and resistance, which in analysis is dealt with by interpretation of the unconscious; in training it is enough if we survive it, showing concern but without reacting to it.

I should like to finish by going back to the idea of giving ego support to students in training. As I have already suggested, we do this in many ways, in teaching, in planning, and through personal knowledge of each student. Students also support each other through the medium of the group, and we all know that group cohesion is an important part of the total experience of training. If the group is to play a constructive part, the students need confidence in the leadership of those responsible for the course, a room of their own in which to meet, and the group must not be too large.

And lastly, I should like to emphasize the importance of parties and social functions in which staff and students meet, eating and drinking together and having ordinary social intercourse. In the kind of training that we are doing, in which students often feel attacked and threatened, these social activities are not just an extra frill or a luxury. They are, in my view, an absolute necessity. For one thing, they reveal to the students that we are, after all, quite ordinary human beings—a good bit of insight to start with!

CHAPTER TWELVE

Development towards self-awareness

(1964)

There is room for all kinds of people in the world, and we find that some have a high degree of self-awareness, and some do not. This state of affairs is all right: it makes for interest and variety between people, but for those who are involved in social work and similar professions which deal with people as individuals, some self-awareness is essential.

Self-awareness implies awareness of others and vice versa. In fact, these two things are two sides of the same coin. When we first become aware of another person, we at that moment become an aware self aware of the other person as distinct from ourselves. And so it is all through life, as we learn about other people, we automatically learn more about ourselves. Those who want to understand other people therefore have to be prepared to understand themselves.

There is no doubt that some people go into social work or become psychologists or psychiatrists or psycho-analysts in order to find out

Presented at a Shotton Hall Conference, Cheshire County Training College, Crewe, 17–19 April 1964. Printed in 1964 in *Challenges, Frustrations, Rewards, for Those Who Work with People in Need: A Report on the 1964 Conference* (Shrewsbury: Shotton Hall) and in 1971 in *Toward Insight for the Worker with People* (Shrewsbury: Shotton Hall).

about themselves or to solve their own problems, although they may not, of course, be aware of this in the early stages. There must be many people who have slipped over into social work (e.g. from administrative), and for these there must come a moment when they stop to consider whether or not they like the increase in self-awareness that social work entails. I would rather warn people off social work than push them into it because of the self-awareness that it involves them in, and self-awareness can be painful. If this comes unexpectedly, the result may be an attempt on the part of the person concerned to make social work into an elaborate form of administration in order to avoid the painfulness of awareness.

Why is self-awareness a painful matter? This question brings us, of course, straight to the question of defences that each one of us has built up in ourselves in order to manage the anxieties which are inherent in life. The personality of each one of us could be described in terms of the pattern of defences which we have each constructed in the process of our development to hold our anxiety and to make life tolerable. If these defences are challenged, we become vulnerable and aware again of the pain which lies behind them. Usually the things we are intolerant of in others are the things we find intolerable in ourselves.

In the development of each individual, anxiety arises from two sources. In the first place it arises from our instinctual drives, which are ruthless and aggressive as well as loving and constructive towards other people. The pain caused by this situation is obvious. It is that arising from the fundamental fear that we shall destroy that which we love. The complex defences which can be constructed against this anxiety cannot be enumerated now. An important one can be the inhibition of all instinct, but I suppose the most common one, and one which I think each of us can recognize in ourselves, is that we divide the world into good and bad people. The good we preserve, and the bad we destroy over and over again and feel justified in doing so.

Most of us can find that we can manage life perfectly well so long as there are certain people or categories of people or things which we do not like. For example, we may not like the people who go fox-hunting, or the "other" religion, or those in authority—or simply people with red hair, etc. In this way, although our view of the world may be distorted, we can save ourselves a lot of pain.

The second source from which anxiety arises in the individual is a more variable one. It is that arising from early environmental failure during the stages of maximum dependence. The developing infant depends on his or her mother or mother-substitute not only for the satisfaction of physical needs but for the continuing idea of him- or herself which is being created by the mother's adaptation to the infant's needs. Any sudden failure in adaptation or care can lead to feelings of insecurity which can amount to fear of disintegration, of impending death, or of annihilation. The obvious defence against this kind of anxiety is an exaggerated degree of self-reliance and/or the permanent search for someone or something to depend upon.

Even if an individual has not had to face serious repeated failure of adaptation in his or her early life, all of us have experienced moments when adaptation was not as good as usual, when something was missing and we suffered some degree of deprivation and sense of loss. These moments are inevitable and are part of the process which leads us towards independence and self-reliance. But this process is nevertheless a painful one, and we defend ourselves from the pain in one way or another. Perhaps we turn to someone else, or to something else, or perhaps we withdraw from the painful situation and re-live in memory the moments when satisfaction was more complete. The way in which we react in these moments sets a pattern and becomes the habitual way in which we deal with similar kinds of situations in the future. In the normal course of events the defences we employ work, and carry us through the difficult patch until we recover and can relax our defences, and so life goes on. On the whole, the more painful, for one reason or another, the original experience, the more rigidly we shall tend to cling to our defences, and this can restrict our capacity for other experiences and further development.

The important thing about defences, therefore, is that they work, and enable us to tolerate our own personal anxieties in a way that does not cramp further development. This may be all right so long as life goes fairly smoothly, but for social workers it never does go altogether smoothly, because they are constantly involved in situations which other people, their clients, find intolerable. Social workers are in a very exposed position in which their own defences against anxiety are always being tested or threatened by the anxieties they see in their clients, and which they must share with their clients if they are to give effective help.

At this point we may ask the question, why is it that social workers put themselves in this vulnerable position at all? Why do they do the job? I suggested earlier that we recognize that many people come into social work in order to find out about themselves or to solve their own problems. Many are aware that they do this, others are not. But anyway, whether they are aware or not, does it matter? Does it mean that they are less good at the job? In answer to this question I should like to say two things.

It seems to me that work which is as demanding as social work must have in it very real rewards for those who undertake it. To find out about other people in order to help them to solve their own problems seems to be a more constructive and socially useful way of finding out about oneself and solving one's own problems than to sit down with one's own problems and to try to solve them in isolation. Another alternative would be to deny the existence of one's problems and to seek an occupation which leaves them untouched.

But social workers are, on the whole, not made that way. They genuinely want to help other people whose problems are usually more complex than their own, but if in so doing they gain more self-knowl-edge and self-awareness and solve some of their own problems, this seems to me to be entirely satisfactory as a basis for work. For one thing, it is, so to speak, economically sound, because work must bring real gain to the worker if it is to be truly productive and if production is to be maintained. Every gain in self-knowledge makes the worker more useful to more people. The drive to solve one's own problems springs from the deepest and most constructive forces in human nature and is part of the healthy urge in us all towards integration and wholeness.

As I see it, a benign circle is established when social workers, in understanding their clients and enabling them to solve some at least of their problems, also at the same time gain understanding of them-selves and solve some of their own problems. The benign circle could, however, become a vicious circle, and this leads me to the second thing I want to say concerning this whole question of motivation in social work.

The danger in social work is not that social workers, by helping their clients, also help themselves, but that they should *fail* to help themselves and to develop through their work. Then indeed a vicious circle would be produced. Although the social situation which each client presents to the social worker is different in every single case, the personal problems which have created the situations are basically the same, because they are part of human nature. They are almost always familiar, both because they have been seen at work in other cases, and because the social worker recognizes the same forces at work in him or herself. There is a need therefore for a constant sorting out of the client's problem and his or her way of dealing with it from the social worker's own feelings about the problem. This work of sorting out must go on all the time, and increase in self-awareness is part and parcel of an increase in awareness of the client and an understanding of his problem.

To illustrate what I mean, I remember a social worker dealing with a difficult family situation. She had, after much hard work, established a good relationship with each parent separately, and the next step seemed to be a joint interview with both parents, but this she was absolutely unable to face until she became aware that all through her own childhood and adolescence she had need (for reasons which need not be gone into now) to keep her own parents separate. Once she had understood the situation, she was able to go ahead with the joint interview, and although it was not an easy interview, it was, in the long run, a productive one, and the social worker felt immeasurably relieved and pleased that she had undertaken it. The bringing together of these two parents was for her like bringing together her own parents at last, and the experience enriched her in a personal way over and above the help that she was able to give to her clients.

Social workers therefore need to be aware of the kind of problem that they are likely to find difficult in their clients, otherwise their insight will be uneven. They will be able to help some people but will fail to help others whose problems touch too closely on their own. Where social workers are unable or unwilling to face a personal problem of their own, they can project themselves, so to speak, into the client, so that in effect they become the client and try to work out in him or her their own problem. This will, of course, solve nothing either for the social worker or the client, because really the social worker is using the client in a ruthless way for personal ends. The need to succeed in this kind of situation can make the social worker controlling and dominating. Moreover the social worker never sees the client as he or she is and will not be in touch with the client's own inner resources and potential for solving his or her own problem. In these cases it could be said that the social worker is using the client's problem to defend him or herself from the full impact of his or her own problem. In other words, self-awareness is not operating, and this blocks the work.

Social workers have to learn to *carry* responsibility for their client's problems without *feeling* too personally responsible for the existence of the problems. In other words, it is a professional responsibility rather than a personal one that we carry. If social workers *feel* too responsible (i.e. responsible in a personal way for their client's problems), we would suspect that a degree of projection onto the client of the social worker's problem is going on, and that it is for their own personal problem in the client that they feel so responsible. Only the self-awareness of the social worker about what is happening can release him or her from the sense of personal responsibility so that the professional work of helping the client can go forward without unnecessary strain.

I do not want to seem to imply that whenever a social worker fails to help a client, the reason is because the social worker's problem is getting in the way. Occasionally this may be so, but far more often than not the nature of the client's problems is such that he or she, although perhaps seeming to want help, has a deep unconscious drive to reject help—or in still other cases, the help has come far too late to be made use of.

It seems then that the capacity for self-awareness is an essential ingredient of a social worker's make-up. But self-awareness, as I have already implied, is not something which is achieved once and for all: rather, it is achieved slowly, bit by bit and often painfully, as we go on facing new situations and developing in ourselves and in our work, and there is no end to it. Self-awareness, however, does not just happen to us. It is not, so to speak, simply one of the perks of the job. We have to work on ourselves as well as with our clients to achieve every bit of it, and we have to give time to this work.

I suggest that there are three ways in which we can further our own development in self-awareness. The first is in our personal lives, the second is through our direct work on cases, and the third is through a study of the theory of dynamic psychology. I have deliberately put these three kinds of experience in the order which seems to me to be the logical one. I should like to comment on them briefly.

First, then, our own personal lives contribute to our self-awareness, because it is in this area of life that we operate as ourselves. We are, within limits, free to choose our friends and our activities. Friendships, reading, and cultural activities of all kinds, and holidays, all enrich our lives and our knowledge of the world and of ourselves. We know that every situation in which we can be ourselves and enjoy ourselves not only adds another dimension to life, but liberates us for further experiences. Our personal life is the base from which we operate and to which we return. The firmer the base, the freer we are to make excursions into the unknown.

The second way in which I suggest we can develop in self-awareness is through our work. Our direct experiences with clients and our involvement in their problems is the raw material out of which self-awareness can be fashioned. We need to give time for the conscious assimilation of our experiences and for the deliberate reconstruction of the case material at leisure and away from the client. We can then take things a step further by comparing one case with another and by comparing our work with that of colleagues and other social workers.

I am fully aware of the difficulty that we all have in finding time to reconstruct our work for ourselves in the way I am suggesting. There is little leisure in a social worker's day. Nevertheless something goes on in us all the time and the experiences with our clients are being unconsciously assimilated, and every now and again we become aware that this is happening. Suddenly quite out of context we will remember something that somebody said or left unsaid, or the way they looked. Possibly, if we tried, we could make more deliberate use of these odd moments of awareness by recognizing their significance and adding them up in a way which will give us more conscious knowledge and a firmer grip on our cases. Time spent in this work of thinking over our cases can save us time in the long run, because when we return to the client, we shall know better where we are with him or her and can make better use of all that has gone before.

I now come to the third way in which we can further our development in self-awareness. As we make the effort to consciously assimilate our experiences and to reconstruct our case material, there comes a point at which we can very usefully turn to the theory of dynamic psychology which can throw further light on our work and enable us to gain a better intellectual understanding of it. Dynamic psychology is concerned with the study of developmental processes in individuals with feelings, conflicts, and defences. The theory can not only enable us to understand ourselves and our clients better, but, most important of all, it can provide a frame of reference which gives us a feeling of confidence. If we have a central structure of theoretical knowledge, we need not be entirely at sea when we face the unknown. Moreover, theory can save us time by helping us to see more quickly what is significant. The point about theory is that it does not have to be complete or final, and it does not necessarily have to be right, but it does have to *exist* and to be there as a starting point, or as something to catch hold of so that we can meet what comes without panic.

It may be obvious that I have not said that in order to become more self-aware, social workers should be psycho-analysed, because I do not believe that this is necessary. Some may need and want this kind of professional help, but that is an entirely personal affair. What I am saying, however, is that we can, if we want to do so, use every means available to enable ourselves to grow up and to further our own development into mature human beings. To grow up means learning to live with ourselves and putting up with ourselves the way we are.

We have to be able to tolerate sometimes feeling awful or confused or ignorant and at other times feeling good or clever or lucky. If we cannot tolerate the whole range of feelings of which we are capable, we can easily become rigid and seek to make everyone else, including our clients, fit in with our pattern and our time. This is the easy way out. Perhaps the most difficult thing in social work is to be the person fitting in with someone else's processes and therefore with his or her time, because processes cannot be hurried. In social work "time not our time rings the bell", and we find that we have to be prepared to wait and perhaps carry the case through long periods of doubt and uncertainty in which we do not know yet what the outcome will be.

In almost every case there is a difficult middle period to be gone through while things are sorting themselves out and we cannot see the end, or even if anything is happening at all. These difficult periods demand all we have got in the way of toleration not only for the client but for ourselves and our uncertainty.

But social workers are only human, and there will be times when our toleration is strained to breaking point. It can happen that all our cases seem to be going through a difficult phase at the same time. Some clients seem unresponsive and others seem negative or hostile. At this point resentment can build up in us, and what are we to do with it? We shall on the whole make every effort to protect our clients from our resentment, but in so doing we can find that we spread it around on to our colleagues and others in office, or onto other social work agencies which we feel to be unhelpful. Maybe this will not hurt anybody very much, but in the interests of our self-awareness perhaps we should at least know what we are doing.

To sum up, what are the positive gains to be had from doing a job as difficult as social work? I hope that I have already suggested some of them, but perhaps the most important thing is that it gives us an opportunity for personal growth which is beyond what we could achieve in our own private lives, because it enables us to share the experiences of others and to add these to the sum total of what we are. This is both a privilege and a responsibility, and it is also exciting, because we are always in a position to gain ever new experiences. In other words, there is no final examination for social work.

PART IV

ON D. W. WINNICOTT
AND PSYCHOANALYSIS

CHAPTER THIRTEEN

D.W.W.: a reflection

(1978)

The editors of this book have invited me to write something of a personal nature about the man whose observations and experience led to the concept of transitional objects and phenomena. In attempting to do this, I shall need to select only those aspects of his life and personality that are relevant to the book. It could seem therefore as if these concepts arose naturally and easily out of D.W.W.'s own way of life. In one sense this is true; but it is only half the story. The rest concerns the periods of doubt, uncertainty, and confusion out of which form and meaning eventually emerged.

What was it about D.W.W. that made the exploration of this transitional area inevitable and made his use of it clinically productive? I suggest that answers to these questions have to be looked for not simply in a study of the development of his ideas as he went along, but essentially in the kind of personality that was functioning behind them. He could be excited by other people's ideas but could use them and build on them only after they had been through the refinery of his own experience. By that time, unfortunately, he had often forgotten the

First published in 1978 in S. Grolnick & L. Barkin (Eds.), *Between Fantasy and Reality: Transitional Objects and Phenomena* (New York: Jason Aronson).

source, and he could, and did, alienate some people by his lack of acknowledgement.

While other people's ideas enriched D.W.W. as a clinician and as a person, it was the working out of his own ideas that really absorbed him and that he grappled with to the end of his life. This was a creative process in which he was totally involved. In his clinical work D.W.W. made it his aim to enter into every situation undefended by his knowledge, so that he could be as exposed as possible to the impact of the situation itself. From his point of view this was the only way in which discovery was a possibility, both for himself and for his patients. This approach was more than a stance; it was an essential discipline, and it added a dimension to his life as vital to him as fresh air.

The question is sometimes asked as to why D.W.W. in his writings seemed mainly concerned with exploring the area of the first two-person relationship. Strictly speaking, this is not true: he wrote on a wide range of topics, including adolescence and delinquency and other matters of medical and sociological concern, and the greater part of his psychoanalytic practice was with adults. However, it could be true to say that his main contribution is likely to turn out to be in the study of the earliest relationships and its application to the aetiology of psychosis and of the psychotic mechanisms in all of us.

I suggest that his study took this direction from two sources. In the first place, he brought with him into psychoanalysis all that he had learnt and went on learning from paediatrics, and secondly, at the time he came to psychoanalysis, the area of study just then opening up was that concerning the earliest experiences of life. Given his personality, his training and experience, and his urge for discovery, it seems inevitable that he would concentrate his researches on the so far comparatively unexplored area of earliest infancy and childhood. His findings, however, are recognized by many as having implications far beyond the immediate area of study. It is the expressed opinion of some that they throw light on all areas of living.

As I have suggested, the essential clue to D.W.W.'s work on transitional objects and phenomena is to be found in his own personality, in his way of relating and being related to, and in his whole life style. What I mean is that it was *his capacity to play* which never deserted him, that led him inevitably into the area of research that he conceptualized in terms of the transitional objects and phenomena. It is not my purpose here to discuss the details of his work, but it seems important to note that in his terms the capacity to play is equated with a *quality of living*. In his own words, "Playing is an experience, always a creative experience, and it is an experience in the space–time continuum, a basic form of living" (D. W. Winnicott, 1971a, p. 50).

This quality of living permeates all levels and aspects of experiencing and relating, up to and including the sophisticated level described in his paper "The Use of an Object" at which, in his own words, "It is the destructive drive that creates the quality of externality"; and again, "this quality of 'always being destroyed' makes the reality of the surviving object felt as such, strengthens the feeling tone, and contributes to object constancy" (D. W. Winnicott, 1971a, p. 93). For him, the destroying of the object in unconscious fantasy is like a cleansing process, which facilitates again and again the discovery of the object anew. It is a process of purification and renewal.

Having said that, I see my contribution to this book as an attempt to throw some light on D.W.W.'s capacity for playing. I expect that readers will be familiar enough with his writings on this subject to know that I am not talking about playing games. I am talking about the capacity for operating in the limitless intermediate area where external and internal reality are compounded into the experience of living.

I hope I do not suggest that D.W.W. lived in a state of permanent elation, because that was far from the case. He often found life hard and could be despondent and depressed and angry, but given time he could come through and encompass these experiences in his own way and free himself from being cluttered up with resentment and prejudices. During the last years of his life the reality of his own death had to be negotiated, and this he did, again gradually and in his own way. I was always urging him to write an autobiography, because I felt that his style of writing would lend itself to such a task. He started to do this, but there are only a few pages, and typically he used this exercise to deal with his immediate problem of living, which was that of dying. I know he used it in this way because he kept this notebook to himself, and I did not see it until after his death.

The title of the autobiography was to be *Not Less Than Everything*, and the inner flap of the notebook reads as follows:

T. S. Eliot   "Costing not less than everything." [Little Gidding: *Four Quartets*]

T. S. Eliot   "What we call the beginning is often the end
And to make an end is to make a beginning.
The end is where we start from." [Little Gidding: *Four Quartets*]

Prayer
D.W.W.:   Oh God! May I be alive when I die.

Following these words, he started on the writing, and it begins by imaginatively describing the end of his life. I shall quote his own words:

> I died.
> It was not very nice, and it took quite a long time as it seemed (but it was only a moment in eternity).
> There had been rehearsals (that's a difficult word to spell. I found I had left out the "a"). The hearse was cold and unfriendly.
> When the time came I knew all about the lung heavy with water that the heart could not negotiate, so that not enough blood circulated in the alveoli, and there was oxygen starvation as well as drowning. But fair enough, I had had a good innings: mustn't grumble as our old gardener used to say . . .
> Let me see. What was happening when I died? My prayer had been answered. I was alive when I died. That was all I had asked and I had got it. (This makes me feel awful because so many of my friends and contemporaries died in the first World War, and I have never been free from the feeling that my being alive is a facet of some one thing of which their deaths can be seen as other facets: some huge crystal, a body with integrity and shape intrinsical in it.)

He then goes on to discuss the difficulty that a man has dying without a son to imaginatively kill and to survive him—"to provide the only continuity that men know. Women *are* continuous." This dilemma is discussed in terms of King Lear and his relationship to his daughters and in particular to the youngest daughter who should have been a boy.

I hope that these quotations give some idea of D.W.W.'s capacity to come to terms with internal and external reality in a playful way, which makes reality bearable to the individual, so that denial can be avoided and the experience of living can be as fully realized as possible. In his own words "playing can be said to reach its own saturation point, which refers to the capacity to contain experience" (D. W. Winnicott, 1971a, p. 52). He was avid for experience, and he would have hated to miss the inner experience of the reality of his own death, and he imaginatively achieved that experience. In conversation he would often refer to his death day in a light-hearted way, but I knew that he was trying to get me and himself accustomed to the idea that it would come.

Having started at the end of his life, I must now go back to the beginnings and relate something about his earlier years and about the years that he and I spent together. I shall limit what I say to an attempt to illustrate the theme of playing, because that was central to his life and work.

First I must set the scene within which he grew up. It was an essentially English provincial scene in Plymouth, Devon, and it was far from London, not merely in mileage, but in custom and convention. When we drove to Plymouth from London, he was always thrilled when we arrived at the place where the soil banked up at the side of the road changed in colour to the red soil of Devon. The richness of the soil brought back the richness of his early life, which he never lost touch with. Of course, on the return journey he was always equally pleased to be leaving it behind. But he was proud of being a Devonian, and that there is a village of Winnicott on the map of Devon. We never actually found the village, although we always meant to. It was enough that it was there.

The Winnicott household was a large and lively one, with plenty of activity. But there was space for everyone in the large garden and house, and there was no shortage of money. There was a vegetable garden, an orchard, a croquet lawn, a tennis court, and a pond, and high trees enclosed the whole garden. There was a special tree, in the branches of which Donald would do his homework in the days before he went to boarding school. Of the three children in the family, Donald was the only boy, and his sisters, who still live in the house, were five and six years older than he. There is no doubt that the Winnicott parents were the centre of their children's lives, and that the vitality and stability of the entire household emanated from them. Their mother was vivacious and outgoing and was able to show and express her feelings easily. Sir Frederick Winnicott (as he later became) was slim and tallish and had an old-fashioned quiet dignity and poise about him, and a deep sense of fun. Those who knew him speak of him as a person of high intelligence and sound judgement. Both parents had a sense of humour.

Across the road was another large Winnicott household, which contained uncle Richard Winnicott (Frederick's elder brother) and his wife, and three boy cousins and two girls. The cousins were brought up almost as one family, so there was never a shortage of playmates. One of the sisters said recently that the question "What can I do?" was never asked in their house. There was always something to do—and space to do it in, and someone to do it with if needed. But more important, there was always the vitality and imagination in the children themselves for exploits of all kinds. Donald's family, including his parents, were musical, and one sister later became a gifted painter. The household always included a nanny and a governess, but they do not seem to have hampered the natural energies of the children in any unreasonable way. Perhaps it would be more correct to say that the Winnicott children successfully evaded being hampered. As a small child Donald was certainly devoted to his nanny, and one of the first things I remember doing with him years later in London was to seek her out and ensure that she was all right and living comfortably. We discovered that the most important person in her life then (1950) was her own nephew "Donald".

There is no doubt that from his earliest years Donald did not doubt that he was loved, and he experienced a security in the Winnicott home which he could take for granted. In a household of this size there were plenty of chances for many kinds of relationships, and there was scope for the inevitable tensions to be isolated and resolved within the total framework. From this basic position Donald was then free to explore all the available spaces in the house and garden around him and to fill the spaces with bits of himself and so gradually to make his world his own. This capacity *to be at home* served him well throughout his life. There is a pop song which goes, "Home is in my heart". That is certainly how Donald experienced it, and this gave him an immense freedom which enabled him to feel at home anywhere. When we were travelling in France and staying in small wayside inns, at each place I would think to myself, "I wonder how long it will be before he's in the kitchen"—the kitchen, of course, being the centre of the establishment—and sure enough, he would almost always find his way there somehow. Actually, he loved kitchens, and when he was a child his mother complained that he spent more time with the cook in the kitchen than he did in the rest of the house.

Because Donald was so very much the youngest member of the Winnicott household (even the youngest boy cousin living opposite was older than he) and because he was so much loved and was in himself lovable, it seems likely that a deliberate effort was made, particularly on the part of his mother and sisters, not to spoil him. While this did not deprive him of feeling loved, it did I think deprive him of some intimacy and closeness that he needed. But as Donald possessed (as do his sisters still) a natural ability to communicate with children of almost any age, the communication between children and adults in the Winnicott home must have been of a high order. Of course they all possessed an irrepressible sense of humour, and this, together with the happiness and safety of their background, meant that there were no "tragedies" in the Winnicott household—there were only amusing episodes. Not so many years ago, when the tank in the roof leaked, causing considerable flooding and damage, they were more excited and amused than alarmed by this unexpected happening.

At this point I should like to quote another page from Donald's autobiographical notes. Before doing so, I should explain that the garden of the Winnicott home is on four levels. On the bottom level was the croquet lawn; then a steep slope (Mount Everest to a small child) leading to the pond level; next another slight slope leading to the lawn, which was a tennis court; and, finally, a flight of steps leading to the house level.

> Now that slope up from the croquet lawn to the flat part where there is a pond and where there was once a huge clump of pampas grass between the weeping ash trees (by the way do you know what exciting noises a pampas grass makes on a hot Sunday afternoon, when people are lying out on rugs beside the pond, reading or snoozing?) That slope up is fraught, as people say, fraught with history. It was on that slope that I took my own private croquet mallet (handle about a foot long because I was only 3 years old) and I bashed flat the nose of the wax doll that belonged to my sisters and that had become a source of irritation in my life because it was over that doll that my father used to tease me. She was called Rosie. Parodying some popular song he used to say (taunting me by the voice he used)
>
>> Rosie said to Donald
>>> I love you
>> Donald said to Rosie
>>> I don't believe you do.
>
> (Maybe the verses were the other way round, I forget) so I knew the doll had to be altered for the worse, and much of my life has been founded on the undoubted fact that I actually did this deed, not merely wished it and planned it.
>
> I was perhaps somewhat relieved when my father took a series of matches and, warming up the wax nose enough, remoulded it so that the face once more became a face. This early demonstration of the restitutive and reparative act certainly made an impression on me, and perhaps made me able to accept the fact that I myself, dear innocent child, had actually become violent directly with a doll, but indirectly with my good-tempered father who was just then entering my conscious life.

Again, to quote further from the notebook:

> Now my sisters were older than I, 5 and 6 years; so in a sense I was an only child with multiple mothers and with father extremely preoccupied in my younger years with town as well as business matters. He was mayor twice and was eventually knighted, and then was made a Freeman of the City (as it has now become) of Plymouth. He was sensitive about his lack of education (he had had learning difficulties) and he always said that because of this he had not aspired to Parliament, but had kept to local politics—lively enough in those days in far away Plymouth.
>
> My father had a simple (religious) faith and once when I asked him a question that could have involved us in a long argument he just said: read the Bible and what you find there will be the true answer for you. So I was left, thank God, to get on with it myself.
>
> But when (at 12 years) I one day came home to midday dinner and said "drat" my father looked pained as only he could look, blamed my mother for not seeing to it that I had decent friends, and from that moment he prepared himself to send me away to boarding school, which he did when I was 13.
>
> "Drat" sounds very small as a swear word, but he was right; the boy who was my new friend was no good, and he and I could have got into trouble if left to our own devices.

The friendship was in fact broken up then and there, and this show of strength on the part of his father was a significant factor in Donald's development. In his own words: "So my father was there to kill and be killed, but it is probably true that in the early years he left me too much to all my mothers. Things never quite righted themselves."

And so Donald went away to the Leys School, Cambridge, and was in his element. To his great delight the afternoons were free, and he ran, cycled, and swam, played rugger, joined the School Scouts, and made friends and sang in the choir, and each night he read a story aloud to the boys in his dormitory. He read extremely well, and years later I was to benefit from this accomplishment, because we were never without a book that he was reading aloud to me, and one Christmas Eve sitting on the floor (we never sat on chairs) he read all night because the book was irresistible. He read in a dramatic way, savouring the writing to the full.

Donald described to me his going away to school. The whole family would be there to see him off, and he would wave and be sorry to leave until he was taken from their sight by the train's entering quite a long tunnel just outside Plymouth. All through this tunnel he settled down to the idea of leaving, but then out again the other side he left them behind and looked forward to going on to school. He often blessed that tunnel because he could honestly manage to feel sorry to leave right up to the moment of entering it.

I have in my possession a letter which Donald wrote to his mother from school which shows the kind of interplay that existed between members of the family:

> My dearest Mother,
>
> On September 2nd all true Scouts think of their mothers, since that was the birthday of Baden Powell's mother when she was alive.
>
> And so when you get this letter I shall be thinking of you in particular, and I only hope you will get it in the morning.
>
> But to please me very much I must trouble you to do me a little favour. Before turning over the page I want you to go up into my bedroom and in the right-hand cupboard find a small parcel. . . . Now, have you opened it? Well I hope you will like it. You can change it at Pophams if you don't. Only if you do so, you must ask to see No. 1 who knows about it.
>
> I have had a ripping holiday, and I cannot thank you enough for all you have done and for your donation to the Scouts.
>
> My home is a beautiful home and I only wish I could live up to it. However I will do my best and work hard and that's all I can do at present.
>
> Give my love to the others: thank Dad for his games of billiards and V and K (sisters) for being so nice and silly so as to make me laugh. But, it being Mother's day, most love goes to you,
>
> from your loving boy
> Donald.

Some who read this abbreviated account of D.W.W.'s early life and family relationships may be inclined to think that it sounds too good to be true. But the truth is that it *was* good, and try as I will I cannot present it in any other light. Essentially he was a deeply happy person whose capacity for enjoyment never failed to triumph over the setbacks and disappointments that came his way. Moreover, there is a sense in which the quality of his early life and his appreciation of it did in itself present him with a major problem, that of freeing himself from the family and of establishing his own separate life and identity without sacrificing the early richness. It took him a long time to do this.

It was when Donald was in the sick-room at school, having broken his collar bone on the sports field, that he consolidated in his own mind the idea of becoming a doctor. Referring to that time, he often said: "I could see that for the rest of my life I should have to depend on doctors if I damaged myself or became ill, and the only way out of this position was to become a doctor myself, and from then on the idea as a real proposition was always on my mind, although I know that father expected me to enter his flourishing business and eventually take over from him."

One of Donald's school friends, Stanley Ede (who remained a life-long friend), had often stayed in the Winnicott household and was well known to all the family. Back at school after a visit to his home, Donald, aged 16, wrote the following in a letter to the friend who had not yet returned to school:

Dear Stanley,

Thank you so much for the lovely long letter you sent me in the week. It is awfully good of you to take such a lot of trouble and to want to . . .

Father and I have been trying consciously and perhaps unconsciously to find out what the ambition of the other is in regard to my future. From what he had said I was sure that he wanted me more than anything else to go into his business. And so, again consciously and not, I have found every argument for the idea and have not thought much about anything else so that I should not be disappointed. And so I have learned to cherish the business life with all my heart, and had intended to enter it and please my father and myself.

When your letter came yesterday you may have expected it to have disappointed me. But—I tell you all I feel—I was so excited that all the stored-up feelings about doctors which I have bottled up for so many years seemed to burst and bubble up at once. Do you know that—in the degree that Algy wanted to go into a monastery—I have for ever so long wanted to be a doctor. But I have always been afraid that my father did not want it, and so I have never mentioned it and—like Algy—even felt a repulsion at the thought.

This afternoon I went an eight-mile walk to the Roman Road with Chandler, and we told each other all we felt, and especially I told him what I have told you now. O, Stanley!

Your still sober and true—
although seemingly intoxicated—
but never-the-less devoted
friend.
   Donald.

It seems that Stanley, one year older than Donald, had taken the line that Donald should do what he himself wanted to do, and that he had offered to broach the question of Donald's future to his father and that he did so. There is a postcard to Stanley, saying, "Thank you infinitely for having told father when and what you did. I have written Dad a letter which I think pretty nearly convinced him."

Donald recounts that when he summoned up courage to go to the Headmaster at school and tell him that he wanted to be a doctor, the Head grunted and looked at him long and hard before replying slowly: "Boy, not brilliant, but will do." And so he went to Jesus College, Cambridge, and took a degree in Biology. His room in College was popular as a meeting place, because he had hired a piano and played it unceasingly, and had a good tenor voice for singing.

But the first World War was on, and his first year as a medical student was spent helping in the Cambridge Colleges which had been turned into Military Hospitals. One of the patients, who became a lifelong friend, remembers Donald in those days: "The first time I saw him was in hospital in Cambridge in 1916 in the first war; he was a medical student who liked to sing a comic song on Saturday evenings in the ward—and sang 'Apple Dumplings' and cheered us all up."

It was a source of deep sorrow and conflict to Donald that all his friends went at once into the army, but that as a medical student he was exempt. Many close friends were killed early in the war, and his whole life was affected by this, because always he felt that he had a responsibility to live for those who died, as well as for himself.

The kind of relationship with friends that he had at that time in Cambridge is illustrated by a letter from a friend who had already joined up in the army and was on a course for officers in Oxford. It is written from Exeter College Oxford and dated 28/11/15:

> What are you doing on Saturday for tea? Well, I'll tell you!! *You are going to provide a big Cambridge Tea for yourself, myself and Southwell* (of Caius) [Caius College Cambridge] whom you've met I think. He's a top-hole chap and has got a commission. If you haven't met him you ought to have, and anyway you've heard me speak of him.
>
> Can you manage it? Blow footer etc. etc. or I'll blow you next time I see you. Try and manage it will you? Good man! It's sponging on you I know, but I also know you're a silly idiot and won't mind. Silly ass! Cheer O old son of a gun and get plenty of food.

Donald could not settle in Cambridge and was not satisfied until he was facing danger for himself, and, coming from Plymouth, he of course wanted to go into the Navy. He applied for and was accepted as a Surgeon Probationer. He was drafted to a destroyer, where he was one of the youngest men on board and the only Medical Officer in spite of his lack of training; fortunately, there was an experienced Medical

Orderly. He was subject to a great deal of teasing in the Officers' Mess. Most of the officers had been through one or other of the Royal Naval Colleges and came from families with a naval tradition. They were astonished that Donald's father was a *merchant*. This was a novelty, and they made the most of it, and Donald seems to have made the most of their company and of the whole experience. He has often related with amusement the banter that went on at mealtimes. Although the ship was involved in enemy action and there were casualties, Donald had much free time, which he seems to have spent reading the novels of Henry James.

After the war Donald went straight to St. Bartholomew's Hospital in London to continue his medical training. He soaked himself in medicine and fully committed himself to the whole experience. This included writing for the hospital magazine and joining in the social life: singing sprees, dancing, occasional skiing holidays, and hurrying off at the last minute to hear operas for the first time, where he usually stood in his slippers at the back of the "Gods".

It is difficult to give any dates in relation to Donald's girl friends, but he had quite close attachments to friends of his sisters and later to others he met through his Cambridge friends. He came to the brink of marriage more than once but did not actually marry (for the first time) until the age of twenty-eight.

Donald had some great teachers at the hospital, and he always said that it was Lord Horder who taught him the importance of taking a careful case history, and to listen to what the patient said, rather than simply to ask questions. After qualification he stayed on at Bart's to work as Casualty Officer for a year. He literally worked almost all day and night, but he would not have missed the experience for the world. It contained the challenge of the unexpected and provided the stimulation that he revelled in.

During his training Donald became ill with what turned out to be an abscess on the lung and was a patient in Bart's for three months. A friend who visited him there remembers it in these words: "It was a gigantic old ward with a high ceiling dwarfing the serried ranks of beds, patients and visitors. He was *intensely* amused and interested at being lost in a crowd and said 'I am convinced that every doctor ought to have been once in his life in a hospital bed as a patient.'"

Donald had always intended to become a general practitioner in a country area, but one day a friend lent him a book by Freud, and so he discovered psychoanalysis; deciding that this was for him, he realized that he must therefore stay in London to undergo analysis. During his medical training he had become deeply interested in children's work and after taking his Membership examination, set up as a Consultant in Children's Medicine (there was no speciality in paediatrics in those days).

In 1923 he obtained two hospital appointments, at The Queen's Hospital for Children and at Paddington Green Children's Hospital. The latter appointment he held for forty years. The development of his work at Paddington Green is a story in itself, and many colleagues from all over the world visited him there. Because of his own developing interests and skills over the years, his clinic gradually became a psychiatric clinic, and he used to refer to it as his "Psychiatric Snack Bar" or his clinic for dealing with parents' hypochondria. In 1923 he also acquired a room in the Harley Street area and set up a private consultant practice.

At the beginning he found Harley Street formidable because he had few patients, so in order to impress the very dignified porter who opened the door to patients for all the doctors in the house, he tells how he used to pay the fares of some of his hospital mothers and children so that they could visit him in Harley Street. Of course this procedure was not entirely on behalf of the porter, because he selected cases in which he was particularly interested and to which he wanted to give more time so that he could begin to explore the psychological aspects of illness.

The sheer pressure of the numbers attending his hospital clinics must have been important to him as an incentive to explore as fully as he did how to use the doctor–patient *space* as economically as possible for the therapeutic task. The ways in which he did this have been described in his writing.

However, there is one detail he does not describe, and which I observed both at his Paddington Green Clinic and in his work with evacuee children in Oxfordshire during the last war. He attempted to round off and make significant a child's visit to him by giving the child something to take away which could afterwards be used and/or destroyed or thrown away. He would quickly reach for a piece of paper and fold it into some shape, usually a dart or a fan, which he might play with for a moment and then give to the child as he said goodbye. I never saw this gesture refused by any child. It could be that this simple symbolic act contained the germ of ideas he developed in the "Use of an Object" paper written at the end of his life (D. W. Winnicott, 1971c). There could also be a link here with the transitional object concept.

In attempting to give some idea of D.W.W.'s capacity to play, which in my view was central to his life and work, I have somehow slipped into an historical or biographical sequence of writing without intending to do so. This is in no way meant to be a biography. What I have been trying to do is to illustrate how he related to people at different stages of his life and in different situations. But I must now abandon the historical perspective which so far protected me, and bring him briefly into focus for myself and in relation to our life together. From now on "he" becomes "we" and I cannot disentangle us.

Many years ago a visitor staying in our home looked round thoughtfully and said: "You and Donald *play*." I remember being surprised at this new light that had been thrown on us. We had certainly never *set out* to play, there was nothing self-conscious and deliberate about it. It seems just to have happened that we lived that way, but I could see what our visitor meant. We played with *things*—our possessions—rearranging, acquiring, and discarding according to our mood. We played with ideas, tossing them about at random with the freedom of knowing that we need not agree, and that we were strong enough not to be hurt by each other. In fact the question of hurting each other did not arise because we were operating in the play area where everything is permissible. We each possessed a capacity for enjoyment, and it could take over in the most unlikely places and lead us into exploits we could not have anticipated. After Donald's death an American friend described us as "two crazy people who delighted each other and delighted their friends". Donald would have been pleased with this accolade, so reminiscent of his words: "We are poor indeed if we are only sane" (D. W. Winnicott, 1945, p. 150 fn.).

Early in our relationship I had to settle for the idea that Donald was, and always would be, completely unpredictable in our private life, except for his punctuality at mealtimes and the fact that he never failed to meet me at the station when I had been away. This unpredictability had its advantages, in that we could never settle back and take each other for granted in day-to-day living. What we could take for granted was something more basic that I can only describe as our recognition and acceptance of each other's separateness. In fact the strength of our unity lay in this recognition, and implicit in it is an acceptance of the unconscious ruthless and destructive drives which were discussed as the final development of his theories in the "Use of an Object" paper. Our separateness left us each free to do our own thing, to think our own thoughts, and possess our own dreams, and in so doing to strengthen the capacity of each of us to experience the joys and sorrows which we shared.

There were some things that were especially important to us, like the Christmas card that Donald drew each year, and which we both painted in hundreds, staying up until 2 A.M. in the days before Christmas. I remember once suggesting to him that the drawing looked better left as it was in black and white. He said, "Yes, I know, but I like painting." There were his endless squiggle drawings which were part of his daily routine. He would play the game with himself and produced some very fearful and some very funny drawings, which often had a powerful integrity of their own. If I was away for a night, he would send a drawing through the post for me to receive in the morning, because my part in all this was to enjoy and appreciate his productions, which I certainly did, but sometimes I could wish that there were not quite so many of them.

Donald's knowledge and appreciation of music was a joy to both of us, but it was of particular importance to me because he introduced me to much that was new. He always had a special feeling for the music of Bach, but at the end of his life it was the late Beethoven string quartets that absorbed and fascinated him. It seems as if the refinement and abstraction in the musical idiom of these works helped him to gather in and realize in himself the rich harvest of a lifetime. On quite another level he also greatly enjoyed the Beatles and bought all their recordings. Donald never had enough time to develop his own piano playing, but he would often dash up to the piano and play for a moment between patients, and invariably he celebrated the end of a day's work by a musical outburst fortissimo.

He enjoyed the fact that I knew more about the poets than he did, and that I could say a Shakespeare sonnet or some Dylan Thomas or T. S. Eliot to him on demand. He particularly enjoyed Edward Lear's "The Owl and the Pussycat" and couldn't hear it often enough. In the end he memorized it himself.

Our favourite way of celebrating or of simply relaxing was to dress up and go out to a long, unhurried dinner in a candle-lit dining-room not so far from where we lived. In the early days sometimes we danced. I remember him looking around this room one evening and saying: "Aren't we lucky. We still have things to say to each other."

For years two T.V. programmes that we never missed were "Come Dancing" (a display of all kinds of ballroom dancing) and "Match of the Day", which was the re-showing of the best football or rugger match each Saturday, or in the summer it would be tennis.

I think that the only times when Donald actually showed that he was angry with me were on occasions when I damaged myself or became ill. He hated to have me as a patient, and not as his wife and playmate. He showed this one day when I damaged my foot and it became bruised and swollen. We had no crêpe bandage, so he said he would go and buy one, and I was to lie down until he returned. He was away for two hours and came back pleased with a gold expanding bracelet he had bought for me—but he had forgotten the bandage.

I was always speculating about Donald's own transitional object. He did not seem to remember one specifically, until suddenly he was able to get into touch with it. He described the experience to me in a letter written early in 1950:

> Last night I got something quite unexpected, through dreaming, out of what you said. Suddenly you joined up with the nearest thing I can get to my transition object: it was something I have always known about but I lost the memory of it, at this moment I became conscious of it. There was a very early doll called Lily belonging to my younger sister and I was fond of it, and very distressed when it fell and broke. After Lily I hated *all* dolls. But I always knew that before Lily was a quelquechose of my own. I knew retrospectively that it must have been a doll. But it had never occurred to me that it wasn't just like myself, a person, that is to say it was a kind of other me, and a not-me female, and part of me and yet not, and absolutely inseparable from me. I don't know what happened to it. If I love you as I loved this (must I say?) doll, I love you all out. And I believe I do. Of course I love you all sorts of other ways, but this thing came new at me. I felt enriched, and felt once more like going on writing my paper on transition objects (postponed to October). (You don't mind do you—this about you and the T.O.?).

It would not be right to give the impression that Donald and I shared only experiences that lay outside our work. It was our work that brought us together in the first place, and it remained central, and bound us inextricably together. Writing to me in December 1946, he said:

> In odd moments I have written quite a lot of the paper for the Psychoanalytical Society in February, and I spend a lot of time working it out. My work is really quite a lot associated with you. Your effect on me is to make me keen and productive and this is all the more awful—because when I am cut off from you I feel paralysed for all action and originality.

In fact, each of us was essential to the work of the other. During Donald's lifetime we worked in different spheres, and this was an added interest, extending the boundaries of our joint existence. We were fortunate that through the years a wide circle of people came to be intimately included in our lives and work, and we in theirs. This was a strong binding force for all concerned, because it provided the community of interest which is the pre-requisite for creative living. How lucky we were in those who shared our lives; how much we owe to them, and how much we enjoyed their company.

Throughout his life Donald never ceased to be in touch with his dream world and to continue his own analysis. It was the deep undercurrent of his life, the orchestral accompaniment to the main theme. His poem called "Sleep" is relevant here:

Let down your tap root
to the centre of your soul
Suck up the sap
from the infinite source
of your unconscious
And
Be evergreen.

To conclude, I want to relate a dream about Donald which I had two and a half years after his death.

I dreamt that we were in our favourite shop in London, where there is a circular staircase to all floors. We were running up and down these stairs grabbing things from here, there, and everywhere as Christmas presents for our friends. We were really having a spending spree, knowing that as usual we would end up keeping many of the things ourselves. I suddenly realized that Donald was alive after all, and I thought with relief, "Now I shan't have to worry about the Christmas card." Then we were sitting in the restaurant having our morning coffee as usual (in fact we always went out to morning coffee on Saturday). We were facing each other, elbows on the table, and I looked at him full in the face and said: "Donald there's something we have to say to each other, some truth that we have to say, what is it?" With his very blue eyes looking unflinchingly into mine, he said: "That this is a dream." I replied slowly: "Oh yes, of course, you died, you died a year ago." He reiterated my words: "Yes, I died a year ago."

For me it was through this dream of playing that life and death, his and mine, could be experienced as a reality.

CHAPTER FOURTEEN

D. W. Winnicott:
his life and work

(1982)

I thought I'd like to talk about the work that [Donald] and I did together in Oxfordshire during the war working with evacuees. But when I came down to it, I thought I wanted to say things first of all about things that influenced him and made him sort of the person he was in the end: things that influenced him, that changed him, made things different, and that showed the sort of person he was.

I thought I'd like to say first of all something about the main influences in his life. The thing that influenced him first of all, of course, is home, which was a very stable, loving home: religious, but not oppressively religious. They all went to the Methodist church down the road, the whole family. But it didn't matter if you didn't go, and there was no kind of pressure on religion like there could be in some homes.

Donald, as soon as he began to go to church, was always allowed the privilege of walking home from church with his father. This he valued very much indeed. He had his father to himself for this walk home even as a toddler upwards, and they discussed life in general.

His father was a very well-known person in the town and in the church. He was Lord Mayor of Plymouth twice, on two occasions. He

---

Lecture given at the Squiggle Foundation, London, 24 June 1982.

was instrumental in getting Lady Astor into the House of Commons. He turned to her when Waldorf had to go into the Lords and said, "Why don't you stand, and we'll get you in." They were a very conservative family. He was chairman of the Conservative Association.

They were a musical family. They were all musical. One particularly, the older sister [Violet], who now at the age of 92 still can play the piano, although she's part blind. She can't read any more. But she can still enjoy an hour at the piano. And she listens to music intensely. It's a great joy to listen with her, and I never miss it if I can help it.

So there's a background of stability. He never doubted he was loved, absolutely never. And later on—and Marion [Milner] will remember this—I used to tease him that he had delusions of benignity, that everybody loved him. But he certainly came right back from this beginning. He was the youngest, much the youngest, member in the family. He was six years younger than the sister next to him, and then there was another sister. There were three of them altogether—two sisters, with a gap of six years between the second sister, Kathleen, and Donald. So he was a very little boy, with these two girls in the family. The mother and the aunt living in the family, the father's sister who was a nurse, who had been a nurse, and there were three maids whom he loved to be with, and his mother used to complain most of the time that he spent more time out in the kitchen than he spent in the rest of the house. You can imagine why. He got all this stuff to eat out there.

He was an extremely lively little boy. Right from the beginning, he was on wheels. He was on a tricycle, on bicycles, which he rode in the house. He used to ride his bicycle around the house. Certain places were not to go. And then motorbikes galore. And then cars galore. One of my first meetings with him was driving with him in a frightful car, which he brought down to Oxfordshire with the roof open. He was sitting on the back of the seat, with a walking-stick on the accelerator and his feet on the steering wheel. Mind you, that was easier to do in Oxfordshire in those days because there was no other traffic. But there was very little traffic in the Oxfordshire lanes, and he would go on for miles like this . . . hair-raising . . . but this is the kind of person he was.

He was the only boy in the family, and all these women in the house. But he escaped, and had a lot of friends, school friends, and they again were on bicycles all the time. He remembers particularly a friend of his called Bruce, and he always said his psychiatric career began with Bruce, because Bruce was an extremely moody little boy. Donald could tell every morning when this child came what sort of mood Bruce was in and would avoid the pitfalls, managed the situation. That friendship broke up—was broken up, actually, by the father, who thought this wasn't a good idea. Bruce was too moody, and later actually committed suicide, much, much, much later.

There were two Winnicott families. There were two brothers Winnicott—Donald's father—and they ran a big business in the town, a hardware business serving all the ships in the Navy and goodness knows what. And the other Winnicott family lived opposite. There were three children in Donald's home, and in the other home there were three girl cousins and two boy cousins. So they were almost brought up as one family.

But what fascinates me, and has fascinated me ever since I've known the Winnicotts, is why are these two families are so different. They lived opposite. They were brought up together, but they are very, very different families. They're just very different. Donald's family was a caring family. They were involved in all kinds of work in the town. So were the other family, up to a point, but they much more grew up into the bridge-playing set who were concerned—I mean, there would be JPs amongst them . . .

But [Donald's] family had a caring feeling amongst it, and a welcome. They welcomed people into the home, and one gets that immediately. I mean, I felt immediately at home in that family.

My sister-in-law, who's 92—she's the only one left now—she still has children, young children, come and see her. All the Winnicotts can get on with children and communicate with children. Kathleen, the youngest sister, ran the Brownies for miles around all of her life, and they used to come to the house. She used to give parties for them. And Violet, this older sister, now has really little friends. I mean, a 9-year-old will ring up and say, "Can I come and play you my new piece of music?" So Julie comes on a Sunday afternoon and plays this music, and Violet will criticize it and say what she thinks about it and discuss—a very serious discussion about the music. So this is the sort of ambience. This is the feeling of the home, and obviously it was absolutely fundamental to the kind of person he turned out to be.

I think it's interesting that they can all get on with children. It fascinates me to watch Violet at 92 and blind talking to Julie and other children. I went and opened the door last summer. Three little kids on the steps said, "We've come to see the old lady." So I said, "You better come in then." And this is quite common, and people still visit this home. It's still a centre, and the welcome is, "Hello, my dear. How are you?" And she'd remember the details of who it is and what stage they're at, and whose grandchild had passed their levels, or son had got his A levels, and who was going to the university. She remembers it. Her mind is completely clear, and this was true for the father. The father, at the age of 93—he died at the age of 93—still doing very complicated income tax returns of his own, didn't have any employee able to do it. So that's the way it was. That's the sort of thing he came from.

I always liked the saying—the sister who is still alive said to me, "You know, there was never a question in our household, 'What can we do?' Nobody ever asked that question. There was always heaps to do and plenty of people to do it with. We were always interested children, and there was always something to do. We never had that feeling that you get from children today, 'What can I do?'" I think that says something, too. There was a lot of imagination. A lot of imaginative play went on in the home.

I think the mother was a lively person, and I think Donald and this older sister very much took after her. The middle sister, Kathleen, was a much quieter, reserved person, much more like father. But mother was very lively and outgoing. I think the thing that perhaps was difficult for Donald in that house [was] that they made a tremendous effort not to spoil him. Mother and sisters made a lot of effort not to spoil him, and perhaps he missed out on something there. I often wondered, and I think he didn't see nearly as much as he would have liked to see of his father. He had this walk home on Sundays, which he treasured very much, but father was out doing business, doing town matters on every possible committee there was in the town. So I think he missed out quite a bit of friendship. He would have liked more friendship with his father.

They were intimate with each other. I've got a whole collection of family letters written, a collection from their house, letters written to each other when they were away from each other—his school letters to his mother, to his sisters, their letters back to him. I've got a huge collection, and there's an extremely warm, teasing feeling about them. And of course they all have a sense of humour. There's a sense of humour in that family, absolutely, without any question. They've got a very wry, very amusing, calm sense of humour.

A very interesting example to me was the younger sister, Kathleen, who was really ill with heart failure. . . . The older one, Violet, said to her, "Now, Kathleen, now we can't have all the things we're used to." I mean they had to live at a much lower level of income than they had been used to. "Now we can't have everything we want. We've got to put up with it." And Kathleen very sweetly said, "But don't I put up with you?" That's the sort of sly touch they've all got, and Donald has certainly got it, and it was very, very important to his work.

Oh yes, there's a lovely story. At the age of nine, [Donald] looked in the mirror and thought, "I'm too nice. I'm too good. I'm too nice. What must I do about it?" So he started blotting all his copybooks, coming at the bottom of the class instead of the top. He really played up, really had a lovely time playing up, just to see how bad he could be. But he got released from that by being sent away to boarding school [Leys in Cambridge], where he settled in and simply loved it.

School days were tremendously important. Again, he was with a lot of boys, away from the influence of all these women. His school days were tremendously important to him. He joined in all the activities, and he used to read a story to his dormitory, the kids in his dormitory, every night before they all went to bed. Now that interests me a lot. Why did he read the story to them all? He always read a story to me when we were married. We were never without a book which he and I were reading together. I mean, if I read to him, he would go to sleep, but if he read to me, I stayed awake. He would enjoy this reading.

He was good at games. He broke the school's record in the mile race, and I've often said to him, "Don't you think that's where your coronary thrombosis started? Could it be right back there?"—because it really was a terrific effort to win the mile race. Then on the sports field he broke his collar-bone—this was a very important incident in his life—when he was about 15. He was in the school sanatorium, and the doctor was looking after him, and he suddenly thought to himself, "If I become ill or hurt myself in any way, I've got to rely on doctors. That's not on. I shall have to be one." I think from then on he really began to build on the idea of becoming a doctor.

The trouble was, of course, that father wanted him to go into the business and promote his side of a very flourishing business. I've got a very amusing letter written by Donald to his father, and father gave in and let him do what he wanted to do. But that was an important moment.

When he went to tell the headmaster that he was going to be a doctor—he often told me this story—the headmaster looked at him and said, "Boy, not brilliant, but will do." So he came out wondering what the headmaster will think now. "Will he change his mind? I don't know." Anyway, Donald always took that very seriously, thought he wasn't brilliant.

Also, when Donald was in the sixth form, he was again brought in touch with children. He and another boy ran a Scout troop of the children in the town in Cambridge, and there were very, very many amusing letters of stories about the Scouts. But I think he was really very attracted to the Scout mistress, it sounded to me, the Cub mistress. Cubs, it was. He was running a Cubs group. But he did that toward the end of his school career, and took them camping, and they did all kinds of hair-raising things in camp, eating the most extraordinary things together, marmalade and baked beans and everything mixed up. But this was an important experience for him. He enjoyed it a lot, and it brought him in touch with children.

There's a lovely letter describing a show that the Cub troop gave at a garden party. It sounds absolutely hilarious. It's written by Donald to his parents, and it's very, very funny.

Well, then he decided to become a medical student, and of course the war broke out. He was in his first year as a medical student when the First World War broke out. So he worked in the Cambridge hospitals which were given over to the military.

And Donald told me how he met a great friend of his who remained a friend for life. Donald describes walking down the ward one day. There was a great, long man sticking out over the bed with these legs out. He was much too tall for the bed, this man with his legs stuck out. He went up to him and said, "Isn't it uncomfortable?" or something. Well, these two became tremendous friends. This man was a Quaker ambulance driver and had been wounded. He was an architect, and they were lifelong friends.

He wrote to me after Donald died and said, "I always remember him as a medical student in the ward sitting down at the piano and singing to us to cheer us all up on Saturday evenings", and this would be very like him. He didn't mind making a fool of himself. He absolutely couldn't care less if they thought he was mad. He didn't mind. Lots of people did think he was mad. As he said, "I remember him singing 'Apple Dumplings', and he cheered us all up."

Another important thing for Donald was the fact that his fellow students who were not in medicine went straight into the war, and so many of them were killed straightaway. He had a great list of intimate friends who were killed, various students, and I think that really affected him profoundly. And he actually has written somewhere, "I always felt I had to live for them all because I survived and they didn't." This is why I'm sure he crammed his life with experiences of all kinds. He mentioned it many, many times: "I thought I had to live for all those who didn't live."

He couldn't stand being back in Cambridge, not in danger as they were. So he got himself into the Navy and was drafted to a ship as a surgeon probationer. After one year [on board, he wrote home that] "I'm the oldest man aboard, on ship, but I'm only here so that all the others can write home and say there's a doctor on board." He was probably right.

Fortunately, there was a very, very experienced medical orderly who told him what to do, lucky for him, but he had an important death on the ship. There was enemy action, and one man died when Donald could have saved him, but he was frightened to give him more morphia. The man kept saying, "Morphia, more morphia", and Donald thought he'd given him too much, and the man died of shock. That profoundly affected him and his belief in morphia, too, and the effect of shock. That made a mark on him.

Another thing that was tremendously important to him during his medical training was that he was extremely ill with an undiagnosed something for three months, and in bed for three months in one of the large wards in Barts [St. Bartholomew's Hospital]. He was immensely interested in all that went on in the ward. He took everything in, learned a great deal. And he always said, "Every doctor ought to have to be a patient in a ward. It really should be part of the training." He had actually an abscess on the lung which nobody seemed to have diagnosed, and he coughed it up one day and that was it. But he was in bed for three months, so he saw a great deal. The thing that cheered him up most was that the Sister gave him her special crockery to have his tea on, and he'd never forgotten that.

Now an important influence in his life was being a junior house physician to Sir John Horder, who was a very great physician. He became Lord Horder and a Queen's physician and all that stuff. But it was Lord Horder who said to him, "Now look. When you talk to a patient, listen to them. Don't go in thinking you know all. Listen to what the patient says. Take careful notes of everything they say. Don't spoil it. Don't go in knowing everything. Learn to listen. Learn to observe changes of mood, attitude, tone of voice, everything."

And he really started off, and that was tremendously important to him. Donald was an exceptionally observant person anyway, but it made use of his powers of observation. Lord Horder really helped him to see the immense value of careful history-taking, and he was a history-taker of all time, actually. He left notes about almost everything. A lot of them were very difficult to decipher because he'd written up here and then down here and then in the middle and then somewhere else about what. . . . He wrote as he thought, but then, of course, would dictate from these notes, and a lot of notes still exist.

And to my amazement, when I laid the foundation stone for the Winnicott Centre three years ago, the professor of paediatrics said to me, "We're still using his notes to teach medical students." So I said, "But surely medicine's progressed since them. You've learned more." He said, "We can really follow the onset and course of an illness through his notes, and we are using them. All right, we treat it differently. The treatment's different, but we're still using his notes." Well, I thought that was astonishing. I don't know what it says for the medical profession at all. But it said something for his careful note–taking, I think.

After he qualified, but actually during his medical training, he did make very, very full use of all the facilities of London, and he joined in everything that went on. He was editor of the Bart's Hospital journal. He wrote for it. He was editor of it, wrote some very amusing articles. He also made use of going to operas. He used to rush out at the last minute in his slippers and stand in the gardens and get a policeman to get him a lift back to Barts. The policeman was very willing to help a medical student get back home, he told me, in those days.

His first jobs were two clinics at Queen Elizabeth Hospital for Children, and that's where the new Winnicott Centre now exists which is a new medical outpatient department. Then he also took a job at the same time at Paddington Green, and he also ran what was then the LCC Rheumatism Clinic for Children. Now he simply soaked himself in clinical medicine with children and made very, very, very great use of it. He did things like . . . In the rheumatism clinic particularly, it was the fashion when a child had rheumatic heart disease, or whatever they called it, the child goes to bed for so long. Well, he began to think, "No. This isn't the answer." And he took risks, medical risks, in not sending kids to bed, which other doctors would attempt today. He stuck his neck out on that.

It began to dawn on him that there were psychological reasons. There weren't always physical reasons for illness in children. Then he wanted to study this more carefully, so he would pay the mothers of some of his children to bring them up to Harley Street in the afternoons, where he could give more time to them. When I told them this at the Queen Elizabeth, they thought it was the funniest thing they'd heard in years. They said, "Well, that would solve a lot of problems in the health service, anybody who did that." But he did do this, and when he felt he didn't know the answer—it wasn't purely physical—he wanted to find out more. He would spend time with children, and he had quite a few coming up and visiting him, which helped him a great deal.

He also started his own analysis. There are two stories about this. He told me that he was with a friend in a taxi and said, "You know, I never dream. I wonder why I never dream." And this friend said, "You want an analysis." So Donald got a book about Freud from a bookshop, and said yes, he did want analysis. It linked up with what he was finding in his children. So he started his own analysis with James Strachey, and it was through Strachey saying to him one day during an analytical session, "Look, there's somebody coming over from . . . Mrs Klein has come over here. She's somebody who's done a lot of work with children and thought a lot about it. You must go and see her. You're working with children."

So he took three of his case histories that he'd written on the children he was working with on Harley Street to Mrs Klein, and she said, "Yes, I'll supervise you on these cases." And she did give him supervision for quite a long time. And he always felt he owed a great deal to Klein's ideas, particularly about the unconscious forces in children . . . the unconscious phantasy of children. He felt her book, her first book, the narrative book. . . . That, I remember, he read straight through it. It was on holiday, and started again at the beginning and read it straight through again. And this really caught his imagination, and he used it, of course, and developed it differently from Mrs Klein, or used it differently, but he certainly always acknowledged and felt he owed a great deal to her for that, and to her for the supervision of his own thesis.

So where do we get to? When he decided to go into psychoanalysis . . . he came into psychoanalysis from a different place than the place that most people come into it from. He came into it with a sort of a long experience of working with ordinary families who've got an ill child, where there's a parent or somebody responsible who brings the child—and this was true in his hospital cases and in his private practice—ordinary families where there's some problem or some illness. I really mean he didn't come into it from pathology.

He came into it from health, building up health, diagnosing and building up health in children, rather than a lot of people who had to come into it from another angle, from adult psychiatry and pathology. So I think this is one of the important things he really did bring to psychoanalysis. And I think this explains quite a lot about his belief in the drive—the biological drive, he would say—for wholeness and health that exists in people if you can only cotton onto it, and only find it and work with it, although he was quite aware that it threw out many symptoms and difficulties en route. You could have many problems en route. But I think this was his basic approach to his work as a psychoanalyst.

And I think his papers in which he formulates this—particularly his one on classification, where he formulates psychosis in terms of failure—[give] vital points in infant care. I think that was a very important paper. It was not liked when it was first read, but I think it will be seen to have a lot of importance. And he couldn't have gotten that, I think, without his experience as a paediatrician. He couldn't have got to that point, followed up when he became a psychoanalyst by working with psychotic patients who threw light on early infantile experiences. So this was his main learning ground.

Now in his clinic work, he often said he avoided taking—if he could possibly avoid it—delinquent children, because he knew he hadn't the skill, the knowledge, and the hospital certainly had not the facilities for dealing with delinquent children. He was working with building up his experience and his knowledge and formulating his knowledge on working with the non-delinquent group, the group that did not have other kinds of problems. And this was quite a deliberate thing.

Of course, he worked in both his hospital clinics. He'd first of all seen measles, and then it would be stealing, or it would be some other problem, bedwetting, or something else. Things got very mixed up in his clinic, but gradually the other doctors in the hospital began to know that he was good with these kinds of problem children, and of course his caseload got built up and ceased to be an ordinary paediatric caseload. But he never lost touch with paediatrics all through his life. He was a founding member of the British Paediatric Association; they awarded him a gold James Spence Medal for paediatrics, and he thought it was important to him to be in touch with medicine and with paediatrics. That went on right to the end.

But, of course, when the war came, he couldn't avoid the problems thrown out by the vast disintegration of family life, the separation that went on, the children sent away. He had to face up to the more difficult problems, and he knew when he took on the consultancy job for the government evacuation scheme, he knew that he was in for something quite different, a quite new experience for him. So he became consultant psychiatrist to the Oxfordshire reception area, where children were sent from London, and he became consultant, really, to the five hostels that were set up to take the children who couldn't be placed in ordinary homes, ordinary families, because they were too difficult. Nobody could manage them.

He'd been in this job for a little while—about a year, I think. I was working then. I had just finished the mental health course, and I was working in Reading with the Minister of Health, and somehow I was told by my boss, "There's a very difficult doctor coming down every week to Oxfordshire hostels. He's very devoted. He doesn't like social workers, and he's making a muddle of things. You ought to go and sort things out." This is what he told me, and we very much liked this introduction we had to each other.

So I just turned up, you know—routine—you do your job. He was at one of the reception centres, and I listened for a while one afternoon and saw things. He was very suspicious of me, and he said, "I shan't want a lot of case histories from you"—you know, social workers who take case histories—and I thought, "Marvellous." He said, "I shall want observation. Can children play? Who do they play with? Can they be creative? Can they play on their own? Can they group? I want observations of what they're like. I don't want a lot of history", looking at me very suspiciously, as if to say, "You know. It's up to you. Can you do it?"

Well, it's interesting to me that before I came into this scheme— before I'd done the mental health course, actually—I had been in what was then a distressed area in Merthyr Tydfil [in Wales] running playgroups for children. I'd run them for a year. I'd actually written a paper on play which I gave to a sort of conference somewhere or other, so I was interested anyway. So I thought, "Well, this suits me fine. This is going to be interesting." But luckily for me I didn't say anything for a very long time. I watched and went round.

He came down once a week, and I would go around to whichever hospital he was at and listen and see what went on, and I gradually could see where I could contribute, because people would say to me afterwards, "You know, he never tells us what to do, and how he leaves us with these terrible children. We never know what to do. He never tells us what to do." Of course, you can imagine he'd never attempt to tell them what to do.

So I thought, "How do we get round this one?" I said, "Well, look, don't you think, he's always in London? He can't tell us what to do down here. He can't be at the moment at which we've got to do something about something. So isn't it best if we do the best we can in the given circumstances, and then we think about it and we tell him about it when he comes next time and see what he says about it? Shall we try it that way round?"

He always says I gave him a place in the scheme, and I think it did help a lot, but we did it that way round. You see, staff were always looking . . . "The doctor must tell us what to do. He's the doctor. He's got to tell us what to do." But of course it couldn't be done that way in this kind of job. So I saw my role, really, as trying to help people to see that it couldn't be done that way, and that we've got to find a way of using him as best we could. Well, you can imagine that these sessions when he came down every Friday and went round to the hostels. We had 90 kids altogether in the whole of them, and these sessions became tremendously important learning experiences for everybody, including him—certainly me and the staff.

Of course, his handling of the staff was the thing that interested me always. The staff would say, "we had this happen this week", and they usually were hair-raising things: you know what kids can get up to. Somebody tried to drown somebody, things like this. And he would discuss it with them, and, you see, he altered the whole thing as to avoid "What should we do about this?" to "Why did so-and-so do this? Let's think why this happened." It just changes the question, and really most of his influence was through asking questions, his way of listening. He was a frightfully good listener, really a very, very good listener. He would not interrupt people. He would listen to the end.

This, of course, goes back to Lord Horder: listen to your patient; listen to people. So he listened to the staff who were in trouble and would ask questions which would illuminate it in some way. I really think I never saw him upset, violate their vulnerability, because they were frightfully vulnerable as staff. They were really exposed to the despair and desperation of these kids all the time, 24 hours. It was a terribly demanding job.

So gradually things began to be talked about in this way. When I first went, he was seeing one child. The staff would say, "We're worried about so-and-so. See him." Well, that took him a lot of time, and often there wasn't time to feed it back, and it wasn't dealing with the staff, either. So in a sense I suppose we did stop him seeing an individual child, although he would do it if we could make time, if we certainly thought it was necessary. But it was really working with the staff and helping the staff to get an attitude so that they themselves could work with a child in a constructive way. And, again, ask the question: "Why is so-and-so doing this?"

I remember, one day they were absolutely fed up with so-and-so . . . reeling off all the bad things this kid had done all week, all the time he'd been there. And Donald said, "Well, look. Let's think its round his way. What's he getting out of being here?" Well, you know, it gradually emerged, not very much, and I think people saw it for themselves. It just sort of emerged that this child was really getting rather a poor deal. He had become the scapegoat, and what we learned about scapegoats.

I was the one who had to deal with the scapegoats, because Donald was in London all the time. I was down on the spot. This whole change-round was a tremendously important one to asking why things happened and not just what we did about it. We would discuss what they did and what doubts they got about it. "What makes you worry about it? What are you worried about, what you did?" That kind of way of talking that didn't upset people.

I remember one funny incident, which I must tell you. When I first went, Donald was giving the most smash-up tea with the staff, not with the kids. I was invited into this tea, and this went on . . . I let this go on a bit. Then I said to him, driving him back to the station in my car, "I suppose you know you've eaten the kids' bacon ration for the week"—or butter ration, or whatever. And he said, "Do you really mean this?" And he hadn't thought of it. Of course, this meant we changed the system. We all had tea together with the kids. That was just an amusing bit. Again, it's the way staff treat the doctor. You always give the best tea you can possibly get to the doctor, whatever happens.

What he and I used to do when we left the hostel, when moving on to the next one, was to try and sum up what we . . . by the way, when he was there talking about the child, he was taking notes all the time. I've got all the notes, lots and lots and lots of notes. He was taking notes and thinking about it as he went along. Then he and I would discuss it, would try and formulate something.

This was a very exciting project to have been in on with him, trying to formulate what was going on, and I think his whole approach to human growth and development was affected by the experience of these deprived children. I think it really made him see things differently. It brought him in touch with this whole question of the "inner" and his paper on the antisocial tendency and the positive factors in the antisocial tendency, and his other paper on delinquency as a sign of hope. But I think right from here he was beginning to see things differently, seeing delinquency in quite a new way by listening to the staff and taking part in the whole discussion. And then we would have a very exciting discussion of it on the way to the next place or back to the station or wherever.

These staff sessions really did affect what happened to children, and the staff had courage to do things that they would have thought rather silly otherwise. For instance, I remember being told by some-body—and she felt really guilty about this—"You know, so-and-so, age ten, really likes to play in the bath. So I bathe him last, so that he can play in the bath. Is it alright? He wants me to swing him up and down and do all the things you do with a two-year-old or whatever." So he, or whoever, or I would say, "It's okay if you can do it. It's fine."

And the 14-year-old child who went to Woolworth's and bought herself a doll's feeding bottle and had to have it to go to sleep with filled with milk. They felt very guilty about this. The staff were worried about it. But talking about it, he would say, "Well, look, if you can let this happen, and if she can do it at the cost of ridicule from all the others, it means a lot to her. Do we have to disturb it?"—just that way of approaching things, that way of talking about things.

I think no miracles happened. We didn't produce miracles, but we did do something, and I have had a lot of pick-up on hostel kids, particularly that one that I told you about who took the bottle to bed every night who became an air hostess learning five languages or something. I picked that up from quite another source. We did hear things back. We did get feedback, but I got more than he did. It's always happening to me, actually. I meet someone whom I met before, and they tell me something about somebody we knew very well. "Do I remember so-and-so?" . . . Will I ever forget them?

I think what we did—we didn't produce miracles, but we did help staff to work without fear to face situations, even pretty drastic ones like setting fire to something, without too much fear and with compas-sion. I think that came into it. "Why is this happening?" "How do I rescue so-and-so?"

And one thing I learned, which is quite beside the point, but mostly I had to do the appointing of staff with the committee because Donald couldn't afford the time to come down and do it. But I learned very quickly that if a man—we always had married couples in charge—if a man looked tall and big and fit, it was a great advantage—it really was, because the kids felt they could be controlled. If somebody was need-ing to control them, somebody could do it. So on the whole I picked the tall one and the big one. I'm only joking about this really, but it was a factor.

We had all kinds of disasters, like the wrong staff being appointed, and everybody running away one night, everybody, everybody. And I was the whole of the night driving around Oxfordshire in my car with no lights, no sign-posts, map reading with a torch, the police telling me where these kids were. The police were picking them up. Some hair-raising things went on, but we survived them. And I think this is one of the things that Donald did help us all to do, to survive things, and that something good could come out of even the most awful crisis if you could survive it and carry on, not give up.

I think as it turned out—thinking of him and me together—I kept the work together, in a way. I was in touch with all the people who were concerned—and lots of people were concerned in the job, the committee, my immediate boss at both County Hall, who was, luckily for me, the Deputy Clerk of the Council. We call them managers now, but I was very lucky not to be in the health department or the education department, because I'd have been stopped doing a lot of things. But I was reporting directly to the Clerk, which was a great help, and he backed me up in things. I often needed a lot of backing up.

You know, somebody rings me up in the morning and says, "So-and-so is on the roof", and this was a very big hostel, a tall building: "So-and-so's on the roof. He's been there for the last hour. Do we get the fire brigade, or what?" So a decision's got to be made. I said, "Well, I'm all for not getting the fire brigade. He'll come down by lunch-time." But I have to check this out. I ring up my Clerk and say, "What about it? I'm taking this risk. Are you going to back me up?" He might say, "What would Winnicott say?" So I said, "I can't get him on the phone anyway, so it's no good. We've got to decide this." Things like that happened, but in a way I think I kept the string.

I kept in touch with schools, and that was a nightmare: village schools landed with a group of frightfully difficult kids on top of their own group, and it was chaos. Always permanent sorting out of the school problem, inviting the teachers to tea, inviting them to join the group, to join our discussions, if they could. And I'm sure you know this kind of setup, but there were many, many people to be placated and kept in touch with if the work was to be allowed to go on. And I did the placing of the children. I took the children to the hostels, and when they moved from the hostel or went somewhere else, I took them away. I was in charge of placing. The decision to discharge was always Donald's and mine and the staff's, but I actually did it.

I think his main part: I kept it together, I said, but he made it work—absolutely made it work. He once said to me, "You know, you could do this job perfectly well without me. There's no need for me to come down here like this", and I said, "Absolutely impossible. Wouldn't work at all. You make it work because everybody believes in you, and they believe in you because they believe in your integrity. That's number one importance. They believe you've got some knowledge, too, but integrity is more important."

I think that's how it did work out. And the staff would really—they believed in him, and this was the means by which they took on his attitudes. We would see these attitudes coming through in other people: attitudes towards children, towards everybody, towards each other. His attitudes became assimilated. They can only be assimilated. Attitudes can only be assimilated. They can't be taught. They can only be caught by experience of them from somebody. I think that was his main contribution. Of course mine was making it possible for him to do it. That's all.

Q: May I take off on this? I often wondered why Donald did just excellent work with children and their mothers. He always seemed to me such an excellent mother, such maternal qualities, and that didn't quite chime in with what you told us about his own mother. I was perfectly at home when you spoke about his relationship to his father, but then I remembered that at the end of one of his papers . . . he wrote, "And about my own mother. I had one."

CW: What's the point you're getting at? Well, "I had a mother", yes. But he would always say to me, "I had a lovely mother. I had a lovely mother." My personal feeling is that she tried very hard to stop everybody spoiling him. And father would spoil him, too. I think he didn't have the intimacy with her that he'd . . . I think she tried not to. I suppose she was so fond of him, she was frightened. That's my feeling.

Q: My question is really how is it when we look at it analytically that a man could become such an empathetic person as a mother unless he had something that he wanted to make up for which perhaps he hadn't had.

CW: It's very hard to know. I don't know what he missed from his mother. He had a nanny, of course, of whom he was quite fond, and I once tried to get his sister to tell me about his transitional object. And she said, "Well, he didn't need anything, because his nanny was with him 'til he went to sleep." Actually, he did have a transitional object. He dreamt about it once. That's a whole other story. But do you feel he's making up for something his mother didn't give him? . . . I know what you mean. I can see what you mean, but he would always say to me when he was talking about his mother, "You know, I had a lovely mother."

Q: And yet his mother didn't like it so much that he spent most of the time with the maids in the kitchen.

CW: Yes. Well, I think he knew where the food was. Yes. He was very spoiled by them all. He was very spoiled by these people. I have a feeling that it was her job to stop Auntie. . . . There was an aunt who adored him in the house. I have a feeling she [mother] tried to not let him get too spoiled. She mustn't be too intimate with him. She wouldn't discuss the question with him, for instance, about whether she'd breastfed him or not, but we know she did. He knew from other people that she did. I see what you mean. She died, of course, unfortunately much too young. She was 47 or something when she died of her heart. He was a medical student and always blamed himself . . . if only he'd been there, she wouldn't have walked down the garden that night. But I think the mother was very much the centre of the whole family. I'm sure. She was the lively one in the family.

Q: Did he regret not . . .

CW: Do we have to say that he's making up for something? I don't know.

Q: I only met him on a couple of occasions. . . . But it was the reality of him. He was so real. He was there, and there was no nonsense. And I, at that age, sensed it straightaway. I always felt that it must be with children. They really felt that here's somebody who takes us seriously, is real.

CW: And he would often—I agree with that very much, and he would often say to me, "You know, I'm a deeply happy person, deeply happy." Many, many times. Not once or twice. He'd often say if something went wrong or something was difficult, "But you know fundamentally I'm a deeply happy person." And that comes out in him.

     I mean his sense of fun. His sense of humour was tremendously important in the hostel job. I meant to bring out stories on that, terrifically important because he'd got a light touch with children and staff and everybody which was serious, and I often do think to myself how true it is, the saving grace of humour, what a lot of things humour can save. It can be real. You can deal with a real issue in a humorous way which people can take, and that doesn't mean making fun of them. There's a very narrow line—not making fun of them, just being a light touch that makes the thing change. They can take it rather than fight it.

Q: I'd like to come in on that, because there was an occasion which always stays in my mind when I was at Paddington Green. [There] was a rather formidable visitor who came. I think she was Swedish, and she sat, and he could work with people sitting in on him—on his cases, as you know. And she kind of emanated a sort of disapproval really, but one could see she was gradually getting hooked. Then we had an interval, and the secretary brought in the usual sort of rather scruffy cups of teas. They were simply cups. Some of them were all chipped and so on, and Donald said—these were handed around—and Donald turned to her and said, "We have invisible saucers here."

CW: We have invisible saucers here?

Q: Yes, of course, only she was so prim and proper to drink tea out of just a cup with no saucer. Quick as a flash, he said that.

Q: Could I just continue with some of that humour, because humour to me is really timing.

CW: Yes, absolutely. Meeting the moment.

Q: Yes, and this being just in his face, and I think you can see humour in the eyes, around the nose and around here, and you could look at him and his face was all alive. Wherever he was, it seemed to me, he was there. I think that's what he meant by being happy. Where life was, he was there, and he was always with it. That's a quote that Donald would say. He was with it, and he always just was able to hook in, it seemed to me, mesh into other people's way of looking at things. His timing, which was his humour, was brilliant, and he was always with the person. And he was so in himself that he could talk to people the way he was so empathetic about it. He was always with it.

CW: Yes. I know what you mean. I had a very nice incident not long before he died. He was seeing a child from a local authority who was in care, a small child, and the mother was there. I was just coming downstairs, and I saw that he was going to open the door. The doorbell rang. So I kept back and waited so I wasn't seen. But I saw him go to the door, and on the door were child, social worker, staff of the home where the child was, and parent—I think only mother— looking terrified, you know, a sotted mass on the doorstep. He got the child's name in his mind. He knew the child's name: Marion, or something. Marion—I'm thinking of you. He said, "Hello, so-and-so. How nice of you to come and see me in your red shoes."

"And my red gloves!" she said. And everybody relaxed. Everybody relaxed.

Q: He knew where to go. He knew just where to go.

CW: He just knew where to go, and he went for the child, you see, too, and this relaxed everybody else.

Q: It's interesting to look for the source of this empathy, which is obviously very unusual, and from my reading he seems to me profoundly feminine in instinct. It's unusual for men, even psychoanalytical men, to understand so profoundly what it's like to be a mother. It must have been something in his experience which gave him the key to that door. Do you know what it was?

CW: Could it be something to do with the fact that he saw 60,000 mothers and children in his career in clinics?

Q: I'm sure it has a tremendous amount to do with it, but I think there's an ulterior question to that, which was what it was that impelled him to be so fascinated in that relationship and to be so good at it.

CW: But you see, it does interest me a lot that the whole family is good with children.

Q: Somebody said that when he was with a child, he was also a child.

CW: Yes, that's true. I think that's true, in a sense, but he was always in control. I do think that his observing of mothers and children. . . . I mean, I think his power of observations was very, very highly trained. I think Lord Horder really put him onto this, but he'd got it in him to do it. I think his observation was very acute and very aware of things that were happening, and I think he would be adding it up, the relationship of this child to this mother. I think his paper on the spatula just shows the. . . . There's another paper where a child learned to play sitting on his knees. A child who wouldn't separate from mother, he dragged away from mother, and it yelled its head off to go back to her. He did it again and again and again, until this child really could accept the situation. But I think he had a very strong empathy. It was the childlike thing in himself that he was permanently in touch with.

Q: Your story about his early background—as a very small child born into that family—I get the impression from listening to you that he knew that he was wanted, right from the very beginning.

CW: Oh, absolutely.

Q: And isn't this a significant factor about his empathy? He really knew that he meant it, and his mother not spoiling him, there was a reality about this. It wasn't pretend.

CW: And that carried on right until he was a medical student and everything. Father would say, "How's your bank balance?" and would cough up a little, and mother stopped it. She really stopped the father doling out money. He's got to go on his own. He's got to learn to get on his own feet.

Q: What was it, do you think, in him that made people want to indulge him so and spoil him?

CW: Well, look. His younger sister, of whom he was most fond of all, Kathleen: I remember her once saying, "I remember him as a dear little boy with warm hands." You know, I'm sure he was. He was immensely lively as a child, immensely lively, and eager, eager.
      He did a lot of nasty things. He went through a nasty phase at school. He went through a nasty phase of torturing flies, doing all these things that kids do do, and he could talk about that for quite a long time, how he deliberately did it. I just think he had a very acute observation somehow, and that came into it somewhere. He would see changes going on, and it just fascinated him.
      And also, you see, just as he was coming into psychoanalysis, it was the area of psychoanalysis that was just beginning to open up after the Freud era, was just beginning to think back into what went on before. It was exactly the phase for him to come into psychoanalysis because he could do it.

Q: Can I just raise a question of the length of his analysis and the length of his analyses? He had a lengthy analysis himself.

CW: Yes. He was with Strachey for a long time. Then, when he had been to Mrs Klein for supervision, he thought he wanted a Kleinian analysis, so he went to Mrs Riviere, for six years, I think, Mrs Riviere. And I think he was about ten years with Strachey.

Q: It was this sort of real lengthy experience of self-exploration with such people that I think prepared him to take on people over a very long time himself. I remember when I was a doctor and psychiatrist, he talked to me—I asked him just, "What's all this about?" Is there any point in it. I felt I could afford to ask a naive question; I really knew nothing. And he said, "Well, there was this girl I saw for 13 years, and she seemed to get a bit better, and then she killed herself." That was really an important thing to tell me about, because he had helped her, he felt. But there were the therapeutic consultations at Paddington Green which really he wanted some research work to demonstrate he had done something worthwhile. He couldn't bear it, because it would mean they'd come back to him.

CW: How do you mean? I haven't got quite . . .

Q: There was always this fantasy that if he had someone really follow up the cases he'd seen, people would say, "Ah, it's just funny you're coming to see me about that", because they're really long follow-ups. They would say, "Ah, yes, I'd like to come back and see you again." It would open up situations again.

CW: But he did follow up his cases, you know.

Q: I know that there were a lot of follow-ups, and on those cases he was very clear that there was a demonstrable result very economically achieved. But what I'm interested in is how far. There's an importance that we have to conduct very long analyses and have very long analyses ourselves. Did he ever discuss the length of analysis, the length of analyses, from a learning and teaching point of view?

CW: I can't answer the whole of that question, but the bit that distracts me—his therapeutic consultations. I mean, to me it's very sad that there aren't more published. I hoped that he and I would together collect them. I wanted the delinquent cases collected where he'd seen somebody once, twice, or three times and completely reversed a delinquent tendency. But we never got round to it.

    I think he felt that the therapeutic consultation, the one like in the book he published, had a future for it, rather than five times a week for a small child, breaking up the family. I think he felt he would have liked to have gone on and conceptualized more about that. It was the last book he did, you know. And I said to him, "When you write the introduction to that book, don't send it before I've seen it."

I was very keen that he would try and spell out as clearly as he could what the value of the therapeutic consultation was and where he thought it would go. And I said to him, actually the night he died, it was that evening, "What about that? Have you sent if off?" And he said, yes. So I said, "You promised me I could see it", and he said, "I couldn't wait. I had to send it. I couldn't wait for you to see it."

But I would have loved it. I mean, I was very relieved when I saw it. It does spell it out quite well, I think, the introduction to therapeutic consultations (Winnicott, 1971b). I think he did feel that that if you could do the thing—the therapeutic consultation, over two, three, or four times, and follow up—this was a more satisfactory thing from a child's point of view unless there was real "it's got to be a five-times-a-week" business. But I think he really believed in this method, and we would have developed it much more.

The other point you said: long analyses. I don't know that I know his view about that. I think he did one or two very long [analyses]. He did one very, very long one which he called his research case, which he learned a great deal from. You can always know, this case is quoted in all kinds of situations. He used that work a great deal. It was a very regressive patient, and he carried her through to something, an independence. I mean, she left London and went away and became an archivist somewhere else in her old age almost. But I think I can't comment any more about that. I don't know what he would think about it.

Q: He would often use the mother as the child's psychotherapist.

CW: If he could.

Q: If he could, yes. And that, too, was very economical compared to, say, five times a week.

CW: Yes, and I know the people who daren't come and see him. I remember somebody ringing him up and saying, "We're Roman Catholics. My husband won't let me bring my child to see you. But he's stealing frightfully badly at school. He's eleven. What can I do about it?" Well, this was someone we vaguely knew, not very well, but we did know. And he said, "Well, come and have lunch with us."

So he had lunch with her—I wasn't there. And discussed with her—she'd got about six children—"Do you ever give this kid ten minutes to himself with you? A quarter of an hour . . . any time at all?"

And there's a letter. She wrote back a letter quite a long time afterwards that she'd done this. She made an effort to go and talk to the child, and, you know, it cleared up the stealing, and she said, "Poor little kid." It's a very, very good letter she wrote back, she'd done it herself. I mean, without him seeing the child.

But I don't want to make out he's a magician. He just used what was there to hand, and if it worked, it worked, and if it didn't, it didn't. I mean, lots of things didn't work. Sometimes it didn't work.

But also I know he had got this very strong maternal identification, but I think he can be a very strong person. He could be very strong indeed. He could confront people, patients, children, very, very strongly if he thought it was needed. In fact, I think one of the last cases he ever saw, I should think very near the end, a young gentleman crook, very much a young gentleman with a very well-known father. He was sent by the father. With a highly organized business of stealing cars and other things, a warehouse to keep them in and means of disposal, doing very well. And this was definitely in opposition to the father. It just couldn't have been more difficult for the father to have this kind of a son. So Donald listened to this story—he'd got a girlfriend—he listened to this story, and at the end he said, "You make me feel very sad. I don't know when I've listened to a sadder story. You're going to watch life behind prison bars." That's all he said, didn't say anything else.

A fortnight later, breakfast time, I rushed down to the front door, and I didn't know who it was. There was this boy come to see him. So Donald said, "Oh, well, yes, I know who it is," as I described him. So we weren't properly up, but he went down to see the boy, and this boy says, "I've come to ask you. I want analysis." Well, I can't think of anyone else in the world who would have done what Donald did on this occasion. He said, "Well, you don't get it from me, and I'm not referring you to anyone else, because you're going to spend the next six years carrying on and blaming your analyst. You face this yourself, or it's an alternative life for you, and I'm very sorry for your girl-friend. You're going to let her down"—or something like that.

Well, I mean, this boy did change. He took the decision and changed. Now that was a confrontation plus plus. There's plenty of money in this home. Most people would have sent him for a long, long analysis. Donald said, "You make the decision. At some point you may want analysis, but that's not the first thing. The first thing is, you're deciding which way you're going to live." And he did get a job, quite an ordinary job, lived in the country and married the girl in the end.

Donald didn't know the final story, unfortunately. I mean, he knew the boy had given up. But I heard later—I had a letter later, addressed to him: they didn't know he was dead—that he was now living in the country and travelling out to London, doing a certain sort of job. I've forgotten what. Now that's confrontation. He could be very strong when it was necessary, when he thought it was the only thing to do.

Moderator: I'd just like to say one thing as one of the original trustees of Squiggle. The Squiggle Foundation grew out of the work in the young family care centres and the nurseries which is a kind of a front-line work very much like your experience during the war. It seems to me that so much of Winnicott's work was in this situation where you were working in social work and so on, and that the Squiggle Foundation has grown from that kind of origins as well. . . . We would hope that you would be supporting one of the most important aims in Squiggle, which is to apply Winnicott's ideas and work . . . for the ordinary mothers and families and the ordinary frontline residential homes and so on. And if we were going to help that a bit, we've done a lot towards that tonight. Thanks.

CW: Don't forget: he did teach social workers for twenty years.

CHAPTER FIFTEEN

Early observations on object relations theory

(1943)

I'm terribly sorry—but I simply *must* say some things to you—in continuation of part of our discussion. At least, I must write it—doesn't matter nearly so much that you *read* it.

About the existance [*sic*] of "good" etc. To make it clear to myself I must sum up a bit first:—

1. The ultimate "good" thing—the experience in which the inner good world unites with the good in the world of reality through some relationship—as you said for a baby this happens when the inner good mother unites with the real mother.

2. It is only possible to attain this experience, of the existance [*sic*] of the inner good world—because only in this way can the *belief* in the goodness be sustained through periods of doubt in the reality situation—you said that for the baby it means that a relationship

---

In this letter to Donald, dated 2 April 1943, Clare passionately explores her own version of object relations theory, undoubtedly influenced by Donald. The admixture of the personal and professional is quite evident, and one sees the emergence of a common language, which sustained their relationship for nearly 30 years. The emphases in the letter are Clare's, originally underlined in the handwritten correspondence.

with the real mother is *only possible* because of the existance [sic] of the inside good mother.

3. So far so good (?)—Now the *importance* of these experiences is that they are the *only* proof there is that one *is good* oneself. In these moments one is entirely good & entirely *safe*.

4. *Difficulties* arise (a): If there is a lack of good relationship one's good world (& oneself) never *become* good: lack of reality. This is a dangerous situation. (b): Only in certain moments is the inner good linked up with reality—so that mostly reality does not really satisfy. And you said that this is the great problem of living & perhaps something which must always be reckoned with (i.e. the hate engendered by frustration).

5. You said—that in facing this problem one must be scientific & say that a good experience happened once & *may* happen again (I said that this sounded hopeless) but there is nothing to say that it will.

6. Now *I* want to say it differently (& *please tell* me if you think I am wrong). If one has a good experience once—it *never ceases* to exist, it is dynamic & creative & enters so deeply into the *fabric* of the personality—that it is independent of *time* & place—& of individuals even—& simply cannot pass like any ordinary event. It is not *only* made up of external reality.

I think that these experiences form part of the background of one's *faith* in life—one's religion, in other words. In this way, they are *stored* up & preserved against the "evil days." And surely this faith *does* help in dealing with reality—(& is not an escape from it). For one thing, there is not the same anxiety about the existance [sic] of good—& of being good—and one is freer to hate—& more independent etc. etc. etc. (heaps so say). But this faith comes *only* to those who utterly trust their *feelings* & *experiences* of good. And it is not a blind faith because it has *reality* behind it.

Well, now just for fun, I want to try your money analogy. I think it will fit rather well! Money—one's experiences of love & goodness which one stored up as an insurance against bankruptcy. It seems to me, that I trust the bank with my money, ultimately I have *faith* in *society*. But you would want to be scientific & say that my money was there yesterday—but it may, or may not, be there today! But surely, to be scientific would be irrelevant?—my faith in society which is based on factual experience—is sufficient to make the whole thing *work*—& that is what matters—(Science couldn't make it *work*).

That money must be in circulation I agree—or it is of no use what-ever. So must one's "goodness" be in circulation in order to enrich life—otherwise, it becomes a millstone (like so many people's religion). One of *the* problems of reality is how to spend one's goodness—isn't it? It takes so much *courage* & so much real faith *in* one's goodness.

This effort has been entirely for my own benefit & in the hope that you may read it & tell me where I am wrong—or where you don't agree. Religion is *so* important to me—that I must get it sorted out a bit.

Good night—shall I tell you 2 lines from a poem by Siegfried Sassoon (can't remember any more of it):

From you, Beethoven, Bach, Motzart [*sic*],
the substance of my dreams took fire.

Isn't that *good*?

Did you know that Wordsworth for most of his life was preoccu-pied with the problem of his great good fortune in that his inner world of imagination linked so much with his real experiences? It was a constant marvel & miracle to him—& he was always seeking the clue to it. Really, that's all.

Clare.

CHAPTER SIXTEEN

A personal tribute:
Dr Lois Munro

(1974)

I first met Dr Munro at a garden party given by Dugmore and Elizabeth Hunter in the summer of 1956. I remember this meeting with the precision with which one remembers an important encounter. At the time I was just recovering from meningitis, and this was the first time I had ventured into any kind of social gathering. Here were people eating and drinking and enjoying themselves, and the sun was shining. It seemed strange to be part of this scene after the life and death struggle in the curtained isolation of the hospital bed.

Many people spoke to me at the garden party, and I to them, but Dr Munro communicated on a different level. She seemed to emerge from the general background and to metaphorically hold out a hand and pull me into the party and into the present. She spoke in a straightforward way about illness, my illness, about life as a patient in hospital, and the dependence that serious illness imposes. She also spoke about how it feels to be back in the world again where time and conventions operate, after being at the back of beyond where there is no time and nothing matters but the next breath. These were her words, and the impact was immediate. A bridge had been made between two worlds. On the way home from the party, Donald told me that Dr Munro herself had been seriously ill in the recent past, and there had been uncertainty as to the outcome. Her reaching out to me at the party not only helped at the time, but it taught me an important lesson: that people who have been through an intense personal experience absolutely need to have this fact acknowledged—naturally and explicitly—if social relationships are to be re-established and maintained in any way that is meaningful. The incident showed Dr Munro's warmth and humanity, and her courageous lack of fear at the human predicament. There was something direct and authentic about her personality; this gave her a strength which was easily communicated to others and which we shall always associate with her.

Since 1956, I had met Dr Munro only rarely at meetings and conferences, but somewhere was preserved the experience of her understanding of what has to be contended with when life is threatened. I was in such a position in September 1971, and I did not hesitate to ask her for help, nor did she hesitate to respond. She took me into analysis then and there. The situation in 1971 was different from that of 1956, but the issues were the same. In the short space of six months I had lost my husband and my work. Immediately after Donald's death I had had to take a leadership role in the dissolution of the work and the working unit I had built up over a number of years in the Children's Department of the Home Office.

The analytic work with Dr Munro was of necessity specifically concerned with the whole process of mourning. Of particular importance therefore was her strength of purpose, which held me firmly and unrelentingly to this task in all its aspects, and firmly within the analytic situation. I knew that she did not under-rate the formidable nature of the task in hand.

Dr Munro spoke infrequently in sessions, but whether she spoke or was silent, she was always a presence, and it was her strength that was experienced and was so much needed in order that new areas of pain could be released, and she had a sure touch in locating pain.

I am very fortunate that the process of mourning had come full circle some months before Dr Munro's death. We both recognized that the essential task was completed because life and death had become a totality—a timeless experience which goes on existing, and which includes all lives, all deaths. At this point I remember saying to Dr Munro that I had an urge to write something about mourning from the point of view of the mourner, and that I should call it "Full Circle" and should dedicate it to her.

Once at the end of a last session before a holiday I made an attempt to thank Dr Munro for her help. I said, "It won't go into words, but I think you must know how much I mean it because I have committed myself to the analysis to the fullest extent of my capacity." She said "yes, yes, I do know it" and then she hesitated and added, "I have always remembered something said by Miss Sheehan-Dare when I was a student at the Institute: at the end of a clinical seminar she reminded us that as psycho-analysts we have a special privilege—that of sharing our patient's experiences." I went away impressed by Dr Munro's humility and her honesty. It rang true.

On Wednesday, December 5th, Dr Woodhead and I attended Dr Munro's funeral in the small thatched hamlet church near to her cottage. It seemed strange to hear again the familiar rubric of the Christian burial service: "I am the resurrection and the life." The words seemed not out of place in this simple rural setting where the lives of the many villagers who were present are governed by the seasons, and where life and death are in close proximity. But deeper than the words was the fact that we were taking part in a universal rite which has been afforded to the dead in one form or another since time began. A rite which bestows a final dignity on the life and death of the individual.

The stark simplicity of the scene and the ceremony was a poignant reminder of Dr Munro's life. There was an essential down-to-earth quality in her wisdom, and no one could have been more unpretentious, more lacking in any form of ostentation, or more direct than she. I talked to her friends in the village and learnt of her generosity to them in buying land so that those who work on it and love it can go on living on it. Speaking in terms of her psycho-analytic work—there are many people who will go on living on land that Dr. Munro helped them to possess more securely.

CHAPTER SEVENTEEN

Fear of breakdown:
a clinical example

(1980)

The case I shall describe in this paper brought alive for me the theory put forward in Winnicott's (1974) paper "Fear of Breakdown". The case also illustrates the use of the false-self defence organization (Winnicott, 1960) as a means of survival, and the use of the transitional object (Winnicott, 1953) in the process of recovery.

It will be appreciated that in a short communication only the milestones in the progress of treatment can be described. Each milestone represents a new level of ego development and integration. What must of necessity be left out of this presentation is the detail of the hard work and often bitter agony that preceded each move forward. However, throughout the long periods of pain and despair I never felt out of touch with this patient's ruthless drive for survival, whatever the cost. It was this that gave the analysis a powerful momentum from the beginning. Previously this drive had maintained the patient's defences against disintegration—but these defences were no longer holding, and the drive for survival had to be invested elsewhere. In the early

Presented at the Thirty-first International Psychoanalytical Congress, New York, August 1979. First published in 1980 in *International Journal of Psycho-Analysis, 61*: 351–357.

stages of the treatment I often felt that the patient might not survive. In her aimless wandering about London, she could easily have met with a fatal accident.

The moment at which I connected what was happening in the treatment with the theoretical formulation in Winnicott's paper "Fear of breakdown" was for me one of those cumulative experiences when everything adds up and comes together. At that moment I saw the *possibility* of a favourable outcome for my patient.

In view of what follows, the main thesis in the Winnicott (1974) paper will be stated briefly. In Winnicott's view, when the fear of breakdown is clinically manifest, this indicates that a previous early breakdown occurred at a time when "the ego cannot organize against environmental failure, when dependence is a living fact" (p. 103). At the dependence stage environmental failure disrupts the ego defence organization and exposes the individual again to the primitive anxieties which he had, with the help of the facilitating environment, organized himself to deal with. This leads to "an unthinkable state of affairs" (p. 103). In fact the word *anxieties* is not a strong enough word, and Winnicott lists what he calls the primitive agonies against which new defences must be constructed. This early trauma will continue to be a threat until and unless the patient is able to experience the original event, now with the help of the ego supporting analyst (mother). Winnicott concludes: "There is no end [to the analysis] unless the bottom of the trough has been reached, unless the thing feared has been experienced" (p. 105).

I shall now describe my case. The patient is a woman, now aged 42, who was referred to me by her General Practitioner. She is a professional musician who trained in England and abroad with the expectation of becoming a solo performer. I will call her Miss K.

One of Miss K's main presenting symptoms was her frequent illnesses, which had led on occasions to hospitalization for investigations and for treatment. Her recovery from illness was delayed, and she was listless and depressed. It was in this state after an illness that she was referred to me. Professionally Miss K did not seem to be making the grade of which she was capable. Her doctor said that Miss K had agreed to see me, but that she was sceptical about "anything to do with psychiatry".

The first interview did in fact turn out to be the first session of Miss K's treatment. She looked questioningly at me with a direct gaze, and I could detect a determination to hold her own in the situation. She started by saying that she had only come here to please her doctor and then proceeded to tell me a great deal about herself. But this was a rehearsed performance, so at length I broke in and said: "I know that you've come to see me because Dr S thinks it's a good idea. But I wonder why you really came? Could it be that you do want some help?" She said: "Well, I don't know about that, but there is just one thing I can't do. I don't know what it is. I know everything about myself, and I always have, and I can manage very well except for this one thing I can't do." I found myself saying: "Well, one thing that you can't do is to *be the other person*." Miss K was visibly taken aback at this idea. It seemed to galvanize her either to ward it off or to absorb the impact. It was touch and go.

Her response was to look at me in an intent searching way for what seemed like a long time, during which neither of use moved or relaxed attention. She was in fact sizing me up, and I felt the question hanging in the air was, would I do as "the other person", and could she possibly risk letting me take that role in relation to herself? At last she relaxed, spoke in quite a different voice, and we made plans to start therapy without delay.

Undoubtedly this first interview laid the basis for everything that has followed and has never been forgotten by the patient. My response had presented Miss K with the opportunity to break through her usual defence of self sufficiency by offering her an alternative way of living which included another person, namely myself, and she decided to try it. The confidence that she has in her own doctor did, I think, contribute to her willingness to take a risk with me.

I learned that Miss K's mother is a high-powered professional woman of considerable influence. Her father was a gifted man in the musical world. He died when she was 14, but by that time had been divorced from her mother for 11 years. Miss K's brothers have made notable successes of their careers. She finally left home at the age of 21 to study abroad and now lives in her own flat in London.

The first part of Miss K's treatment was directly based on "the other person" theme, which she took up immediately. She told about the recent break-up of her relationship to her lover, which had lasted three years. She remembers leaving him one evening knowing that this was the end. The next thing she was aware of was waking up at home in bed in the middle of the next day. She said: "I had a complete amnesia for the whole of that time, and it was a great shock to me." I said that it looked as if the amnesia covered up something that she didn't want to remember, something from a long time ago perhaps, that had also been a shock to her. She did not react to the idea but seemed to consider it, and it led to the next step in her therapy.

One day when Miss K had had enough time to build up some confidence in the analytic process (by working through some of her negative feelings with regard to dependence), she told me of her recurring nightmare. She remembers this dream from her early days at boarding–school, and at the time of telling it was still operative. She dreams that *she is in a desert which is a vast empty sandy space. There are animals but no people in the desert. The animals don't seem real, although they are familiar. Some are two-dimensional, made of wood or cardboard. They all begin to sink into the sand until they have completely disappeared, and she is alone and very frightened and wakes up.*

I began to think of the animals as her nursery toys which had ceased to have meaning for her because at some point she had lost touch with the good internal and external object (mother). I commented that she must have been angry with the animals to send them all away. It seemed as if they were her familiar nursery toys, and for some reason she didn't love them any more, so she pushed them down out of sight. But this meant that she was alone, which was intolerable, so she woke up. Miss K said in a surprised way: "Oh, you think I sent the animals away, do you?" I said: "I am suggesting that you got rid of them because you didn't love them any more, so they became bad unreal cardboard things, without any meaning, so you got rid of them, and then you were alone and the world had become a desert."

Miss K came to the next session bringing the early family photograph album which she has secretly kept for years. She showed me a picture of a child of about 2½ years standing framed in the doorway of the cottage where her family had lived. The child was cringing and withdrawn, clutching her dress and sucking her thumb. I thought, "autistic child". Miss K said: "They tell me that's a photograph of me. I simply can't believe it. I can't recognize anything of myself in it. But my mother says, "Don't be silly, of course it's you—who else could it be?"

Eventually after a pause I suggested that she could have brought this photograph to me so that I should know about that part of herself which she herself did not know about and could not recognize as herself. I also said that the child looked terrified, as if something quite intolerable had happened to her. I thought that she had kept this photograph hoping that someone would help her to join up with that bit of herself which she had lost and could not recognize.

In this connexion I also referred to "the one thing she couldn't do" of the first interview; she said that it could have something to do with joining up the terrified distressed child part of herself with the rest of her. She needed my help to do this. Miss K listened intently with the whole of herself to what I had been saying, and it seemed to mean something to her, although she again denied recognizing herself as the child in that picture. I said I knew that she couldn't recognize that child, but it was important to her that I knew of the child's existence. This session was a memorable one, and I consciously linked what had gone on with Winnicott's paper on "Fear of breakdown". I also thought how fortunate I had been in having the patient's problem laid before me so clearly. Moreover, because the patient had brought the picture to me, it must mean that she was ready to start to look at this fact of early breakdown.

Quite unexpectedly one day Miss K reflected on her relationship to me, saying it was different from any other that she'd ever known: "You don't press me into any kind of shape. You give me elbow room and space to move around in." I commented that she felt that the space included me—it was the space between us, and this was different from emptiness—the emptiness of the desert.

The reconstruction of the facts about the early breakdown has taken time, and we are still discovering more about it. To sum up the facts: she was about 2½ when the war started. The *au pair* girl who had looked after her from birth was German and disappeared. Her brothers, the youngest of whom was 6, were sent away to relations on the other side of the world, and were away for six years. The cottage filled up with evacuee children for a short chaotic time, during which Miss K's father finally left home after many comings and goings, and she seldom saw him after that time. Recently Miss K remembered starting head-banging in her room at that cottage, and this symptom continued well into her school days.

Painfully in one session with me Miss K recovered a memory that she had completely lost. It must have been when she was about 3 that she was taken from the cottage by her mother, and they went a short journey out to tea with her mother's friend. After tea her mother was no longer there, and she slept the night alone in a big bed. Next day she was taken to the boarding school where this friend worked as a Matron. She stayed at this school until she was 9, more often than not spending the holidays there, including Christmas, because her mother was working. Effectively, she was left by her mother from the age of 3 until she was 9, and later on she had another period at boarding school.

Miss K remembers the headmaster of the first school, and his wife, with affection. At 3 she was very much the youngest child, and they were good to her. This enabled her to use the school to organize herself to deal with the trauma resulting from the complete disintegration of her world. The way in which she did this could have been predicted. She used her very good I.Q. and her strong personality to organize the school around herself, and this she seems to have done with considerable success, but in so doing the broken-down child was sacrificed and became split off and defended against. In other words, she developed a successful false-self to deal with the situation.

Here also two of Winnicott's primitive agonies can be mentioned: (1) *the loss of the sense of real*: the defence against which is the exploitation of the world in support of the individual's primary narcissism, and (2) *falling forever*: the defence against which is self-holding. From this very early age on Miss K increasingly managed her own life by organizing her teachers, her friends, and the mothers of friends to do the bits that she herself could not manage. She eventually planned her own career and largely paid for it by winning prizes and scholarships. Her musical ability was spotted at an early age and special teaching provided.

Not surprisingly, while working out the details of the past, Miss K went through periods of severe depression. She visibly lost weight in a short time and seemed on the verge of collapse. Often at such times I would wonder if I should ever see her again. I always related these depressive phases when she lost touch with me to the feelings of despair that she was not able to experience following the breakdown at the age of 2½ when her whole life collapsed; that she was feeling this now, and blaming me now for deserting her and inflicting all this pain on her. She easily agreed that she blamed me. The analysis made her feel worse, not better, and she would go to see her doctor. Gradually she would come through these phases, and after one such episode came an important dream.

Miss K dreamt that she was in bed at home in her flat. *At the foot of the bed on the right side was a huge pile of coal, which gradually disappeared in front of her eyes. While this was going on, she noticed at the other side of the bed opposite to where the coal had been there was a camel. She was very pleased to see it because she knew that it was me. She had brought a drawing of this dream showing the black coal and the yellow camel.* As she woke up, she was saying to herself: "She's sended it away. She's sended it away." She knew that this meant the nightmare, and that she would never have it again. She said: "I was filled with a sense of joy. As I lay there I thought: 'where's my teddy?'—and I very much wanted him, but I knew he wasn't in the flat, so all I could do was to go and fill a hot water bottle instead." Miss K reported this dream in a tone of voice that indicated surprise and pleasure.

I was aware of the idealization of me in the dream and the handing over to me of omnipotent powers. She said that the camel in the dream was different from the animals in the nightmare, because it was real, and she recognized at once that it was me. The two humps reminded her of breasts. I said it seemed that she recognized me as a mother therapist who could feed her, and a special camel mother who had enough food stored up to take her across the desert.

During the next few minutes I was able to see and to say that she felt I had special powers and could send away her depression, which was represented by the pile of black coal. The coal had disappeared when she recognized me as the camel. It seems that when I am present, her depression goes away, but if I am not there, she is left with the broken-up bits of coal, which are like the broken-up bits of me because of her anger that I am absent. I reminded her of all the broken-up relationships she had told me about recently, and how much she wanted to get rid of them. Miss K said that her teddy-bear had been part of her life for as long as she could remember and had been her favourite possession, outliving all others belonging to her childhood. She went home (a very long way) and collected it at the weekend and brought it to her Monday session sitting it on a chair facing us both— a much–used, much-battered object with whom she was obviously pleased to be reunited.

It seems that when Miss K could accept me as a good feeding mother she could bring to life her teddy-bear which was her transitional object. By getting in touch with her transitional object (a child's first-loved possession which becomes the symbol of the mother's breast and the early mothering experiences, if they have been good enough to allow the symbolization), Miss K was able to re-establish the relationship to the early mother before the breakdown at 2½. I tried to put this into words so that Miss K could make the connexions and grasp the sequence for herself.

Her response was to say that her mother did in fact breast-feed her and she probably did it well, because she is a warm person, even if somewhat overpowering. She added: "I think I survived because I'm tough, like my mother's side of the family." I felt these words indicated Miss K's recognition that her survival had depended on having re-ceived something positive from her mother at the beginning of her life.

Following this dream in which Miss K got into contact via her transitional object with the early mother before the breakdown, there were changes in the patient's attitude not only to the treatment, but in her life generally. She always refers to this episode as a landmark because from then on she knew that she didn't want to die. She refers to it as "the time when I began to want to live", and she has never yet gone back from this position in spite of quite severe depressive phases which include hostility and loss of contact with me, which to her are extremely painful and alarming.

Miss K gradually moved forward to take up the theme of *wanting to live*, to spend time considering her career and her place in the world. She had made a reasonably successful début as a solo performer but in spite of pressure from her friends could not follow it up because although she had worked hard to acquire all the professional techniques of remembering music and they were now part of her, the fear of forgetting and breaking down was overwhelming. She knew it was ridiculous, but there it was, she couldn't help it. I suggested that she could be afraid that other frightening memories might come in and cut across the memory of the music. The cut-off, ill part of herself might take over. Miss K seemed unable to take this further, and I thought this was because the summer holiday was upon us.

Miss K went abroad for the holiday, staying with the family with whom she spent her student days, which was perhaps the happiest time in her life. She is very much at home with this family.

On her first session back, Miss K reported two dreams which had occurred fairly early in the holiday. She dreamt that *she saw that child in the picture standing in the doorway of the cottage, only it was real, not a picture. As she looked at the child, it began to lift its arms slowly in jerks, as if it were clockwork. It seemed to want to move but wasn't sure that it could.* Here the dream ended. The very next night she had the dream again exactly as before, except that this time *the child moved its arms more easily and lifted them towards her. She thought: "that child wants picking up, so I'd better go and do it". She picked up the child, put her under her arm and walked down the garden path towards the gate.*

Miss K seemed pleased with these dreams and told about them in an animated tone of voice. I said that it seemed that she now felt strong enough with my help to go back and pick up and carry that distressed child part of herself from which she'd been cut off for so long. I also said that it seemed that the child was now no longer frozen, but was ready to move and come alive and to be part of her (Miss K's) grown-up self.

At her next session two days later Miss K told me that when she got home after last time, she started to play, as usual. Getting home for her means getting back to her music, and it has been while playing that all her thinking about her analysis goes on. While she was playing, to her surprise, she suddenly said to herself: "I shan't be afraid of forgetting my music any more. In fact I've never been afraid of forgetting, I've been afraid of remembering."

She was silent, and after a pause I said: "Remembering what?" And as she didn't seem sure, or wasn't able to say, I suggested that it could be remembering the agony of that child in the picture which would be so terrible that she would not be able to go on playing. She would want to retreat and hold herself together as the child in the picture had done to prevent herself from falling apart. She seemed to accept this and said: "You see, I shan't be *afraid* any more, that's the point; I may forget the music, but it won't matter, I can go on playing until it comes back." I suggested that since the dream of picking her up, the child in the picture no longer seemed to be a threat to her—because she had now become part of her.

Miss K's relationship to her music and to her music teachers would be an interesting study in itself. Her music, which includes her image of herself as a musician, is certainly the most important thing in her life. It provided the only continuity that she knew and enabled her to function somehow in spite of the unpredictability and deprivation to which she was subjected.

It did not surprise me that some two months or so after the session just described, Miss K asked in a matter-of-fact voice, "And when am I coming to play to you?" And a time was arranged.

I suggest that the degree of ego integration which Miss K has achieved during treatment has in fact freed her music to be used differently. It could now be shared, and I knew that I would be the first person with whom she would take this risk. The question of her playing to me again has never arisen, and she was able to find a partner with whom she gave several recitals. As far as her therapy is concerned, whether or not she becomes a recognized performer is incidental. What matters is that her music is available for her to use as she wants. Not long ago she was asked to play at a big party, and in the middle of so doing had thought to herself: "Now, isn't that nice, I am really enjoying myself."

The most recent phase of Miss K's treatment has been concerned with reconstructing her father's life and death. She went home one holiday determined to find out from her mother all she could about her father. But her mother categorically refused to speak of him. After an argument, Miss K became so angry that she "froze to the spot". She remembers the scene at that moment with the clarity that shock gives to it. She returned to London and stayed with a friend, and it was here that she had what she called another amnesia. The friend called Miss K's doctor. It took some time for her to recover from this confrontation with her own anger amounting to murder of her mother. I related this to the fury and anger that she had not been able to experience at the time when her world disintegrated at the age of 2½. I suggested that the force of today's pain and shock belonged not only to today but to that early time, the difference now being that she has me to be angry with about it and her doctor to look after her. From my point of view this episode was "the bottom of the trough" mentioned in Winnicott's paper. It was from this point that her recovery became a possibility.

As part of her recovery, Miss K spent the next six months finding out all she could about her father. This is a remarkable story of ingenuity, initiative, and persistence. When she had completed this task as well as she could, there then gradually set in a process of mourning for her father and all that she had missed by not knowing him. She almost deliberately set about this work of mourning. She sent her man friend away so that she could be undisturbed for as long as she needed. To me she said: "I suppose it's my usual autumn depression." But in fact it had more significance: she was mourning her father consciously for the first time.

Eventually she related the following dream: *she was back near her home walking in the country. She was following a path through a wood and came to a bridge across a stream, and walking to meet her across the bridge was her much-loved dog who had been her companion for 11 years and who disappeared when she was 19. In the dream he was very much alive and pleased to see her, and she was delighted to find him again looking so well.*

I said I thought the bridge represented the joining up of two parts of herself; the despairing depressed part that had lost not only her dog but had also lost her father and everyone she knew, and the other part of herself which could bring people to life by re-experiencing what they had meant to her, as she had done in the dream of the dog.

This dream was the beginning of the lifting of her depression, because soon afterwards she announced that her depression had not lasted so long this time. She was also able to talk about the value of depression: how one needs to muster one's resources, because life is

difficult, awful things happen which have to be dealt with somehow.
After a pause she said: "Looking back over the last four years it feels as
if I've had one long breakdown on and off all the time." I agreed with
her that she'd been having the breakdown that she wasn't able to have
when she was a small child in the picture. She finished by saying
"Well, things feel very different, I no longer feel I will disintegrate."

PUBLISHED WORKS OF CLARE WINNICOTT

Published under the name Clare Britton

1945   Children who cannot play. In: *Play and Mental Health* (pp. 12–17). London: New Educational Fellowship.

1946   Remarks in "The Oxfordshire Hostels Scheme". *Report of Child Guidance Inter Clinic Conference* (pp. 29–35, 42–43). London: National Association for Mental Health.

1950   Child care. In: C. Morris (Ed.), *Social Work in Great Britain* (1st edition). London: Faber and Faber.

1954   Child care. In: C. Morris (Ed.), *Social Work in Great Britain* (2nd edition). London: Faber & Faber. (Mostly identical to the chapter in the 1st edition, but with some significant revisions.)

1955a   Casework techniques in the child care services. *Case Conference, 1* (9): 3–15; *Social Casework,* 36 (1): 3–13. Reprinted in: C. Winnicott, *Child Care and Social Work* (pp. 7–27). Hitchin, Hertfordshire: Codicote Press, 1964.

1955b   Methods of care. *Accord, 1* (1): 11–19.

1955c   The "rescue motive" in social work. Letter in *Child Care Quarterly Review, 9* (July, No. 3): 120.

1956   The "rescue motive" in social work. Letter in *Child Care Quarterly Review, 10* (January, No. 1).

Published under the name Clare Winnicott

1959a   Child care and society. *Proceedings of Tenth Annual Conference.*
         Association of Children's Officers, G1–9. Reprinted in C.
         Winnicott, *Child Care and Social Work* (pp. 83–96). Hitchin, Hert-
         fordshire: Codicote Press, 1964.

1959b   The development of insight. In: P. Halmos (Ed.), *The Problems
         Arising from the Teaching of Personality Development. Sociological
         Review, Monograph No. 2.* Keele: University College of North Staf-
         fordshire. Reprinted in: C. Winnicott, *Child Care and Social Work*
         (pp. 71–82). Hitchin, Hertfordshire: Codicote Press, 1964.

1962a   Casework and agency function. *Case Conference, 8* (7): 178–184.
         Reprinted in: C. Winnicott, *Child Care and Social Work* (pp. 59–70).
         Hitchin, Hertfordshire: Codicote Press, 1964.

1962b   Casework and the residential management of children. *Accord,* 7
         (4): 4–14; *Residential Child Care Association Newsletter,* 4–14. Re-
         printed in: C. Winnicott, *Child Care and Social Work* (pp. 29–39).
         Hitchin, Hertfordshire: Codicote Press, 1964.

1963   Face to face with children. In: *New Thinking for Changing Needs,* ed.
         J. King. London: Association of Social Workers. Reprinted in C.
         Winnicott, *Child Care and Social Work* (pp. 40–58). Hitchin, Hert-
         fordshire: Codicote Press, 1964.

1964a   *Child Care and Social Work.* Hertfordshire, Codicote.

1964b   Development towards self-awareness. In: *Challenges, Frustrations,
         Rewards, for Those Who Work with People in Need* (A Report on the
         1964 Conference). Shrewsbury: Shotton Hall, 1964. Republished in
         Toward Insight for the Worker with People. Shrewsbury: Shotton
         Hall, 1971.

1964c   Communicating with children (I). *Child Care Quarterly Review, 18*
         (3): 85–93. Republished in: R. Tod (Ed.), *Disturbed Children: Papers
         on Residential Work* (pp. 65–80). London: Longmans, 1968.

1965   Training for practice. *Accord, 10* (3): 17–26.

1970a   Early one morning. *Case Conference, 16:* 503–504.

1970b   A toast to ACCO. *Commemorative Report: 1949–1970.* London: As-
         sociation of Child Care Officers, The Oxford House.

1970c   The training and recruitment of staff for residential work. *Residen-
         tial Child Care Association Newsletter:* 16–23.

1972a   Comment: Residential work within the context of the social serv-
         ices and some training issues involved. *Social Work Today, 3* (7
         September, No. 11): 2–3.

1972b   Comment: Social work in the residential setting. *Social Work Today,*
         3 (21 September, No. 12): 2–4.

1972c   Foreword. In: E. Holgate (Ed.), *Communicating with Children*. London: Longmans.

1977a   Communicating with children (II). *Social Work Today, 8* (26), 7–11. Reprinted in: *In Touch with Children: Work Book*. London: British Association for Adoption and Fostering, 1984; *Working with Children: Practice Papers*. London: British Association for Adoption and Fostering, 1986; and in *Smith College Studies in Social Work, 66* (1996, No. 2): 115–128.

1977b   Foreword. In: *Working with Children Who Are Joining New Families: Training Aid*. London: Association of British Adoption and Fostering Agencies.

1978a   D.W.W.: A reflection. In: S. Grolnick & L. Barkin (Eds.), *Between Fantasy and Reality: Transitional Objects and Phenomena* (pp. 15–33). New York: Jason Aronson.

1978b   Introduction. In: D. W. Winnicott, *The Piggle: An Account of the Psychoanalytic Treatment of a Little Girl*, ed. I. Ramsy. London: Hogarth Press.

1980   Fear of breakdown: A clinical example. *International Journal of Psycho-Analysis, 61:* 351–357.

1984   Introduction. In: D. W. Winnicott, *Deprivation and Delinquency*. London: Tavistock.

1986   Preface (with R. Shepherd & M. Davis). In: D. W. Winnicott, *Home Is Where We Start From: Essays by a Psychoanalyst*. New York: Norton.

Authored jointly by D. W. Winnicott and Clare Britton

1944   The problem of homeless children. *The New Era in Home and School* (September–October): 155–161.

1947   Residential management as treatment for difficult children. *Human Relations, 1* (1): 2–12. Reprinted in: C. Winnicott, R. Shepherd, & M. Davis (Eds.), *Deprivation and Delinquency*. London: Tavistock, 1984; New York: Methuen, 1984.

REFERENCES

ACCO (1970. *Commemorative Report, 1949–1970*. London: Association of Child Care Officers, The Oxford House.

Aichhorn, A. (1925). *Wayward Youth*. New York: Viking.

Albemarle Baptist Church (1965). *Church Centenary Booklet*. Scarborough-on-Sea.

Bowlby, J. (1944). Forty four juvenile thieves: Their characters and home life. *International Journal of Psychoanalysis, 25*: 19–52.

Bowlby, J. (1951). *Maternal Care and Mental Health*. Geneva: World Health Organization.

Brierley, M. (1951). *Trends in Psycho-Analysis*. London: Hogarth Press.

Britton, J. (1934). *English on the Anvil: A Language and Composition Course for Secondary Schools*. London: John Murray.

Britton, J. (1970). *Language and Learning*. Coral Gables, FL: University of Miami Press.

Britton, J. (1988). *Record and Recall: A Cretan Memoir*. London: Lightfoot Publishing.

Britton, J. (1994). *The Flight-Path of My Words: Poems 1940–1992*. Bristol: Loxwood Stoneleigh.

Britton, J. N. (n.d). *"To Be or Not to Be."* London: Kingsgate Press.

Britton, K. (1953). *John Stuart Mill*. London: Pelican.

Britton, K. (1969). *Philosophy and the Meaning of Life*. Cambridge: Cambridge University Press.

Brown, N. (1980). Mirroring in the analysis of an artist. *International Journal of Psycho-Analysis, 61*: 493–503.

Burlingham, D., & Freud, A. (1942). *Young Children in Wartime: A Year's Work in a Residential War Nursery*. London: Allen & Unwin.

Burlingham, D., & Freud, A. (1944). *Infants Without Families*. New York: International Universities Press.

Carvel, J. (2002). Split of services for children and elderly: Milburn announces reform of council social care. *The Guardian* (17 October).

Clancier, A. (1984). An inimitable genius: Interview with Serge Lebovici. In: A. Clancier & J. Kalmanovitch, *Winnicott and Paradox: From Birth to Creation* (pp. 133–138), trans. A. Sheridan. London: Tavistock, 1987.

Cooper, J. (1993). *Speak of Me as I Am: The Life and Work of Masud Khan*. London: Karnac.

Curtis Committee (1946). *Report of the Committee on the Care of Children*. London: HMSO.

Dockar-Drysdale, B. E. (1961). The problems of making adaptation to the needs of the individual child in a group. *Magazine of the Residential Care Association, 9*.

Donnison, D. (1965). *Social Policy and Administration Revisited*. London: George Allen & Unwin.

Dyer, R. (1983). *Her Father's Daughter: The Work of Anna Freud*. New York: Aronson.

Fraiberg, S. (1952). Some aspects of casework with children: Understanding the child client. In: E. Holgate (Ed.), *Communicating with Children* (pp. 57–71). London: Longmans, 1972.

Freud, A. (1936). *The Ego and the Mechanisms of Defence*. London: Hogarth Press and The Institute of Psycho-Analysis, 1937.

Fromm, M. G., & Smith, B. (1989). *The Facilitating Environment: Clinical Applications of Winnicott's Theory*. Madison, CT: International Universities Press.

Giovacchini, P. (Ed.) (1989). *Tactics and Techniques in Psychoanalytic Therapy III: The Implications of Winnicott's Contributions*. Northvale, NJ: Aronson.

Goldberg, E. M., et al. (Eds.) (1959). *The Boundaries of Casework* (2nd edition). London: Association of Psychiatric Social Workers.

Goldman, D. (Ed.) (1993). *In One's Bones: The Clinical Genius of Winnicott*. Northvale, NJ: Aronson.

Goodman, Y. (1992). A reflection on James Britton. *Teachers Networking: The Whole Language Newsletter, 11* (4): 3.

Grolnick, S. (Ed.) (1990). *The Work and Play of Winnicott*. New York: Aronson.

Grolnick, S., & Barkin, L. (1978). *Between Reality and Fantasy: Transitional Objects and Phenomena*. New York: Aronson.

Grosskurth, P. (1986). *Melanie Klein: Her World and Her Work*. New York: Knopf.

Halmos, P. (1958). Personal involvement in learning about personality. In: *The Problems Arising from the Teaching of Personality Development. Sociological Review, Monograph No. 2*. Keele: University College of North Staffordshire.

Hamilton, G. (1940). *The Theory and Practice of Social Work*. New York: Columbia University Press.

Hartshorn, A. (1982). *Milestone in Education for Social Work: The Carnegie Experiment, 1954–1958*. London: The Carnegie United Kingdom Trust.

Heimann, P. (1975). Obituary, Lois Munro, 1907–1973. *International Journal of Psycho-Analysis, 56*: 99–100.

Holgate, E. (Ed.) (1972). *Communicating with Children*. London: Longmans.

Holman, B. (1995). *The Evacuation: A Very British Revolution*. Oxford: Lion Publishing.

Holman, B. (1998). *Child Care Revisited: The Children's Departments 1948–1971*. London: Institute of Child Care and Special Education.

Holman, B. (2001). *Champions for Children: The Lives of Modern Child Care Pioneers*. Bristol: Policy Press.

Holmes, J. (1991). *A Textbook of Psychotherapy in Psychiatric Practice*. Edinburgh: Churchill Livingstone.

Hopkins, L. (1998). D. W. Winnicott's analysis of Masud Khan. *Contemporary Psychoanalysis, 34*: 5–47.

Howe, D. (1986). *Social Workers and Their Practice in Welfare Bureaucracies*. London: Gower.

Irvine, E. (1966). Review of "Child Care and Social Work". *British Journal of Psychiatric Social Work, 9*: 23–24.

Irvine, E. (1973). The role of Donald Winnicott—Healing, teaching, nurture: A review article. *British Journal of Social Work, 3* (3): 383–390.

Isaacs, S. (1941). *Cambridge Evacuation Survey*. Methuen: London.

Jacka, A. (1973). *The ACCO Story*. Birmingham: The Society for the Promotion of Education and Research in Social Work.

Jacobs, M. (1995). *D. W. Winnicott*. London: Sage.

Jeremy, D. J., Barfield, J., & Newman, K. S. (1982). *A Century of Grace: The History of Avenue Baptist Church, Southend-on-Sea, 1876–1976*. Southend-on-Sea: Avenue Baptist Church.

Kahr, B. (1996). *D. W. Winnicott: A Biographical Portrait*. London: Karnac.

Kanter, J. (1988). Clinical issues in the case management relationship. In:

M. Harris & L. Bachrach (Eds.), *Clinical Case Management* (New Directions for Mental Health Services, No. 40, pp. 15–27). San Francisco, CA: Jossey-Bass.

Kanter, J. (1989). Clinical case management: Definition, principles, components. *Hospital and Community Psychiatry, 40*: 361–368.

Kanter, J. (1990). Community-based management of psychotic clients: The contributions of D. W. and Clare Winnicott. *Clinical Social Work Journal, 18* (1): 23–41.

Kanter, J. (Ed.) (1995). *Clinical Studies in Case Management* (New Directions in Mental Health Services, No. 65). San Francisco, CA: Jossey-Bass.

Kanter, J. (1996). Case management with long-term patients: A comprehensive approach. In S. Soreff (Ed.), *Handbook for the Treatment of the Seriously Mentally Ill* (pp. 257–277). Seattle, WA: Hogrefe & Huber.

Kanter, J. (2000a). The untold story of Clare and Donald Winnicott: How social work influenced modern psychoanalysis. *Clinical Social Work Journal, 28* (3): 245–261.

Kanter, J. (2000b). Beyond psychotherapy: Therapeutic relationships in community care. *Smith College Studies in Social Work, 70* (3): 396–426.

Kastell, J. (1961). *Casework in Child Care.* London: Routledge & Kegan Paul.

Klein, M. (1940). Mourning and its relation to manic-depressive states. In: *Love, Guilt and Reparation and Other Works, 1921–1945: The Writings of Melanie Klein, Vol. 1* (pp. 344–369). New York: Free Press, 1984.

Klein, M. (1984). *Love, Guilt and Reparation and Other Works, 1921–1945: The Writings of Melanie Klein, Vol. 1.* New York: Free Press.

Kris, E. (1956). Insight in psycho-analysis. *International Journal of Psycho-Analysis, 37*: 445–455.

Lambrick, H. M. (1962). Communication with the patient. *The Almoner, 15* (7).

Martin, N. (1994). An intellectual adventurer (Obituary of Jimmy Britton). *Times Educational Supplement* (11 March).

Memoirs of Ministers and Missionaries (n.d.). The Baptist Handbook.

Middlemore, M. P. (1941). *The Nursing Couple.* London: Hamish Hamilton.

Milner, M. (1969). *In the Hands of a Living God: An Account of a Psycho-Analytical Treatment.* New York: International Universities Press.

Milner, M. (1985). Obituary: Clare Winnicott. *Winnicott Studies, 1* (1): 4.

Phillips, A. (1988). *Winnicott.* Cambridge, MA: Harvard University Press.

Read, H. (1943). *Education Through Art.* London: Faber & Faber.

Ribble, M. (1941). *The Rights of Infants.* New York: Columbia University Press.

Rodman, F. R. (1989). *The Spontaneous Gesture: Selected Letters of D. W. Winnicott.* Cambridge, MA: Harvard University Press.

Rodman, F. R. (2003). *Winnicott*. New York: Perseus.

Searles, H. (1975). The patient as therapist to his analyst. In: *Countertransference and Related Subjects*. New York: International Universities Press.

Spitz, R. (1945). Hospitalism: An inquiry into the genesis of psychiatric conditions in early childhood. *Psychoanalytic Study of the Child, 1*: 53–74.

Stevenson, O. (1954). The first treasured possession. *Psychoanalytic Study of the Child, 9*.

Tibble, J. W. (1958). Afterthoughts on the 1958 Conference. *The Sociological Review, Monograph No. 1*. Keele: University College of North Staffordshire.

Tod, R. (Ed.) (1968). *Disturbed Children*. London: Longmans.

Towle, C. (1945). *Common Human Needs*. Washington, DC: National Association of Social Workers.

Waldron, F. E. (1958). Methods of teaching personality development. *The Sociological Review, Monograph No. 1*. Keele: University College of North Staffordshire.

Winnicott, D. W. (1943). "A Doctor Looks at the Psychiatric Social Worker." Unpublished manuscript.

Winnicott, D. W. (1945). Primitive emotional development. In: *Collected Papers: Through Paediatrics to Psycho-Analysis*. London: Tavistock, 1958.

Winnicott, D. W. (1949). Hate in the countertransference. In: *Collected Papers: Through Paediatrics to Psycho-Analysis* (pp. 194–203). London: Tavistock.

Winnicott, D. W. (1953). Transitional objects and transitional phenomena. *International Journal of Psycho-Analysis, 34*: 89–98. Reprinted in: *Collected Papers: Through Paediatrics to Psycho-Analysis*. London: Tavistock, 1958. Also in: *Playing and Reality*. London: Tavistock, 1971.

Winnicott, D. W. (1954). Two adopted children. *Case Conference, 1* (2): 4–11.

Winnicott, D. W. (1955). A case managed at home. *Case Conference, 2* (7).

Winnicott, D. W. (1957a). *The Child and the Family*. London: Tavistock.

Winnicott, D. W. (1957b). *The Child and the Outside World*. London: Tavistock.

Winnicott, D. W. (1958). *Collected Papers: Through Paediatrics to Psycho-Analysis*. London: Tavistock.

Winnicott, D. W. (1959). On envy: Book review of M. Klein, *Envy and Gratitude*. *Case Conference, 6*: 177–178.

Winnicott, D. W. (1960). Ego distortion in terms of true and false self. In: *The Maturational Processes and the Facilitating Environment*. London: Hogarth Press, 1965. Reprinted London: Karnac, 1990.

Winnicott, D. W. (1961). Effect of psychotic parents on the emotional development of the child. *British Journal of Psychiatric Social Work, 6* (1).

Winnicott, D. W. (1963). The mentally ill in your caseload. In: J. King (Ed.), *New Thinking for Changing Needs* (pp. 50–66). London: Association of Social Workers; also in: D. W. Winnicott, *The Maturational Processes and the Facilitating Environment.* London: Hogarth Press, 1965.

Winnicott, D. W. (1964). The value of depression. *British Journal of Psychiatric Social Work, 7* (3): 123–127.

Winnicott, D. W. (1970). One fine morning. *Case Conference, 16*: 504–505.

Winnicott, D. W. (1971a). Playing: A theoretical statement. In: *Playing and Reality.* London: Tavistock.

Winnicott, D. W. (1971b). *Therapeutic Consultations in Child Psychiatry.* New York: Basic Books.

Winnicott, D. W. (1971c). The use of an object and relating through identifications. In: *Playing and Reality.* London: Tavistock.

Winnicott, D. W. (1974). Fear of breakdown. *International Review of Psycho-Analysis, 1*: 103–107. Reprinted in: C. Winnicott, R. Shepherd, & M. Davis (Eds.), *Psycho-Analytic Explorations.* London: Karnac, 1989; Cambridge, MA: Harvard University Press, 1989.

Winnicott, D. W. (1986). *Home Is Where We Start From.* New York: Norton.

Winnicott, D. W. (1987). *Babies and Their Mothers.* New York: Addison-Wesley.

Winnicott, D. W. (1988). *Human Nature.* New York: Schocken.

Winnicott, D. W. (1989). *Psycho-Analytic Explorations.* Cambridge, MA: Harvard University Press.

Winnicott, D. W. (1993). *Talking to Parents.* New York: Addison-Wesley.

Winnicott, D. W. (1996). *Thinking about Children.* London: Karnac; New York: Addison-Wesley.

Winnicott: D. W. (2002). *Winnicott on the Child.* New York: Perseus.

Women's Group on Public Welfare (1943). *Our Towns.* London: Oxford University Press.

Wyatt-Brown, A. (1993). From the clinic to the classroom: D. W. Winnicott, James Britton, and the revolution in writing theory. In: P. Rudnytsky (Ed.), *Transitional Objects and Potential Spaces: Literary Uses of D. W. Winnicott* (pp. 292–305). New York: Columbia University Press.

Younghusband, E. (1978). *Social Work in Britain, 1950–1975.* London: George Allen & Unwin.

INDEX

Abram, J., xv
ACO: *see* Association of Children's
Officers
ACCO: *see* Association of Child Care
Officers
Adler, A., 13
adolescence, 69, 109, 238
adoption, 97, 98
adult, role of in child's development,
114–115
aggressiveness, fear of, and inability
to play, 120
Aichhorn, A., 74
Albemarle Baptist Church, 4
Ambache, S., 53
Anderson, J., xv, 90, 91, 92
angry child(ren), communicating
with, 193
Anna Freud Clinic, 55
Anthony, E. J., xiii
antisocial child(ren), hostels for, 106,
107
antisocial elements in society, 126
antisocial tendency, 124, 223, 266
Applegate, J., xv

Applied Social Studies Course, LSE,
25–29, 42, 48, 89
Ashdown, M., 13, 222
Association of Child Care Officers
[ACCO], 27, 28, 43, 45, 62
Association of Children's Officers
[ACO], 42, 43
Annual Conference, 1963, 42
Association of Psychiatric Social
Workers, 89
Auterinen, P., xv, 60, 93
Avenue Baptist Church, 4, 6, 7, 13
Axline, V., 203

Bach, J. S., 251
backward child(ren), hostels for, 108
Balint, E., 55
Balint, M., xix, 37, 55
BAP: *see* British Association of
Psychotherapists
Barfield, J., 4, 6, 7
Barkin, L., 54, 237
Barnett, B., xv
bedwetting (clinical vignette), 81
Beethoven, L. van, 251

305